ALSO BY LACY CRAWFORD

Early Decision

Notes on a Silencing

Notes on a Silencing

A Memoir

Lacy Crawford

Little, Brown and Company

New York   Boston   London

Little, Brown and Company
Hachette Book Group
1290 Avenue of the Americas, New York, NY 10104
littlebrown.com

First Edition: July 2020

Little, Brown and Company is a division of Hachette Book Group, Inc. The Little, Brown name and logo are trademarks of Hachette Book Group, Inc.

The publisher is not responsible for websites (or their content) that are not owned by the publisher.

The Hachette Speakers Bureau provides a wide range of authors for speaking events. To find out more, go to hachettespeakersbureau.com or call (866) 376-6591.

ISBN 978-0-316-49155-6
LCCN 2019947036

10 9 8 7 6 5 4 3 2 1

LSC-C

Printed in the United States of America

For girls on the stairs
and for S, N, and T

I told you I wanted to live in a world in which the antidote to shame is not honor, but honesty.

Maggie Nelson, The Argonauts

Author's Note

This is, among other things, a story of slander, of how an institution slandered a teenage girl to coerce her into silence. To survive, the story of slander must resonate. An entire community is therefore implicated, and also burdened. I believe this is especially true for a school. We were young. The institution was always the greater power.

Most names and identifying details have been changed, particularly those belonging to my schoolmates.

Notes on a Silencing

1

October 1990, Fifth Form

One evening around eleven o'clock, a young man called a girl on the phone. This was a few decades ago, and they were students at a boarding school, so he called the pay phone in her dorm from the pay phone in his. Someone answered and pounded up three flights of stairs to knock on the girl's door. She was not expecting the call. He was a senior—a grade ahead, but a couple of years older— and he was upset. Crying, she thought, but it was hard to tell, because she barely knew him. He said something about his mom, swallowing his words. He wanted the girl's help. Please.

She knew the senior because she had helped his friends in math class. He'd joked in the hall to her once that maybe she could help him sometime. It had been a surprise that he'd sent his attention her way, and this phone call was a bigger surprise. Something must have happened, she reasoned. Something very bad.

She had no roommate that year and lived across campus from her friends (an unfortunate turn of the school housing lottery). Her parents were a thousand miles west. It will tell you something about her naivete, and maybe her character, that to her the strange specificity of the senior's request—for *her* help, and no one else's—is what made his summons feel important, and true.

School rules forbade leaving the dorm at that hour, but she knew, as they all did, how to let the back door close without rattling the latch. She skirted pools of lamplight where campus paths crossed. His room was in shadow. He pulled her up through the window. She landed, in his hands, on a mattress, and she felt and then dismissed surprise—beds could sit beneath windows, of course, there was nothing wrong with that.

His roommate was on the bed too. She didn't know the roommate at all.

Neither of them had shirts on. Neither of them, she saw, as her eyes adjusted, had pants on.

She said, "What's wrong?"

They shushed her and gestured toward the wall. Each student dormitory incorporated at least one faculty apartment, where the head of the dorm lived, sometimes with a family. Mr. B.'s apartment was right there, they warned. Her voice through the wall would bring him in, blazing.

He would catch her (she realized) after hours in a male dorm with two undressed seniors on a bed.

Suspension. Shame. Her parents' shame. (College!)

There was a moment while she waited for the one who had called to tell her how she could help him. He pressed her down. When his roommate did this too, she understood that she could not lift these men and would have to purchase her release a different way.

Four hands on her, she said, "Just don't have sex with me."

Instead they took turns laying their hips across her face. Their cocks penetrated her throat past the pharynx and poked the soft back of her esophagus, so she had to concentrate to breathe. The repeated laryngeal spasms in her throat—the gag reflex—caused her throat to narrow and grip their dicks rhythmically.

Someone unbuttoned her jeans and stuck his fingers inside her.

When they were finished, she climbed out the window and walked back to her own dorm, keeping to campus roads this time. There were two security guards who patrolled the grounds in a white Jeep. The kids called them Murph and Sarge, and they saw everything. But they did not see her.

She found the door as she'd left it, gently ajar.

After a long shower, she slept.

This happened in the fall of my junior year in high school, when I was, as we said—using the English terms—a *fifth former* at St. Paul's School in Concord, New Hampshire. I have told this story, or some version of it, dozens of times since then. I have told it to parents and friends and therapists and boyfriends and lawyers and strangers. I have been recorded telling it to detectives. I have written it in fictionalized form, work that took years and went nowhere. I have gone years in new cities not telling it at all.

It's not a remarkable story.

In fact, it's ordinary. A sexual assault at a New England boarding school. (A boarding school! I was assaulted in privilege; I have survived in privilege.) What interests me is not what happened. I remember. I have always remembered.

What interests me is the near impossibility of telling what happened in a way that discharges its power.

I like to imagine there was a moment, maybe immediately afterward, when my sneakers hit the sandy soil beneath their window and I was free to go, when I might have grabbed the incident by the tail and whipped it around to face me so I could see exactly what was in its eyes.

I had a therapist once, in my early twenties, who suggested that I might describe the event to her and then "never tell it again," positing a future in which I would have no use for it, which is a way of saying that the assault would have no use for me. She was talking about moving on. I was still mired in the search for remedy.

A note on terms: it took a very long time to find the right name for what happened to me. I was too stunned to think *rape* when I pleaded with them not to have sex with me, though *rape,* in the traditional sense, was precisely what I meant to avoid. I had been raised to believe that by every metric, the most serious thing a girl could do was have a penis in her vagina. Not even Mary the mother of Jesus had done that. Certainly I had not. It had not occurred to me what else these two boys might do.

Rape was serious, and I thought—and wanted to think—that what happened to me didn't really count. I did not understand how the boys' violation was of *me,* rather than only a part of me; I did not understand that self-esteem and safety weren't held like treasure between a girl's legs, but could be plundered in other ways. This conclusion was neatly congruent with my sense of my body and in particular with a wordless marrow urgency that pulsed, in those first days, with forgetting all about it. I had no purchase even on a name.

For years thereafter, I envied the monosyllabic force of the word *rape*. Say *rape,* and people get it. People know the telos of the encounter (intercourse) and the nature of the exchange (nonconsensual). Whereas I had no label. I did not think *rape* applied, and in any case I refused it, as my private way of caring for other girls; I considered it important to reserve the word for those who would use it to describe their own assaults. I meant this as a form of respect.

Twenty-five years after I'd left St. Paul's, a detective with the Concord Police Department sent me the 1990 New Hampshire criminal statutes. The terms for the penetrative events of that night were *felonious sexual assault* (because I was under sixteen) and *aggravated felonious sexual assault* (because I was held down). I found some satisfaction in this clarity, but only some. I read the statutes over and over. Nowhere in them does the word *rape* appear. Legally, in New Hampshire as in many other jurisdictions, there are only degrees of assault— descending circles of violation. This is a marker of evolving jurisprudence, because the legal term *rape* originated to describe a violation of property, not person, which is why it applied only to intercourse, and only to women.

I was looking for it, though. I was looking for the word for the worst thing. For the thing that had not quite happened to me, but which would, when it happened to a girl, trigger rescue, awaken the world, summon the cavalry. As an adult I knew better than to think *rape* would do it, but still I must have believed it was out there. Still.

Assault conjures violence, not violation. Hence the necessary modifier, *sexual*. But *sexual assault* puts sex right in the front window, even though the encounter isn't, to the victim at least,

7

about sex at all, but about cruelty exacted in domination and shame. And this leaves the listener to wonder: if it wasn't rape, then what exactly went on? Which means a person, however kind and concerned for you, hears the term *sexual assault* and is left either guessing or trying not to guess which part of you was violated and in what ways or what you did or how far it (you) went.

So, *assault*. There are also *encounter, incident, event, attack, happening, situation, night in question, time in that room*. Little-known fact about victims: they can tell whether you believe them by which term you use when you ask what happened to them.

Victim is a whole other kettle of fish.

When I woke up the morning after the assault, my throat hurt. This often happened. We were five hundred teenagers in a New England boarding school dominated by architectural grandeur and mediocre plumbing. The buildings were either icy or boiling. In the cavernous bathrooms, we learned to yell "Flushing!" before the surge of cold water into the john caused every running shower on three floors to scald. Our windows breathed frost. We woke to glazed lawns and ran across them, athletes, with hair that was always wet. We ate like rats at the back of a bakery, arriving in Chapel with buttered bagels in our pockets. We were wealthy (except for the few, obvious, who were not), well-turned, and in the process of refinement, and our homesickness was a small candle beside the hard-banked fires of our own becoming. Our headmaster, the rector, told us from the pulpit that ours was a "goodly heritage." Senators, bishops, authors, barons, moguls, ambassadors, peerless curators of life of all kinds had preceded us—schoolboys then! We dragged our fingers along the letters of their names, carved in paneled halls.

Once, during my time there, a man pushed through the double glass doors of the reading room in late morning. We looked up from books and peeked around red leather chairs. The man found the student he was looking for and bent to talk to him, and then he left. The room exploded—appropriately, of course, which meant quietly enough, in rapt whispers. The man was George Plimpton, and he had come to say something to his son, who was a student there.

My point is that we were a room full of teenagers in the early 1990s who knew George Plimpton on sight. That was our job. His appearance on a weekday morning was like a pop quiz from the world.

We were blessed with excellence, and excellently blessed, and our schoolwork and sports teams and choirs and clubs and shoulders thrummed with the Calvinist confidence that is actually a threat: if you do not become spectacular, it means you are not us.

We got sick a lot.

For the most part we ignored it. The ladies at the infirmary, sweet and ineffective, distributed aspirin in pleated cups. I didn't bother, and anyway, what would I have said? "I was impaled by two dicks, ma'am—may I please have a lozenge?"

My throat got better. I did not tell my friends what had happened. I did not intimate or tease, or do the things people do when they claim to want to keep a secret but really just want to seduce with the lovely shape of their almost-telling.

I did not catch the boys' eyes in Chapel. I did not let myself look for them.

All that stuff I just said about money and power—that's not just setting. It's about character. I'm trying to show what I would have given up, what I thought I would have been forced to give up, if I had gotten caught in the boys' room. I'm trying to argue my side. That's why I didn't scream, see? That's why I didn't claw their eyeballs out, or bite. I was trying to find my place in that moment, and I could not admit to myself that the moment was violent. Also I was trying to claim my place in what seemed to me, at fifteen, to be the test of my life. I already knew the colleges on offer for those of us who excelled. I had begun to work out the reason for the tiny pauses in conversation before and after people spoke my class- mates' last names. I had learned when it was acceptable to ask where someone had spent the summer, and when you should already know. Whose father held a Nobel and whose was under indictment; whose had just been sworn in and whose laid to rest with televised honors. I imagined our adolescent channels of envy and rapport to be the headwaters of the adult currents of law and policy and finance and education and the arts that you could not, once they were deep and running fast, jump into if you missed them now. I was the older of my parents' two children, their girl, born to a small family in a small northern suburb of Chicago, and while Mom and Dad would never have said, precisely, that St. Paul's would be the making of me, when we had toured the place the autumn I was thirteen, my parents had been so undone that I had seen them, for the first and only time in my life, holding hands. I understood this to be my chance to find my way into my own life. Into *history*. Do you see?

I know I'm stacking the deck in my own defense. Which I should not have to do, because I was a minor and the boys were eighteen and there were *two of them*—one of whom was on that night almost a foot taller and a hundred pounds heavier than me. I was a virgin. They pushed me down and—

I'm doing it again.

The boys, however, talked.

By supper (which four nights a week we attended in formal attire—suit and tie, dresses or skirts) there were eyes on me that the previous day had been unseeing. It had been a steady source of frustration for me that I was unnoticeable, in spite of the assurances of my parents and friends that I was lovely and so on. I was particularly invisible to the boys whose attentions appealed to me: athletes, mostly, but also the occasional shaggy-haired poetic genius. Now several broad-shouldered seniors were looking at me. This was from across a room crowded with students, and as people passed unknowingly between them and me, I caught shadows of respite from the heat of their eyes.

The tradition after Seated Meal was to gather with coffee or tea in the common room outside the dining halls, a sort of proto–cocktail party training. The boys who had assaulted me were not looking at me, but their teammates stared. These boys' eyes, when I dared to meet them, were incredulous, afire. It seemed to me the best approach was to map the threat; to determine, with quick surveying glances, which boys knew and which did not. Then I'd simply avoid the ones who knew.

In case I was uncertain *what* they knew, one of them called a word in my direction:

"Threesome?"

The term hadn't occurred to me. No term had occurred to me. The event had hardened into wordless granite, silent and immobile, and I intended to go around it.

My friends had not heard. But already I was being asked to admit or deny, so that standing there, saying nothing, willing my aching face to be still, I felt complicit in a lie. A space opened between my friends and me. I could all but hear the crack of ground giving way.

In the days that followed, I watched the news pass from student to student, like that horror movie where the villain hops from stranger to stranger on a city street, awakening in each civil soul a demon.

I understand. School days were long and exhausting, but the claustrophobic nature of boarding school, hothouse that it is, tends toward ennui: every morning, at breakfast, *These people again?* The nation was at war in the Persian Gulf. The Berlin Wall was coming down. But we at school knew little of anything, since there was only one television in each dorm's common room, and it was often broken. In any case we had little time for television. No internet. The only cell phone was a satellite phone the size of a woman's handbag, owned by the son of a scion, and you had to go to his room during visiting hours to check it out. Nothing much was happening. And even if there had been something of interest to discuss on that night or any other at Seated Meal, how often did you have a prudish junior girl, a strawberry-blond chorister who had never had sex or much of a love life at all, just up and cruise to a senior boy's room around midnight to suck two cocks in one go? It was good stuff. I'd have been talking about it, too.

Especially good gossip, no matter how outlandish, contains the sense of its own inevitability. How unlikely I was to have become, of a single night, a prep-school porn star! The illogic of my fall made its own case for truth. *Stranger things. She just cracked.* I wondered, when everyone was so quick to believe what the boys claimed, if this proved that it was my fault. There was something ugly that they had all seen in me, but I had not.

I was young for my class, having entered St. Paul's as a high school sophomore—a fourth former—aged only fourteen. I'd started my period a few months prior and was still surprised every time it happened. I was freckled. Just barely had the braces off. I had the knees and spindle of a girl.

In my very first week at the school, I had been taken up by two classmates, also fourth formers, who trailed urban sophistication (Washington and New York) and Samsara perfume. They thought I was hilarious and sweet. I thought they were holograms. One of them wore Chanel suits and pearl-drop earrings, the left earring white and the right one black. One of these girls came with a boyfriend from Bermuda, who was blond and had sapphire eyes and a comical jaw, like the wrong prince in a Disney movie. When we walked into Seated Meal, when the great studded doors opened, he set his hand on the small of her back to guide her in, as though they were forty.

At Parents' Weekend that first fall, over supper at the nicest restaurant in town, this girl's mother leaned close to my mom and said something, and my mother, pale with fright, excused herself to the bathroom. Later Mom told me she'd been asked if I was on the pill. The other mom had started her own daughter on it, she offered, so her daughter could "enjoy herself."

By Thanksgiving my fabulous fuckable friend had dumped her beach prince and taken up with a senior, and new opportunities beckoned. One plan was to steal the *newb book* from her boyfriend's dorm. This was an actual stapled booklet of names, home addresses, and birthdays of the new students, typed neatly beneath thumbnail photographs. (The pejorative *newb*, derived from *new boy*, had not evolved after almost twenty years of coeducation.) It took some sneaking around to get hold of the newb book belonging to a popular sixth-form boy, but my city friends knew schedules and corridors. Giggling, we thumbed the pages. Her boyfriend and his senior chums had rated all the girls from *1* to *10*, to two decimal points. I was happy to see that many of the girls I was coming to know, and whom I liked a good deal, were *7*s and *8*s. Some assessments struck me as harsh: a curvier girl was graded ruthlessly, and a few African American girls not at all. Other girls, shy but clear-cheeked, had pleasingly high marks. My friends were *10*s, natch.

We found my name. Under my picture someone had written: "If a fart had a face."

"It's just not a great photograph," said my New York friend, and turned the page.

Twenty-five years later, in California, I was having dinner with a classmate from St. Paul's who herself had been raped while a student there, though her attacker was a much older alumnus who liked to take advantage of the fact that there were no locks on our dorm-room doors. We laughed about this, drinking red wine a quarter of a century later. Imagine that— Gothic piles full of sleeping girls, unlocked doors each to each, in the middle of the New Hampshire woods! The country roads we ran on to train for our sports seasons rose and fell along decrepit stone walls, the asphalt shattered from ice and salt. The view was in all directions forested and gave onto an occasional dimly screened clapboard house. It is pure Stephen King country, adjacent to his native Maine. My friend poured more wine and said, "Imagine the book *he* could write!"

I told her about my assault for the first time that night. She'd known about it but not *known* it, she said, and she thanked me for telling her. Her boyfriend was with us, and because he is my husband's dear friend, I filled in some of the story: how the boys had called me on the pay phone of my dorm, and how surprising this had been. "You have to understand," I told him, adding detail he would not have known, "that these guys had girlfriends. Beautiful, athletic women..."

My friend interrupted me. "Cool," she said, nailing it. "They were cool girls."

But they too were used, as surely as the threat of the faculty member catching me there, to lure me in and silence me afterward. The leap of self-preservation my mind made when the boys pushed me down was that no one could ever know about whatever this thing was that was going to happen, *because they had girlfriends.* (That was also, not incidentally, the chief reason why it never occurred to me that the boy on the phone wanted my body. He dated a beautiful senior, a girl way beyond my measure.) If it were ever known that I had *scrumped*

15

with these two—the term we students used to describe what happened between boys and girls—I would be shunned. Basic social arithmetic. At the level of my thoughts, at least, I was more in thrall to those girls than I was to myself.

That my reputation vis-à-vis their girlfriends was my concern tells me that I had immediately arrived at two conclusions: first, that a physical assault, whatever form that was to take, was assured. And second, that nobody would believe it wasn't my fault.

Another note on terms: the two males might be called *boys* or *men,* and I use the words largely interchangeably. They were both eighteen years of age, so legally they were adults. Men. But they were high school students, and in high school we were not *men* and *women* but *boys* and *girls.* They lived in boys' dorms and they played on boys' teams. They were members and, in several cases, between the two of them, captains of the varsity boys' soccer, football, ice hockey, basketball, and lacrosse teams.

I can't call them *guys* because there is a friendly familiarity in the word that evokes a certain forbearance of behavior, as with *lads,* and I won't give them that.

Perpetrators does nothing for me. *Assaulter* is not a word. *Attackers* is useless because they were not Gauls, and so is *accused,* because I am not here accusing them, nor have I ever accused them. I eventually talked about what happened in that room, but so did they—long before I did, and in much more salacious terms. Nobody has ever disputed what happened between us, what body part went where. By the time I broke my silence, everybody knew, and everybody believed it was my fault. I thought that a good girl—the one they were accusing me of *not* being—would agree. My assumption of guilt was my defense against guilt.

Girl works for me. I was fifteen.

Two days after the assault, I was walking down the vaulted corridor that led from the dining halls, the place where all the names were carved, when a slovenly ice-hockey player behind me muttered, "I heard those freckles can fly." I turned and looked at him: stained khaki pants, last year's red-and-white letter jacket, a spray of blond hair in a near-mohawk, like the ghost of a rooster's comb. Then I turned my eyes forward. I was walking alone, though students filled the hall in groups of twos and threes.

"It's true, isn't it?" he pressed. The shorter jock beside him guffawed. "Freckles everywhere."

I did not turn around again. I heard their enormous sneakers scuffing the tile and I kept a measured pace as I pressed out the doors and walked down the hill toward Chapel and class, moving the way every bullied child in history has ever walked, eyes stinging, back on fire, wishing to vanish into another world.

They stopped hassling me. But I made note of the incident— I was taking the pulse of the community's awareness, and it was quickening by the hour.

And yet the girlfriends appeared not to know. This, wondrously, given my fears, persisted. They appeared not *ever* to know. One of them was in my grade and on my tennis team, and we remained as friendly as we had ever been. The other was a neutral stranger in the halls, to my eyes a nearly mythical beauty, shrugging back her long, glossy hair and twining her fingers with her boyfriend's on the way out of breakfast. It was impossible that his hand could hold hers after how it had held me down. It was impossible that these girls had not heard the news that I had cruised to their boyfriends' room and gotten them both off.

Particularly in light of what came later, I have wondered if the girlfriends' refusal to come after me was a deliberate act of grace. Plenty of people vilified me, but these two never did— at least not to my face.

"Maybe it happened to them too," offered a classmate in graduate school. She was writing a dissertation on various versions of the embodiment of pain.

The queer theorist beside her said, "Then that's bullshit, because they needed to rally behind you."

This latter thought had never occurred to me. What a wonder. Can you imagine? We don't expect such things of girls, from girls, for girls. I was beyond grateful to be treated to simple silence.

A few days after he'd first heckled me, again I found myself in a hall alongside the boy with rooster hair. His shuffle. His sidekick: shorter, same hair, also shorter. They had shed their other buddies this time, which is why my skin tightened when the taller one said, "Hey." Without an audience, he must have had a different purpose in calling out to me. Something he meant to convey.

I slowed.

This hallway, which ran from the dining halls the length of the largest building on campus, was a glassed-in cloister, and the high windows streamed with morning sun. On the inside wall were affixed wooden panels carved with the names of more than a century of alumni, form by form. Individually they were fun to read, but collectively they gave a creepy impression of silent watchfulness, not unlike a cemetery. Sometimes I liked to try to guess, as I walked to and from meals, whereabouts on that hallway the line between life and death would fall. Which classes were mostly gone by now? Which still hanging on? Time's shadow, tracking along. I was selfish with youth. We all were.

The wooden benches in front of the panels were heaped with backpacks and jackets hurled by kids on their way to dine. Periodically, entryways opened onto dark staircases that led up to the three dorms that together made up this broadside length of the building. We called these dorms North, Center, and Wing. When I was there, they were respectively for boys, girls, and boys. It was somewhere around Center when the taller boy called out to me. I am not sure if it's a trick of memory that all the other students seemed to fade away, or if he chose a moment when no one else was there, but it was just the two of them, tall and short, walking behind me for a good span of the red tile in the morning light. We were heading to Saturday classes, only a half day, and no Chapel. There was release in the air.

I turned around and walked backward, keeping my distance.

The taller boy smiled. He had a full, smug mouth and an ordinary name that nobody used, preferring the nickname "Budge." There was never a day he didn't wear his hockey jacket, but I doubt he had reason to sport anything else—he was a hockey thug. These boys were fixtures. St. Paul's considered itself the American cradle of the sport, and prospective families were shown the pond where the first sticks and pucks had been used in a little nineteenth-century game called shinny. Our hockey fable culminated in the dashing figure of Hobey Baker, Form of 1909, the Philadelphia Main Line boy who became a legend on the ice at St. Paul's and Princeton, and later a World War I flying ace. People always said that Hobey Baker "had it all," meaning it was rare to find supreme athletic talent in a blue-blooded body. By the time I was at St. Paul's, the school seemed to have settled on admitting blue bloods and recruiting athletes. These dueling cultures were clear. Budge the hockey player listened to heavy-metal rock ballads and shaved the sides of his head, while the squash-playing heirs, feeling similarly restless, grew silky locks, wrote sonnets, and traded Dead bootlegs. Budge was without subtlety. I admired this, and I felt a little bit sorry for him. Also, he had a girlfriend, a girl a grade behind me who played on my soccer team. She spoke of him as though he was a wayward stray. Everything Budge said was sarcastic, everything a joke. Was he in on the fact that he was there only for what he could do on the ice? Was this the reason for the hair, the nickname, the filthy pants and semaphore jacket?

"Budge," I said.

"What's up?" he replied.

His sidekick was grinning.

Budge said nothing more, so after a moment I turned back around. This sort of thing happened with Budge—he liked to provoke you and then let the clock run out. It left you wondering if you were supposed to have done something differently.

"Hey," he said again. "I'm gonna pop your cherry."

I kept walking. Autumn light streamed in. The panels of names were honeyed with sun. *Pop your cherry.* That ugliness rattled around the majesty of the place, a horsefly trapped in a cathedral. The beauty was immune to the puerile, and the puerile unmoved by beauty.

"Okay, Budge," I said, without interest. "Whatever."

"Okay?" His voice tightened. "You mean it?" Two paces, three. His buddy chuckled and I startled. They had closed the space behind me. "You said okay."

My back to them, I shook my head and rolled my eyes. *Sure. Whatever.* But I was losing my grip on the casual. Because how did he know I was a virgin? Why did he care? What about his girlfriend? If he was not worried about her, what other rules would he transgress?

"I'm serious," called Budge. I heard heat in his voice, and his buddy fell silent. "I'm going to be your first."

He wanted me, because he knew that for me, now, there would actually be no *first.* Whatever had been innocent was gone, and this was why he was trailing me down the hall on the way to math class, to loot what was left after the smashup. I hated him. If my virginity had been a ring, I'd have ripped it off and hurled it at him right there, to get it the hell off my hand. I'd have let it clatter to the floor.

"I'm gonna do it," he said, as I pressed through the doors and out into the morning.

Around this time, in the first days and weeks after the assault, I became aware of a curious mind's-eye perspective I had never held before. I saw myself as if from high above, moving across campus, going from dorm to Schoolhouse and back again. Whenever I crossed a quad, I saw the top of my own head, way down there, progressing right to left. When I approached the Schoolhouse or chapel, buildings with their own gravity, I watched myself as a tiny figure being pulled in, as though I were about to be swallowed up.

I was always so far away as to be featureless, almost a speck, and my vulnerability was clear. How exposed I was, walking the paths! My progress across campus seemed terribly slow; it took me forever to get back inside. Why didn't I run? The tiny-self moved about her days, oblivious to danger, almost automated in her ignorance.

But there was also the self up here, perched aloft and fretting. And there was the rapacious threat that I sensed for my self-on-the-ground, born in my own mind, the way that all of our nightmares are entirely our own. So that when I saw myself push through the doors of Wing and head out into the morning, sugar maples burning themselves alive on either side of me and sky blue blue blue, I willed myself to get away from Budge as fast as I could. But also I imagined turning and taking him on. Also I imagined *being* him, and how easy it would be to ruin me. Maybe, if that happened, this tiny person would go away, and I could be free?

Several days after the assault—maybe four, maybe five—I began to feel properly ill. Feverish, achy, my neck wrapped in painful lumps that rose up under my ears. I welcomed such persistent, credible sensations of dis-ease. I would have to take care of myself.

There was pleasure in the untethered focus that proper flu

demands. This did not mean slacking off my classwork, or failing to deliver assignments. It was more an unshackling from constant vigilance of my own performance. I did not care who was looking at me on the way to class—I had a fever, I was deep in a scarf. I did not care whether a missed hello was intentional—I was unwell, I might not have heard. Shivering suited me. There were things I was trying to shake off, after all, and I sat there quivering like a dog in my chapel seat, letting my eyes go soft over the rows of faces in the long pews across the way. Our chapel was among the oldest and largest examples of Gothic ecclesiastical architecture in the nation. It seated eight hundred and was nowhere near capacity even with all of us in our assigned spots, four mornings a week and occasional Sundays. Its majesty seemed always to contain some rebuke. We gathered, I felt, like pebbles at the bottom of a deep lake. You could never amass enough to reach the daylight.

In my line of sight was a stained-glass window with biblical script:

> *Now get up and go into the city and you will be told what*
> *you must do*
> *The knowledge of the secrets of the Kingdom of God has been*
> *given to you.*

It scans well, and I tried to take in its almost-pragmatic message of encouragement. Walking the path to classes, I had its beat in my head: *Now get up and go. Now get up and go.* There was no city, but I substituted a hazy notion of future. I liked to think there was a direction for me, however much solitude it might demand, however much loneliness.

In the library one evening after Seated Meal I pulled out a Bible, alive with silverfish, and looked it up.

The lines, as it turns out, are a biblical mashup. The first, *Now get up and go,* is Acts 9: the voice Saul hears on the Road to Damascus when, thrown to the ground by the light of God, he looks up at the sky and asks, "Who are you, Lord?"

Jesus replies:

I am Jesus, whom you are persecuting. Now get up and go into the city, and you will be told what you must do.

Saul becomes Paul—the apostle and great teacher of first-century Christianity, and not incidentally the patron saint of my boarding school.

In spite of my illness and sense of crisis in those days, I liked that there was a window telling the story of Saul's transformation. We were all of us being exhorted to become somebody better, somebody new, at that school. It was nice to see a founding narrative quietly waiting to be discovered, to be reminded that we weren't the only ones.

The second line in the window, about the knowledge of the secrets of God, is from Matthew. As Matthew tells it, Jesus has just finished teaching the parable of the sower, which is a challenging one. In the telling, seeds are scattered over paths and rocky places—shallow soil and soil choked with thorns— and nothing grows. Only the seeds that fall on rich land will produce. Presumably the Word of God, just so, will be wasted on improper hearts. I always wondered why God didn't just help people understand. And anyway, is there not also a place for paths and rocky places and thorns? Is this not Creation too?

The disciples agreed with me. They ask Jesus why he teaches in tricky parables, and he replies, "Because the knowledge of the secrets of the kingdom of heaven has been given to you, but not to them."

But not to them. They left that part off the bright glass.

Do you really need it?

This chapel window offered up the school's soul: the commanding of a divine mission backed by an assurance of superior knowledge. The light fell through it and jeweled my entire row.

2

Fall 1989, Fourth Form

Our first year at school, our fourth-form year, my urban friends, Washington and New York, shared a double room beneath the eaves of their dorm, with sharply slanted ceilings, and we used to sit on their sofa and talk about things boarding school could not deliver. Because of the alcove space, the room was long and dark. One high dormer window above the sofa opened over the roofs of other dorms and the crowns of the trees, so we could hear voices coming up from the quad but not see their owners.

What was grim about it made it fabulous. Lovely girls trapped in a tall tower—we could work with that. The girl from New York stroked her long hair with a Mason Pearson hairbrush ("You don't have one? Don't you know the others will break your hair?") and the girl from D.C. practiced tying scarves to sit just so across her collarbone. They applied face creams. "Here, touch, see how soft," said New York, presenting her face to me like a child. Her forehead was entirely smooth, where mine was stippled with acne. Had she noticed my skin? The way she presented herself, her surfaces, for my inspection and my touch, stunned and soothed me. She was not comparing us or judging me. We were always looking only at her.

She took me into the bathroom to teach me how to make myself throw up: "Just open up and take it all the way in. Like you're giving head." I made accommodating gagging noises from my stall alongside hers. *Fellatio* was what she meant. I was to stick my hand down my own throat. Why would I want to make myself puke? "Cool," I told her.

Plans were afoot for them to sign out for the weekend and travel with their boyfriends to Martha's Vineyard, to stay in someone's parents' house. Lies would be told. Parents were not consulted. This was astonishing to me. The trip involved plane travel, and I was not even sure that was legal—weren't there officials of some kind to monitor these things? But New York picked up the pay phone in the hall by the back door and read the numbers off her credit card. If I asked who Martha was, my friends laughed and laughed, watching me for the tell. When it didn't come, they laughed even harder and said, "Oh my God, you're so cute!" I did not ask the things I really wanted to know: What happened when you spent a weekend with a senior? What did you eat? What happened at bedtime? Did you brush your teeth, your hair? What did you wear?

"We have to get you a boyfriend," said New York.

D.C. had ideas. None of them were good.

"Let me talk to Russ," said New York, of her new beau. "He'll come up with someone."

He did. A senior on the wrestling team who was game to "hang out" with me. This boy, Shep, was cute—blue-eyed, with a too-thin top lip that gave him a rabbit smile, but it was sweet, and he was growing into it. With a bit of insouciance, it would have made for a nice come-hither curl. Analogies were prominent in our classwork, *this* is to *this* as *that* is to *that,* of angles or adjectives, and I understood that Shep was to Russ as I was to New York. There was no romance to this but the geometry of high school popularity. I thought it was a fine idea.

Shep had a caveat.

Her name was Shyla, and she was a fourth former too. She looked, to my eyes, like a pinup model: glamour-puss lips, blinky blue eyes so large and bright you thought they might close automatically when you laid her down. She was oddly independent, not falling in with the sort of crowd her looks would suggest. I had yet to work out the catch here, the reason why she wasn't considered a bombshell. Was she poor? Was she too smart? Was she crazy? She did wear this bulky wool coat, with wooden-toggle closures and a fur-lined hood, when the done thing was a light outdoorsy sweater or (arms crossed, refusing the shiver) nothing but short sleeves. Did someone know her from before, such that she trailed a horrible home-town tale?

I liked Shyla. She smiled and said hello, and lots of people didn't.

So, my New York friend told me, Shep was going to choose one of us. We were each to write a note explaining why we wanted to be his girlfriend and place these notes by lunch-time in his student mailbox at the post office at the center of campus. He would come to the library that night and tell us who had won his favor.

Odd, that we, the girls, were the suitors, and the older boy the prize. Even I sensed that something was off. But what did I know? My friend was smiling her perfect, delightful, seed-corn smile, and rubbing her hands together as if to warm them before setting them on chilly me. "Let's do this," she said. "He will choose you."

I wrote:

Dear Shep,

I hope to see you tonight at the library.

Lacy

I folded the notebook paper and addressed it to him. He had a famous name, and I thought it might appeal to him that I was an ordinary person, not afraid to use normal words and say simple things. Maybe he'd think I was unimpressed, which would make me impressive. Besides, I didn't know what else I might have said. I hoped my brevity conveyed sophistication.

After dinner I went to the library and waited. Other students filed in one at a time—the shy or exceptionally studious. The more gregarious among us were involved in activities or clubs, practicing debate and rehearsing shows, or visiting each other's dorms. According to the practice of "intervisitation," a girl could visit a boy's room and vice versa, but three rules applied: door open, lights on, three feet on the floor.

I remember how my mother laughed when she first heard this rule, at orientation that fall. The laugh escaped her throat and floated free, and other mothers turned to look. I didn't understand their curiosity because I didn't understand the rule. Nowhere in my imagination was the implied danger—namely, kids on the dorm-room bed. Instead, hearing "three feet on the floor," I dreamed up a student standing one-legged, like a flamingo. Would it be the boy or the girl? I was gulping down information in those first days, and with particular urgency in the hours before my parents kissed me good-bye and drove back down to Boston for their flight home. Impressions burrowed deep. When I remember "intervis," my mind still conjures teenagers balancing in the raw-bulbed light of a dormitory single.

At the library, aged fourteen, waiting for Shep, I wasn't sure what I was supposed to be doing, so I wandered the poorly lit reading room. A set of black books on a low shelf were stamped with red swastikas. I reached for one and let it open in my hand. Tiny print described a scene from a Nazi killing field that remains to this day the most horrifying thing I have ever read. I have never again seen a description of that same grotesque act forced upon the condemned. I grew dizzy and the print swam. Could this be real? Could any of this be real? I closed the book on my thumb and looked up and around. I had forgotten about Shep. I forced myself to reread the page, and then again, and then, nauseated and terrified and very far from home, I went to the bathroom and tried to make myself throw up.

Shep didn't show.

My New York friend explained the next day: Shyla had tucked into his post-office box a blue satin bra and a note that read, "If you want to see the other piece of this set, meet me in my room tonight."

Even New York was impressed.

Blue satin bras and killing pits were ever after twinned in my mind. The one, in its self-conscious cupidity, limned the depths of the other. All at once I appreciated the depravity and banality of the human animal. I was positively wearied by wisdom. Shyla's bra, my friends and I discussed at length. The horror page stayed secret in my mind. Silly gorgeous girls, they weren't ready for that sort of knowledge. Not yet and maybe not ever.

I got my bras on hometown outings with my mother to Mimi's, which was pronounced "Mimmy's" and did not sell blue satin anything. The ladies made Cs with their wrinkled fingers and pressed them to my rib cage. Baby hangers tinkled like xylophones. The place smelled like peonies.

The Holocaust was more interesting to me than bras or Shep or, for that matter, sex—unless it was, as it might have been, an elaborate unconscious substitution for the threat of sex. (You, a girl, are waiting to meet a boy. Which book do you pick up? One that looks inviting, or one that looks forbidding?) Death for sex, terror for maturation—there's a well-traveled path there, of course. At fourteen, I suppose, I found what I imagined of war less frightening than the possibility of a boy's body on mine.

I beheld Shyla's triumph without regret or envy. The entire experience was clarifying. I was not a girl who belonged to boys. I had known that already. Nor did I long for what such girls had: men to squire them to island retreats when it all got too dreary, badger-bristle brushes for their hair.

I went back to the library. This was the school's old library, which was decommissioned a year later, following the completion of the enormous Robert A. M. Stern–designed new library across the way. The old library was squat and gray, all stone, and built so close to the edge of the pond in the center of campus that from many angles it appeared to rise out of the water. I never picked up the Nazi book again, though I kept my eye on it from the couches, the way you watch a spider on the wall. The library took me in most nights that fall. In the cold blaze of novelty of the first months at school, I had forgotten this simple thing about myself: that I loved books.

There was something else new, too. If I played my cards right, this school might offer the world—devastated and astonishing—to me.

Among all the silly questions and squirrely concerns traded with my two friends that first semester at St. Paul's, there was one thing I said that caused them to stop and listen: I mentioned, casually, that a man wanted to fly his plane up to see me.

"Wait, who is he?" asked New York. She had been filing her fingernails with a silver emery board, and now the *zip-zip* sound stopped. Her head was tipped, her lips pink, and she was looking right at me.

A nascent instinct for seduction told me not to give his name. "He works with my dad," I said. Not true—he was one of the sons of a storied financial institution, and back home in Chicago my dad worked for an investment arm of that institution. I wasn't sure if this man worked at all. "He takes me to lunch in the city."

This was true. I had taken the train downtown the previous summer with my father, who then went on to the office. Mr. Lane chose an Italian restaurant in the gallery district, hip and loud. I drank iced tea and concentrated on not spilling on my dress. I had gotten everything right: I remembered to

32

kiss him on both cheeks, the way he preferred to be greeted; I remembered to thank him for everything, I remembered the books I was reading when he asked. (St. Paul's had assigned *The Unbearable Lightness of Being* as summer reading. This is incredible to me now—that this novel, with its themes of loveless sex and careless coupling, could have been required reading for sophomores—but Mr. Lane seemed unsurprised. He nodded and sipped, and smiled wet teeth.) I made him laugh.

"It's important," said my mother, "to have adults like that in your life. It's an honor that he wants to spend time with you."

New York nodded coolly—lunch with a man did not impress her. My mom was right, then—one had to have adults like this in one's life.

My Washington friend was Catholic, the daughter of a European mother. "Is he like a godfather?" she asked.

The Lanes had surged into our world once my father joined the firm that bore their name. We'd moved to a bigger house closer to town and begun to meet different sorts of families from the city, where Dad now worked. He spoke of having gotten a late start to his career, and his path in early adulthood formed a founding narrative for my brother and me, since the story was about fairness, luck, and the value of education. As a senior in college my father had been awarded a Rhodes Scholarship, but in spring 1968, a few months before he was due to head to England, President Lyndon Johnson ended graduate-school deferments for men seeking to delay service in Vietnam. Dad's hometown of St. Louis had already been under pressure regarding the inequitable use of student deferrals. He was told he'd be classified 1-A and called up immediately.

Dad abandoned his Rhodes and presented himself to a Navy recruiter. He and Mom spent the first years of their marriage in Fairfax, Virginia, where Dad was able to take advantage of an unusual program for enlisted men who possessed special skills in urgent demand: his then-esoteric fascination with the first mainframe processors had prepared him for work programming shipboard computers. He never so much as set sail as a Navy man, but what did disappear over the horizon was the life he had imagined would follow his Oxford degree. I'd grown up hearing about Dad's fellow Rhodes honorees—chief among them young Bill Clinton—who had secured exceptions to the new draft rules. There was always the sense thereafter of catching up to where my parents felt we belonged.

Mr. and Mrs. Lane were a sign that all was in order. They adopted my parents very much the way my first St. Paul's friends adopted me: immediately, with the conviction of rescue, and with all attendant expectation of gratitude. Never mind. It was an invitation to the ball. His name was a monument and she was even better, a tiny heiress who had grown up adored in the hills of North Carolina.

The Lanes were sponsors, in a way, of my leaving for boarding school. If they had done it, then this was how it was done.

"He's sort of a godfather," I told Washington. "He wasn't there at my christening, but he's really involved now."

New York said, "Married?"

"Definitely."

"Do you like her?"

"I love her," I told my friends.

I thought Mr. Lane hardly deserved her. They lived in a five-story brownstone on the loveliest of Chicago's Gold Coast streets, but she answered the door barefoot, with no makeup, and took you by the hand. No child was made to feel like a child and no woman was made to feel unwelcome. She gave terrific gifts, silver cases and blown-glass bottles nestled in striped boxes. I've rarely seen her conspiratorial blend of secrets and goodwill. Her circle was clever and close. Her children, younger by a few years than my brother and me, were lucky devils.

Mr. Lane's beard bothered me. I was unimpressed by his story of racing sports cars without headlights over country roads in Michigan. (I was more interested in my mother's report of how he had bitten into a chocolate truffle at a dinner party and, finding half a pistachio inside, excused himself to the bathroom to inject himself with epinephrine before he died. It was a startling example of an adult's vulnerability, which I did not often see. It was also, of course, a story about what a person might do without disrupting a dinner party—about what manners could conceal.) But my father thought he was great fun, and can I blame my parents for thinking it a kind of triumph when my dad was asked to join the small group of men who crewed on Mr. Lane's yacht each August, cruising the Aeolian Islands?

It was really something, that he had taken me to lunch. And I had done so well that he'd said he would fly his plane to New Hampshire to take me to supper, once I had begun at St. Paul's. I hadn't even taken this idea seriously before now. Why hadn't I seen the riches in my hand?

"What kind of plane?" asked New York.

"I don't know. He flies it himself."

She worked on this for a bit, then said, "You should do it. When's he coming?"

Behold the grammar of entitlement: from the imperative *should* to the present progressive, from the provisional to the certain, just like that.

Could you do that, and have the world obey?

"Christmas," I said. Christmas sounded good.

"Oh, great. Can he take us to the Vineyard?" asked Washington.

"Don't be silly," said New York. "He's coming to see Lacy. It's amazing."

The girls looked at me differently after I told them about Mr. Lane. If I'd known, I'd have mentioned it the first day they invited me to sit with them at our welcome picnic. I'd have pinned it to my newb name tag. I'd have written that on my note to Shep.

Mr. Lane never did fly to me. But at a party that Christmas, after he'd presented me with a ribboned hat box that contained a bowler hat, his wife opened her satin clutch to allow me to peek at the pearl-handled Derringer she carried with her in the evenings. It was the first handgun I had ever seen. You will not see it again, in spite of Chekhov's imperative.

May I suggest a substitution? The gun will not go off. It will be the man.

When I called home that fall, I never asked when Mr. Lane would fly up to take me to supper. Instead I sobbed and begged my parents to let me come home. This had to be done from the pay phone behind the gym rather than the one in the basement of my dorm, because I didn't want other kids to hear. I crossed the road and stood beneath the fluorescent lights, bugs whapping and zipping, and cried until three minutes to ten, when I hung up, wiped my face, and crossed the road back to check in for the night.

My mother would get very quiet when I called from the pay phone in tears. My father would step up. "You have to give it a try. You need to stick this out."

What could I say that would sound the alarm? As a parent, I can imagine heaps of tips: Shyla's bra or my lone Holocaust investigations or purging lessons in the girls' bathroom. The full bottles of vodka that I weighed in my hands in my urban friends' room, the brands the kids loved in those years, lettering bright as aquarium fish through the liquor (not for nothing was Aleksandr Solzhenitsyn's son, who lived across the quad, nicknamed "Stoli"). What if I had mentioned the newb book, and how the girls in it were rated to two decimal points each? This was the semester my big-city friends were wild-eyed with the news that a new student in their dorm—a doll-sized cross-country runner who was as kind as she was fast—was getting beaten up by her sixth-form hockey-star boyfriend. I am trying to remember if I knew already that the dance instructor told his girls, pre-professional ballerinas, that having sex would improve their turnout. I'm trying to remember if this was the fall that sixth-form boys swapped peroxide for shampoo in the bottle belonging to a black student, so that his hair glowed as orange as the maple trees. If this was the fall they held down an American Sikh student and pried off his dastaar.

The private devastations I reported left my parents unmoved. I described the day when I heard a fifth former blasting my favorite song, a Kate Bush dirge, a floor below me and I went down onto her hall to tell her I loved it, and she just gaped at me—positively stone-ass blanked me—until I cottoned on that I was not supposed to even *be* on her hall, much less *talk* to her, because I was a new student. She continued staring as I turned around and let myself back out through the fire door, back upstairs to my newb bed in my newb room with my newb sensibilities, where I belonged.

My father said, "Oh, that's too bad."

"Maybe she's just shy," said Mom.

"Maybe she didn't hear you. You said her music was loud."

"Do you want me to call your adviser and talk about it?"

Mom would have let me come home, but Dad had a rule. "One year. You have to make it through the year, then we'll reevaluate."

I threw out my best shots: my roommate was mean, and when I got dressed the other day, she watched from across the room and told me she wished she could merge our bodies so that she had my tits and tummy but her thighs and butt.

"Maybe she meant it as a compliment."

"Yes, she envies you."

"I don't have a boyfriend."

"Well, does *everyone* have a boyfriend? I should think you'd be concentrating on your studies."

"I can't make friends."

"What about those lovely girls we met at Parents' Weekend?"

"They go to the Vineyard every weekend with their boyfriends."

"That seems inappropriate."

"Yes, better you stay at school. Use the time to meet people!"

"I don't belong here."

"Oh, but you do. The school said as much when they admitted you. How bright and capable you are."

It was cold, by then, at the pay phone. I kicked frozen gravel.

Mom said, "By the way, did you hear about Cecily?" A classmate of mine from grade school, who was among the small group from my hometown to start boarding school that fall. She'd gone to St. George's in Rhode Island. "She just came home. Gave up. She couldn't hack it."

When Thanksgiving break finally arrived and we were free to travel home, I shared a car to the airport with Gaby, a fifth former from my hometown who had gone to my small elementary school. Gaby wore her red hair cut bluntly just below her chin, and when I scooted into the back of the livery car, on the opposite end of her seat, she did not peek out from behind it, much less smile at me. I was too exhausted to care. Besides, she was taciturn in a way that I appreciated— she seemed cynical, which suggested some individuality. Also, I knew a curious fact about her: she liked to wash her feet in the sink at night. I'd learned this the year before from a ninth-grade classmate, Connor, who had spent middle school loving her hopelessly. The closest he'd gotten to dating her was a nightly telephone call of the endlessly wandering, knotted-cord sort we engaged in then. During those calls, Connor told me, Gaby washed her feet in the sink. He heard the water splashing and the slap-squeaking of her soapy hands. After Connor hung up with Gaby, he would sometimes call me just to talk about her.

I didn't mind. I wasn't interested in Connor, and in any case

I was struck by the image of Gaby, balanced before her sink, phone pressed between her shoulder and her chin, washing her feet one at a time. I was strictly a shower girl, because I was a competitive tennis player, which meant I spent summer days scalloped with crusts of sweat and sunscreen. I had never washed only my feet. It had never occurred to me. To wash only your feet struck me as so luxurious it might be inappropriate. And to do this alone, in the summer evenings, every night? It was almost a ministry of self. I loved imagining it.

Sometimes, on the phone with Connor, I'd tried putting my own toes under the faucet, but the bathroom was small and the narrow pedestal sink high, and I ended up slipping. My mother, coming up the stairs, paused on the landing. "You're not on the phone in the john, are you?"

Before I'd left for school, she arranged a lunch with Gaby and another Chicagoland Paulie, Helena, during that summer of the foot washing. Helena was the daughter of a powerful Chicago philanthropist who chaired the boards of hospitals, schools, and museums. Like Gaby, Helena was a rising fifth former. As an older girl, a returning student, and the child of a famously giving mother, she would be welcoming and kind. I would meet Helena and Gaby downtown, where Helena lived, and have lunch with them in the city. Then Gaby and I would take the Chicago & North Western commuter train an hour back north, to our hometown, and I, before even setting foot on school grounds to begin my fourth-form year, would have two friends.

It didn't turn out that way. In the parlor of the charity matron's mansion, Helena asked me who my "old girl" was— the sixth former assigned to be my advocate and buddy through my first year. I'd received a nice letter from the girl chosen for me, welcoming me to the school community. She'd heard I played tennis and wanted to introduce me to her roommate, who was number one on the team. She promised to find me as soon as I arrived on campus to help me learn my way around. When I named this girl, Helena and Gaby aimed red faces at each other, then fell to laughing.

I couldn't think what I'd done to cause this response. Maybe there was no one there by that name? Maybe I had said it—*Susie*—wrong?

"Nothing," said Helena, finally. "She's just kind of a loser."

"Oh."

"She's kind of . . . big."

"Oh."

I was either too young or too impressionable to respond to cruelty with anger. Instead I set about recalibrating my world. I concluded that the sixth former who had written to me was not in fact kind and inviting, but a big loser. I'd get to school and I'd work out why.

Then they asked what dorm I'd been assigned. Warren House, I told them, pleased that I remembered what had been written on the white form letter mailed to my home. This time their faces stayed aghast. Could it be any worse? Was I marked for misery in some way?

"No, nothing," said Helena again. "It's just a new dorm, way out away from, like, everything."

Well, at least I'd know where the center of campus was, and where it was desirable to be.

"I don't know anyone in Warren," added Helena, as if I weren't clear on who she was by now.

Gaby turned to her. "Kelly got shafted into Warren."

This was the girl whose music would summon me down to her floor, and whose icing would send me wordlessly straight back up again. The knowledge of it would drop into my mind like a coin into a slot as I stood there staring at her staring at me. *Kelly. Of course. You got shafted into Warren.* She was a friend to these girls, but I knew nothing about any of it sitting there in Helena's living room, waiting to head out for a summer lunch.

"Oh, right," said Helena. "That sucks."

On the way to the restaurant, Helena took Gaby's arm ahead of me on the sidewalk. I kept up so I could hear them talk. "Wow, Gab," she said. "We're fifth formers now."

I could think of nothing to say. I was obsessing over big Susie and my hopeless dorm. The cold exhilaration of total uncertainty had been replaced by the certainty of gloom. After lunch, which was in the café of the Neiman Marcus store on Michigan Avenue (my mother had zipped a few twenties into my little canvas purse to treat), Helena hailed a cab. I guessed Gaby and I would head back home. It was sooner than I'd hoped—nothing good had happened, and I had hoped for something good—but I'd be relieved to settle onto the train. Maybe Gaby and I could talk. We had Connor in common. We had summer evenings in our small town in common. And this big New Hampshire school, which I was slated to begin.

Helena stepped forward to open the taxi door for me—so polite, so adult—here, finally, was the daughter of the mother I'd heard so much about. I slid onto the seat. With Gaby on the pavement beside her, she called out "Chicago and North

Western Station," slammed the door, and the driver pulled away from the curb. They were rid of their charge.

The city block slid along the windshield, slipped so easily across its face as we moved forward. I was surprised by the back of the driver's head. Would he talk to me? What should I say?

It was fine. What fourteen-year-old can't take the train alone? Still, I piped up and asked the driver to take me to the address of my dad's office in the inner Loop instead. Nobody but Dad expressed surprise to see me there, alone at midday, so I waited, reading in a chair, until I could ride home with him.

Now that I was an actual fourth former, in my faraway crappy dorm with my loser old girl, poor Gaby still had to ride with me back and forth to school. Our mothers had arranged this, and I felt sorry for Gaby that she had to suffer it. I'd have been happy to take the bus into Boston and transfer to Logan Airport by myself, finding solidarity in the apathy of public transportation, but that would have terrified my parents. Early on the morning that we were released for Thanksgiving, I climbed into the livery car to find not only Gaby but her boyfriend, too. He was the son of the scion, and the car was his treat.

"Huh. You're Lacy," he said.

I said hello. The leather seat was delicious—deep gray and soft as a cat.

"You're also from Lake Forest," he said.

His stating the obvious made me nervous—like he was calling my bluff. What was I supposed to say to these things?

But this boy, Stewart, was smiling. "Another Lake Forester," he said. "Another little Lake Forest redhead." Cajoling. I saw now why he was smiling: it *was* silly, how similar we all were, the Waspy girls from the same towns.

I nodded. "I am."

"Lake Forest is like the Greenwich of the Midwest," he mocked. Stewart was himself on the way home to Connecticut. "You guys are so sweet to be proud of your snooty little prairie town." He nudged Gaby, and I saw through the scrim of her hair how her cheeks rose in a smile. "I always tease Gaby that she lives in a junior-varsity suburb. You're JV Greenwich. You guys aren't starters. But that's cool. We like you anyway."

I loved him for saying this. I loved him for finally calling out one tiny corner of the vast labyrinth of hierarchies that ruled the world of St. Paul's School. Status was our first language, one that had to be learned, instantly, if you did not arrive fluent (and many students did); and it functioned like some primitive, instinctive form of communication beneath the surface of every exchange. We knew the grammar of privilege (lacrosse over track and field, low-slung corduroys over khakis, old station cars over luxury vehicles) and could infer from silence where the greatest power lay. You could not discuss the hierarchy, and in any case we had no words for it. In fact, where it held sway, there *were* no words. No student from an old Boston Brahmin family would ever admit to knowing her name was iconic, or that it was, say, carved on a lintel beneath which we passed every day. This is why they laughed so hard when I asked who Martha was, and where you could buy her wine.

Say what you will about Stewart's father, he actually worked for a living. The taurine jowls of the man's face, pixelated on A1 of my dad's newspaper, were still boyish cheeks on

44

Stew, and the son's eyes were round and sympathetic. Just the fact of being a known quantity set Stewart outside that first, almost royal set of Paulies—kids who passed without any wake through the halls that held their granddaddies' ghosts, winning prizes and gaining admission to Ivy League schools and needing nothing, troubling nothing, admiring nothing. Their families summered on islands where homes cannot be bought. Their fathers worked, if at all, with silent currents of cash. When you discovered that someone's mom's name was Abigail Adams, well, believe it. There were no accidents.

"Tom Buchanan had his polo ponies brought up from Lake Forest," I told Stewart. I'd read *Gatsby* right around the time my family moved from a small development to a larger home on a main road, the summer I was twelve. Across the street was a country club that had at its founding been a polo club. I liked to imagine that Daisy's horses had been stabled there, beneath the trees I could see from my window—enormous oak and ash crowns that moved softly at night.

"Yeah," said Stew. "He bought them in Lake Forest and got them the hell out of the Midwest."

Gaby hit him, and after he flinched, he reached, laughing, and took her fist so he could unfold her fingers and hold her hand.

In Stew's limo we escaped the gates of the school with its demure white sign, and traveled down Pleasant Street toward Concord and the river, and from there to the highways. I kept my face to the glass to give the couple space. I saw each clutch of forest and granite escarpment for the first and last time, dignified it with my seeing, and bade it all farewell. St. Paul's just wasn't going to work out. I was thinking about the ponies, was my problem. I wanted to understand *them* (How were they chosen? Who loaded them into the trailers? Who rode east with them? Who greeted them when they arrived?) when I should have been, like everyone, smitten with Daisy, and the whisperings and the champagne and the stars.

"It's the Crawford Curse," said my mother about my dorm assignment, my old girl assignment, my infelicitous roommate situation. "Things never work out for us."

That hadn't been the case before St. Paul's, as I remembered. And to most anyone observing my family from the outside, things were working out quite well indeed. So the problem was me. Was I.

My parents always did say I was *sensitive*. "You're being very dramatic," said my dad, finding himself unable to imagine what I felt. I learned from a young age to anticipate moments when I was likely to come in for this response. In the eighth grade, I'd been subjected for a short while to a particularly ingenious bit of bullying from a male classmate who used a portable tape recorder to record me in class and then replayed awkward moments over and over to a clutch of other boys in the hall. They held themselves and shook with laughter. I went home hived from crying. My father called the boy's mother, who ordered her son to produce his tape recorder. I sniffled politely while Dad listened through the phone, so assured in my indignation that I felt almost sorry for the tape-recording monster.

But Dad's face settled, then brightened. "Oh," he said. "I see." He turned to me, relaxed and frank: "There's no reason for you to be upset. I heard the tape. It's just recordings of you answering questions in class. You sound very bright. I'd actually be proud."

"Dad," I said, still crying, still twelve years old. How could I explain? "This makes me want to kill myself."

He frowned. "I don't think that's a solution."

Then there had been a period, following eighth grade, when for six weeks or so I became inconsolable just as the sun began to sink toward late afternoon. This was in summer when I could find no clear reason for sorrow. Long light on the oaks and elms. Two parents, a younger brother, some toy spaniel dogs (we bred them, so for a few years there were puppies). Tennis lessons and afternoons at the pool and church on Sundays. Yet that summer, I watched the sun begin to set and grew nauseated with terror. I was aware that the crisis concerned death, but I had no way of working with that awareness. What frightened me was not the idea of an ending—mine or anyone else's—but the glimpses I thought I was catching, in panicky micro-bolts, of nothing. *Nothing!* The idea of it sent my belly dropping like a trapdoor. The universe tended toward nothing. Relentless nothing. Arcs of cold white bending away to invisible warps in space-time (I had read Stephen Hawking, at my dad's suggestion) and nowhere, not anywhere, a hand or a heart. The terror was unsolvable because no light could survive that dark. It awaited me. I had no choice.

"That's *Huis Clos,*" said my mom, when I tried to describe my crisis. *"No Exit."* Mom had grown up in Europe, where her stepfather worked. She spoke five languages and read four. She had her hands in a bowl of fruit salad when she told me about Sartre, tossing everything but bananas with a generous snow of sugar, orange juice, and a splash of Grand Marnier. She popped a blueberry into her mouth. "It's about the trap of mortality. I think we even have it in the library."

I walked, weeping, down the hall. Our small den was walled with bookshelves and had a window that faced east, where the yard was in dusk. There were no soft last beams of light here. Just a shaggy hedge, friendly, settling in for the night beneath a cover of gnats. Maybe I was wrong—maybe what terrified me was not darkness but the relinquishing of light, the letting go. I stood for a moment watching the cool yard, and then I searched the shelves for *Huis Clos* so I could get this death thing sorted out.

The bookcases were terrain I knew well. My father's sections: photography, physics, chess openings. My mother's: fiction, classics, theology. Half a wall of *Encyclopædia Britannica,* an ancient family Bible, and, in the cabinet beneath, my mother's portfolio from her days as a model, in London, before she married my dad. She'd been a ringer for Kate Moss, but with better teeth. I'd lie on the carpet and turn pages of her. This was the only room in our house where I was allowed to roam. Every new discovery introduced a complication, but it's ever thus with knowledge: I'd read *Roots* in the fifth grade and spent weeks feeling almost betrayed that my mustachioed science teacher used the word *flux* to refer to simple scientific variability when, in this magnificent book, it meant diarrhea suffered by slaves. Everything I knew about sex came from the *Clan of the Cave Bear* series, the orphaned white woman raised by Neanderthals finally finding the lone white man who is wandering prehistoric Earth, looking for her. In a somewhat related investigation, I'd stolen the instructions from a box of Tampax in my mother's bathroom cabinet and, finding no correlation between the illustration and my own body, snuck the page into the den to look for clues in the anatomical transparencies in the *A* volume of the *Encyclopædia*.

Sartre was not present on my parents' shelves, but (in the French section now) I thought *Les Fleurs du Mal* sounded right. For the next few days I worked the poems with my French-English dictionary. Baudelaire did not help. "I find comfort in knowing that I will be with my Lord in heaven," said my father, which also did not help. Sitting in my lit closet with the door closed while the night murdered the day sometimes helped.

This season of fear when I was thirteen lifted as mysteriously as it had lowered. I was able to eat again. I took new comfort in the way my mother left radios on in various rooms and switched on the network news every night promptly at five-thirty. Other adult things began to make sense: cocktails, fast cars, the prattle of gossip. I reshelved Baudelaire.

I knew it marked me, to be this vulnerable, but I couldn't stop the questions from coming into my mind, nor the sadness that followed them like fish on a line. My only hope had been to bury it all beneath sweetness and hard work. I was resigned to be a pretender.

But St. Paul's was shrewd. The wheels of the school's fates picked out my darkness and assigned me a lonely old girl and a lonely dorm room and a lonely and angry roommate, and the stone library offered up not dates but death scenes. There was a shaking out to the place, a reckoning of the sort that spiritually dynamic spots—mountains, graveyards—are known to deliver. I could not thrive, I thought that first fall, and my parents would not let me come home.

At the airport, I thanked Stewart and then walked purposefully alone into the terminal so Gaby could kiss him goodbye.

I didn't see her again, not checking in for our flight or on the plane to O'Hare, not in the terminal, not at the curb where my mother waited in the car. How did Gaby do that, just disappear into the world like any other adult on her way home? If I was going to stay at St. Paul's, something would have to change.

I found my answer in my parents' house the afternoon I arrived for Thanksgiving break, in a glossy magazine on the kitchen counter. This was the year *Vanity Fair* ran William Styron's essay about his suicidal depression, and the headline, "Darkness Visible," spoke to me as if by name. I snatched the magazine and took it into my closet and closed the door.

Mom had warned, looking at the magazine in my hand: "Styron writes about a woman who has to choose which of her children will die in the Holocaust."

I knew he was my guy. In particular I was struck by this:

The fading evening light—akin to that famous "slant of light" of Emily Dickinson's, which spoke to her of death, of chill extinction—had none of its familiar autumnal loveliness, but ensnared me in a suffocating gloom.

Solemnly, so as to preserve credibility, I waved the magazine at my mother and said, "This is me. I'm chemically depressed."

I am not surprised that she agreed. My sobbing phone calls from St. Paul's would have exhausted and unnerved her. Within days I had an appointment with a top adolescent psychiatrist who was—my luck!—enrolling patients for a study. How convenient it would have been to determine that my brain was the problem. I wished this, too: much easier to take a drug than give up our dream of my schooling. And it was an interesting problem I'd introduced—chemical depression was then still new, still a bit fancy. "Maybe things are starting to turn around for you," said Mom, after securing the appointment at Northwestern Memorial, in downtown Chicago. "Things are looking up."

Dr. Derek Miller was British and had worked alongside Anna Freud in London. His accent alone would have sunk me, but the gravitas of his dark suit and hard squint made me want to be the best depressive I could possibly be. The study was to investigate the effects of brand-new Prozac in adolescent patients. There were actual Rorschach tests, white cards with black splotches. I proposed that one was a butterfly on a windshield. I thought I was reaching a bit when I described another as a mother holding her dead child. But hey, Styron! Dr. Miller mentioned this last one to my mom in his private conversation with her following my assessment. When she repeated it to me—*cradling a dead child!*—she sounded almost proud.

The doctor agreed that my marked clinical depression and associated lack of self-esteem were unlikely to abate on their own. The cause was almost definitely some combination of a strong biological predilection and certain environmental conditions, the specifics of which were unknown to him. We didn't stay long to talk.

Dr. Miller wrote to Ms. Shay, my adviser at school, to work out how I could retrieve my medication. The school didn't want me to keep it in my dorm room—Prozac was new then, and the school worried about pills getting lost or stolen. It was determined that the infirmary would hold the bottle, and

I'd visit once a week for seven capsules in a matchbox-sized manila envelope. I kept them in the top drawer of my school-issue dresser, beneath my socks and underwear and alongside the dish towel–sized remnant of my baby blanket, Nigh-Nigh. Almost every newb had some transitional object hidden away. Get to know someone well enough and you'd discover a bear in a jacket pocket or the frayed rabbit that lived beneath the pillow. I even knew boys with Legos that they said were for math class somehow.

I told no one about my Prozac. There was no need. After all, I wasn't seeing the school counselor, the way some students were, for emotional distress. I certainly hadn't been referred to the psychiatrist who visited campus a few days a week to see more troubled students. Dr. Miller thought I was well supported. He wrote to Ms. Shay that he did not feel I needed to see a psychotherapist at that time, but that I should be discouraged from calling home at all hours in tears. Perhaps I could call him instead, he suggested. I never did.

Anyone well-versed in narratives of sexual assault might sense here the gathering contours of a familiar landscape: this girl is a damaged girl. She's damaged in a way that makes her needy, that will cause her to seek out the inappropriate, transgress the proper, and probably lie. I mean, come on, the kid was on Prozac before Prozac had even been approved for use in children! There's something just off about her already. We catch the wobble. Would it surprise you that this child came in for trouble in the coming months? Wouldn't you expect just that?

This bias sits as brightly in my mind as anyone's. I hesitate to mention Dr. Miller. And it's true that I would not have considered him part of this story, had the school not later done what it did. After those winter consultations I never saw the doctor again. But when we send a child into someone else's care, we take pains to detail *everything* that our child might possibly need, every possible reaction or concern, as a defense against the unknown. My parents let the school know all about Dr. Miller's assessment, and how he'd prescribed Prozac for me. The school, acting *in loco parentis,* therefore had a record of my every possible vulnerability. I took my pill once a day, as directed, and felt certain, because they'd told me this, that no one would ever have to know.

3

Fall 1990, Fifth Form

Ten days or so after the assault, just before Halloween of my fifth-form year, my throat began to hurt in a jagged way, as though I had swallowed a piece of glass and it would not go down. In the dining hall, I sipped ice water onto my tongue and then tipped my head back to let it run down my throat, because the act of swallowing caused the glass-edge to grind into me again. When I got really hungry, I did this with skim milk. The milk filled me up more than water did.

Back in Brewster House, where I was assigned my fifth-form year without any of the friends I had signed up to live with (unfortunate lottery, said the school; Crawford Curse at work again, said Mom), I went to the bathroom at odd hours so I could be alone to lean over the sinks, put my face right up against the mirror, and open my mouth as wide as possible.

There was never anything to see. I'd close my mouth and look at my reflection, as though there might be traces visible on my skin. Instead, I saw my whole family staring back at me. I had my father's eyes, hazel and smaller than my mother's, and not wonderfully wide-set like hers. I had his mouth and chin, too, with thin lips. My high forehead was from my mother's mother—a mark of intelligence, she claimed—and already I saw in my squared jaw my father's mother's profile, held in lamplight over her needlepoint. Entirely mine were the remnants of an underbite that, until it was corrected via years of orthodontic procedures, gave me the dogged expression of a TV orphan—in every photo from my earliest years, I look determined as hell. My brother pulled from our grandfather the light blue eyes. But I got Mom's cheekbones, and from the redhead genes that hopscotched through the generations on my father's side I'd lucked into the strawberry-blond hair that my mother called "glorious." It was my great-great-grandfather George Lacy Crawford who'd last had red hair, and I was given his name.

However imperfectly they all came together in me, I was theirs, and they wanted this school for me. So much so that my parents had been willing to send me across the country to receive what they believed was, hands down, the best education the nation could offer. Saliva accumulated in my mouth. I'd spit in the sink and then open my mouth again, wider, and peer down my nose until my eyeballs ached because there had to be *something* there. If I could find it, I could deal with it.

I understood that this was happening because of what I had done. I just didn't understand how. I knew the morality but not the mechanism. It didn't matter. I accepted completely that if you suck two dicks in a boys' room after hours, you will end up with a Pharaonic visitation in the part of your body they rammed.

This seems an appropriate time to mention that my mother was (is) a priest.

To be precise, she was the first woman from Chicago to be ordained a priest in the Episcopal Diocese of Chicago, in 1987, the year I was twelve.

We had always been churchgoers, every Sunday at 9 a.m., unless you were actively vomiting. My father was a regular reader of the lessons and served on the vestry. I was baptized in the same church where my parents were married and my grandparents would one day be buried. Our fealty was total. Our piety was of the Episcopalian sort that places great importance on the clothes you wear to worship Jesus the homeless Jewish carpenter before driving straight from church to the country club for brunch among other families who, like you, are white, Anglican, wealthy, and heteronormative, because nobody else is permitted to join.

"What is there to understand?" said my father, when I was finally adult enough to ask. "I'm a Christian, and this is my club."

Discreetly, Dad wore a metal cross on a cord around his neck, never visible beneath his Turnbull & Asser shirts and Hermès ties. Nights he read to my brother and me, and after switching off the lights we recited the Lord's Prayer and our God Blesses, naming every member of the family and all pets, teddy bears, bikes, blankies, and assorted teachers and friends. When Dad ran in the mornings, his five daily miles before dawn, he told me, he prayed. He talked to Jesus about his life, his family, his questions. He'd come home and have breakfast with the papers and make the 7 a.m. train to the city, returning twelve hours later to a beautifully cooked supper from his wife, who, the year my brother was born, when I was almost five, decided to begin seminary.

Of the two of them, Dad was by far the more devout. He talked about God and the church without irony or ambivalence. Mom worried about getting her nails done before celebrating the Eucharist. She chafed at the constant use of the male pronoun in the Book of Common Prayer, and would loudly sing, at the doxology, "Blessed is *she* who comes in the name of the Lord." She was willing to spill wonderful details from the back-of-house operations, such as the silent jockeying that went on, when more than one priest was presiding over a service, to determine who would have to polish off the wine in the chalice (because no blood of Jesus could be spilled) after it had been passed through the entire crowd. "There are actually *things* floating in there," she told us. "It's vile." I knew which deacons wore heavy metal concert T-shirts beneath their cassocks, and who at the altar had Oreos under his seat. Mom let us peek inside the tabernacle, where the spare communion host was kept once it had been sanctified, when the little red light burned to signify the presence of God. I watched boxes of wafers, not yet holy, being unwrapped, simple as saltines.

Over pots in our kitchen Mom practiced breaking the bread. She worked on the clarity of her enunciation in prayer, and labored over her preaching, which was praised by her seminary professors. I recognized this pride. I'd always seen it. It was the same high focus with which she cooked and served us dinner, in deep pasta bowls warmed in the oven and topped by a chiffonade of basil leaves grown on her window-sill. We ate with rigorously enforced manners and directed our conversation over a centerpiece hand-arranged from her own gardens.

When might vanity become devotion? Or was the question better posed the other way around? Because it was never an option to do things differently, not for her and not for us. Clothing had its own taxonomy. So did dining and travel. So did women. There were wonderful people out there. Mom loved a classy lady, dignified and reserved: look for her in vintage Lagerfeld or Halston. Mink in winter. Wool bouclé in spring. Linen or silk in summer. She ate a chopped salad and sent an engraved card the next day, even if she had treated. Nonetheless, iconoclasts were welcome—Mom's best friend in seminary was a defrocked nun. There was also a category for ditzes and one for fools, and one—characterized as best I could tell by bleached-blond hair and hard eye makeup—for women who, Mom said, "looked rode hard and put away wet."

And then she'd go out there on Sunday mornings and turn crackers into the body of Christ. There was no higher form of rightness than righteousness. Beyond that, I never knew the nature of Mom's calling, but I'd have been comforted to hear something of her conviction. Those years she was in school, part-time because we were so young, my brother and I learned not to take the bait when certain other adults in our community tipped their heads and said, "So, your mom's gonna be a priest, huh?" There were people, we knew, who did not want to be blessed by her. There were people who thought her horrible for thinking she might bless anyone at all.

As for myself, I gave up on God as Mom progressed through seminary. Not because I didn't believe, but because I considered myself undeserving. In church we were told that Jesus listens to us and weeps with us. I was the chorister who sang, a cappella, the first verse of "Once in Royal David's City" to open the Christmas Eve service, standing at the back of the darkened sanctuary in my robes and trying not to vomit from nerves. I took to heart the message that Jesus suffered like we did so that God might show us understanding. But I did not have much claim to suffering. If indeed God listened to the cries of the world, I thought, he ought to handle the hearts of several billion people before he tuned in to me. My own form of devotion was to avoid asking for anything at all.

The lone exception fell when I was nine and our choir director announced a new music education scheme that meant medals would be awarded to top choristers. We saw them in advance, silver medallions on silky blue ribbons. The medal for head chorister was even larger and threaded on scarlet satin. That it was mine, should be mine, was as clear to me as the ribbon was bright. I was good. I could sight-read. I worked with a hymnal privately at home. Rehearsal was my favorite hour each week.

On the night before medals were to be announced, I got down on my knees. I moved away from my area rug and onto the hard floor so it would count more. I asked clearly, kindly. I felt a new presence as I prayed, as though my willingness to make a request opened something in my heart. I would be an even better Christian now, an even better girl.

Sunday morning we were gathered in our robes around the altar, and the director, smiling widely, slipped a blue ribbon over my head. She awarded head chorister to my classmate Elizabeth, a mild girl with sea-glass eyes who always sang a tiny bit off-key, and whose father was our parish priest. Standing right over us, he beamed.

"Well, *of course* Elizabeth got it," said my mom, on the way to brunch. "Her dad's the boss. Really, you can't get worked up about stuff like that."

The lesson was that, in some things at least, prayer is no match for politics. But I concluded that I had been remiss in my desire. I'd made a foolish request. If I'd been named head chorister, after all, the other girl would not have been. It was a zero-sum game, and my request therefore concealed a selfishness that could not be forgiven. This was why it hadn't worked out. I had a jealous heart. I hadn't noticed, but the Lord had. In the same way, I stood before that mirror in the second-floor bathroom of Brewster House, aged fifteen and almost unable to swallow, and determined that somehow my desire was to blame.

St. Paul's School is an Episcopal school. The head of school is the *rector,* and for a century and a half almost all of the school's rectors have been ordained priests. The rector during my time there, Kelly Clark, had previously been head of the divinity school at Yale. "In today's dark and dangerous world," Reverend Clark said, on the occasion of his 1982 appointment to St. Paul's, "the graduates of St. Paul's are summoned to a steward-ship of light and peace." School language soared in the direction of an Anglican heaven. Priests were our chaplains and teachers, and bishops served as trustees. Many were also the parents of my peers. When she sent me there, Mom sent me into her new world. In my files is the release form I signed, months after the assault, so the Concord Police Department could retrieve my medical records. My name is first, and below it, because I was a minor, is Mom's signature. THE REVEREND ALICIA CRAWFORD she wrote in all caps, showing them who she was, who we were, and above all, who she imagined me to be.

Already, looking in the mirror, I knew this was a lie.

I'd like to think that it was an impulse to self-care that sent me to the infirmary to get checked out, but I know it wasn't. Only a fool walked into what I had walked into. In my memory of the night, which I experienced in strobe fashion (bright still shots rather than a running tape), I saw myself held against one damp crotch by the arms of the other man. Disposable, flimsy. A damsel, a whore. I hated the girl who had done those things. The last thing I would do was align myself with her needs. I did not think I deserved to get better, but I was a girl with a firm sense of doom. The Crawford Curse was mine. Whatever was going on with my throat was only going to get worse—I could lose the ability to swallow; I could suffocate—and I needed help to make it stop. So after Chapel I cut left out of the door, away from the students and teachers streaming up toward the Schoolhouse, and headed along the brick path to the infirmary perched on the hill.

Already there in the little chairs (had they run up from Chapel, or skipped it altogether?) were a Japanese exchange student I recognized from my dorm and two third-form boys. In a different universe, I'd have gone to them and said hello, recognizing their homesickness through the flushed cheeks and tired eyes. But I was on fire, and contaminated; it was a kindness to them to keep my distance.

"There's something really wrong with my throat," I said.

The nurse took my temperature (normal) and told me strep was going around. She selected a tongue depressor. "Let's have a look."

There was no other way. I opened my mouth to let the horror out. I imagined everything I had suppressed coming at this small woman. A ball of spiders, a cup of maggots. Vile things were nesting in my throat, and this was it—she was going to see it all.

"Ahhhh," I said. I gargled the sound. My eyes were pressed shut. The other kids sat there quietly.

"Try again," she instructed.

I really went for it. "AHHHHH!" She pressed my tongue down with her wooden stick, and when she did I felt the tug of the back of my tongue where it met my throat, and how even that hurt. Tears escaped the corners of my eyes and ran along my hairline, into my ears.

"Hm," said the nurse. "Okay, you can close."

I opened my eyes.

"Nothing there," she told me. "Tonsils normal, perfectly clear. Maybe just get a little more sleep?"

I walked the brick path back to class.

My throat was always worst first thing in the morning, when, it seemed to me, the act of lying down all night had allowed the raw skin to adhere to itself. By the afternoon it was modestly improved, and by evening I could join my choirs in rehearsals that met in the chapel after supper. I had gained places in the full school choir, which was not terribly selective, and in the Madrigal Singers, which was more so. Years of childhood choir paid off in my inclusion in a group with a proper musician for a conductor and other students whose voices were remarkable. (At least three of the kids I sang with went on to careers as vocalists.) Our director, Mr. Fletcher, modeled our sound on the old madrigals of the Anglican tradition. We often sang a cappella—mostly motets and Ave Marias, in four parts. As with English church music, the girls' voices—sopranos and altos—were meant to be piercing but steady, without vibrato, so that we sounded like the little boys for whom our parts were written, purity of tone representing purity of heart. There was one chorister, Nina, whose father was director of liturgical music at the Cathedral of Saint John the Divine in New York, who could make these sounds just by opening her mouth. The rest of us had to direct our voices up into our heads, behind our noses, to focus the tone and remove any hush or wobble or wisp of air. "I want you to feel your cheekbones vibrate," said Fletch, who was forever sweeping his hands up, open-palmed, trying to raise the sound from our chests. He would swish in his robes right up to the choir rail and press a finger good-naturedly in the spot between our eyebrows. "It's right *there.*"

Then Dr. Schmidt, hopelessly underutilized at the piano bench, would pick out a chord in four notes, and we'd summon all of our energy into that delicate place at the heart of our faces, as though we were trying to illuminate.

I did not have a good singing voice, but I had a good ear. What was particularly wonderful for altos was how we came in, usually after the sopranos, to complicate the sound—this was true for tenors too. It was harder to hit and hold the soprano notes, but their line was almost always the easier one, the melody. There was no harmony without us. We rehearsed in a small choir room off the transept that felt, with its wooden paneling and wooden pews, warm and unified, as if carved from a single source. Beyond us the enormous chapel lay dim and vacant, and above us the bell tower rose up. When I read, in class, Shakespeare's Sonnet 73, with its "bare ruined choirs, where late the sweet birds sang," I gasped. I knew the carved pews. I saw the loss. I recognized the feeling of being a bird, lower and throatier, darting among the soprano line.

Maybe, I considered, I was just losing my mind. Maybe

I was going crazy and imagining that something was wrong with my body. It was a hysterical reaction. Quite dramatic. Very me, in a way. The sort of thing you'd expect from a kid already on Prozac.

When I sang, I took myself up and out of my own throat. I hit the right notes. The sound we made together was often beautiful, and I belonged.

A few days after I saw the nurse who saw nothing, I woke up tasting blood. I sat up in bed, back to the frozen windows, and forced myself to swallow. I felt the tug as clots pulled away, and I felt myself swallow them. Then the blood ran free. It was warm, deep in my throat.

I went back to the infirmary. Things were becoming impossible: running on the soccer field, in air just above freezing; swallowing anything solid; singing without crying.

This time they sent me to see an ear-nose-and-throat doctor in Concord, a proper physician. I took a taxi from the infirmary into town and back again, with a referral page clutched in my hand and a scarf wrapped tight around my neck. I have no memory of this visit, except that it explains why, for as long as I could remember, I had the word *otolaryngologist* available in my mind. According to the physician's report, the clinician in Concord was able to numb my throat and look past my tonsils to see that the hypopharyngeal space, where the esophagus meets the trachea, was badly abscessed. But that's all the notes show. He did not take swabs to culture. He did not test me for any diseases, sexually transmitted or otherwise. He did not ask me if anything had entered or wounded my throat. There's no mention of a proper diagnostic process at all.

The diagnosis recorded on my St. Paul's infirmary referral form was "aphthous ulcers." Canker sores. Remarkable, given that I had not a single sore in my mouth. It was recommended that I gargle with a tonic of Kaopectate, Benadryl, and Maalox to soothe the throat and counter inflammation. Follow-up as needed.

Drinking Maalox didn't help, because two days later I was back at the infirmary, feverish, swollen-necked, still unable to eat. I had lost almost ten pounds. My mother was calling my pediatrician at home, terribly worried, and looking into plane tickets to bring me home.

The pediatrician employed by the school to come in and care for us in the infirmary saw me briefly that day, and wrote on my chart, "See outpatient report. Has herpetic lesions. Will start Zovirax." He underlined the prescribed medication three times.

It would be more than twenty-five years before I learned what he'd written that cold afternoon.

The pediatrician did not talk to me about herpes simplex virus, those "herpetic lesions" he meant to treat with Zovirax. Had he done so, I'd have been floored. Herpes was an STD, and STDs were acquired through sex, and I had not had sex.

He did not tell me and he did not tell my parents and he did not tell my doctors. Not then and not ever. And that "outpatient report" he referred to from the ENT in Concord was never shown to me or to anyone who cared for me, and it is now lost to time—or, as documents would come to suggest, to more pointed interventions.

Reading his shorthand more than twenty-five years later, though, I can hear the nib of his pen. I'm there on the bed beside him, inpatient at Armour Infirmary, attempting to sip ginger ale. I don't remember, but I can imagine. I'd have been articulate and compliant, but not forthcoming. I'd have been quite thin, with lank hair and not a lick of makeup. I was likely agitating to get back to class. He'd have had me open my mouth to say *Ah,* just because, and I can see him clicking the penlight and putting it back in his jacket pocket. Just like he was then, I'm looking for something I'm not going to be able to find. He was a pediatrician, after all. His job was to care for children. Certainly he could not have meant to lie to me. Is it possible that by writing *herpetic* he meant only to describe the appearance of the lesions, which he, without appropriate tools, could not even see? If so, who described them to him? How did they decide to give me Zovirax, and why did he underline this indication alone?

And what did it say on that outpatient report?

Information faxed much later to my pediatrician at home indicates that I was started on a range of medications: the Zovirax, yes, but also antibiotics, and throat lozenges and cough drops—everything you'd use if you didn't know what a patient had and meant to cover all bases.

Except that it seems that they knew. The ENT in Concord. The school's physician. And at some point soon, via some process of privileged intrusion that would never be explained to me, the administration would know.

Now. Here is a fifteen-year-old girl swallowing blood. The suspicion is that she has a sexually transmitted disease so deep in her throat it cannot be seen during a normal exam. You hold this suspicion strongly enough to make this note in her chart and indicate that she will begin the proper treatment for it. Her bafflement, coupled with the disease's ferocious presentation, strongly suggests that she has just contracted it. Her body has never seen this virus before and is mounting a mighty response. Because she lives on campus—and, like all of her peers, is not allowed to leave without written consent from the vice rector—you can be reasonably sure that she contracted it from another student (or, I suppose, from a faculty member or an administrator). Therefore, there are at least two students at this school with a painful, infectious, incurable, and highly contagious disease. And here before you is a girl, a thousand miles from home, who cannot eat. You are, legally and ethically, *in loco parentis* of them all.

And you say nothing?

Hiccups, head colds, herpes, ho-hum?

Maybe, said my physician years later, it was just that the sores were so deep. Herpes is very unlikely to present that way—that is, in the hypopharyngeal space and nowhere else. To introduce the virus only there would have required an aggressive act, and maybe that was unimaginable? You'd be surprised what a clinician can miss.

To which I'd reply: *You'd be surprised what a kid can find it unimaginable to say.*

By this time my pediatrician, psychiatrist, and an ENT at home in Chicago were discussing whether the Prozac might be making me sick. They couldn't think what on earth was wrong with me. There was no record of it in the literature, said Dr. Miller, reached by phone, but the drug was so new that they supposed it might be possible, and neither the ENT in Concord nor the pediatrician at St. Paul's had given them anything to go on. Also included in the differential were lupus and erythema multiform, a rash related to certain immune disorders. Blood work was ordered. It was decided that I would stop Prozac, just in case, and to the antibiotics and antivirals they added Vicodin for the pain.

Not quite a week later, the records tell me, I went with my mother to see an ENT in Chicago. I have no recollection of this visit at all. My parents were so worried that they flew me home, but I don't remember this—not the airplanes, not the night in my own bed, not the doctor's questions. Certainly not my mother looking at me and my needing to hide what was there. I'd have been terrified. I *was* terrified. I went to the doctor dutifully because I knew I was already being punished mightily. God was taking care of business. No reason to make things worse by breaking my mother's heart.

By that time I had been on the Zovirax for several days, and the initial outbreak was finally subsiding. The ENT I saw in Chicago noted that the hypopharyngeal lesions were healing. He offered no diagnosis. I was instructed to continue the course of medications and follow up with a physician in New Hampshire if things got bad again.

"Thank you for referring this interesting patient to us," wrote the Chicago ENT to my pediatrician. "I am most gratified to report that the problem seems to be improved."

Prozac-free, with occasional Vicodin to help me eat, I was returned to school.

I have files a few inches thick, each off-center page reproduced from the scanned originals, that record my passage from place to place, opening my mouth in the hope that someone would see.

Perhaps I was just being dramatic. This is what my father would have said, and it's not wrong: I wanted the injury to speak for itself. I thought it *was* pretty damn dramatic, in fact. What happened in the boys' room seemed to me both monolithic and so obvious as not to require revelation, like a compound fracture or a dangling eyeball, the sort of thing that makes someone wince and say, "Oh, shit, okay, don't move, I'll call someone right away."

And no one saw.

That feeling was not limited to my throat. Watching myself troop up and down stairwells, changing for soccer and then changing again into a dress for Seated Meal, racing across high stone bridges before the chapel bells rang, I thought, *Can't you all see this girl is ruined? Isn't anyone catching this?*

The boys saw, of course. But everywhere else, I was waiting for it to be revealed. I had been waiting to be discovered since the moment I left their room, when I walked back as slowly as I could. Beneath how many streetlights did I linger?

In the boys' room, I had been unwilling to get caught and give up my perfect record and all I had achieved at school. Moments later, back on the path, I'd made a new bargain: I'd leave school altogether, as long as I never had to say what had just happened to me.

My plan was to be found by a security guard out of my dorm after hours and brought, as I would be, before a Disciplinary Committee (the dreaded "D.C."), which I would politely but firmly refuse to address. The committee was run by a chemistry teacher and lacrosse coach with a military bearing and a theatrical nickname, "The Rock." He'd expel me, and still I'd say nothing. It was Bartleby's defense, of *Bartleby the Scrivener:*

I'd simply decline to participate in the world. *I would prefer not to,* I'd say, and they would throw up their hands and tell my parents to book a plane ticket, none of us the wiser. There were fine high schools in Chicago.

I make no claims for the logic of my intended rescue. What I find remarkable is that I set up an encounter of this shape, in which I would be apprehended by a guard, a man in power in a place where I did not belong, and be forced to give something up—in this case, an explanation for what I was doing out after hours—as a means to my own release. I intended this to happen immediately after leaving a dark room in which exactly this sort of transaction had taken place.

It did not once occur to me to seek my own remedy: to call someone or knock on a midnight door. I believed in rescue only if it was forced upon me, and only if I did not say what was true.

When the security guards did not find me, I turned to doctors and nurses, and opened my mouth wide so they would force the telling out of me.

But even fulminant viral disease failed to do the job. I thought, for years, *Because I could not stop to tell, the telling kindly stopped for me.* What was left, if not the bleeding throat? I would have no choice but to fall apart.

4

January 1990, Fourth Form

I had returned to St. Paul's in January of my fourth-form year
on a tear. Having solved what I believed was wrong with me—
my early-teen expression of clinical depression—I was a girl
mightily fortified, if in placebo power alone, by the powerful
new drug Prozac. In his limo on the way back from the airport, Stewart asked me how the ponies were doing in old Lake
Forest. "Fantastic," I replied. "Whinnying like champs." As we
drove up onto the frozen school grounds, Gaby emerged from
her hair and said, "Hey."

"Yeah?"

"I like to do this thing. Every time I come back, I think
that the first person I see will dictate how the next stretch of
school will go. So, like, if it's someone I love, I'm going to
have a great term. And if it's someone hein, it's going to suck.
People you travel with don't count. So, okay: Go."

She turned intently to look out her window, and I turned to
mine. It was too cold for students to be gathering on the lawns.
I let my eyes move lightly along the grounds and rolled in my
mind that word *hein:* it was campus slang, short for *heinous,* and
a worse insult than the complete word would have been. *Hein*
things were *buzzkills,* or *bks,* and if something was really *hein,*
it might not only *k your b* but actually become a *bad vid,* an

71

experience that kept going for some time. *Hein* was an insider's word, a true Paulie term. Gaby had tossed it at me like something she'd borrowed and was giving back. Easy as that.

The first person I saw was a fifth former named Leighton Huhne. He was very tall, ursine, with a surprisingly childlike face and bowl-cut hair. I didn't know him at all, but he ambled along in a friendly enough way, and he mostly hung out with the *buddies,* the group of boys who were still huffing the fumes of the Beats like old cigarettes their dads had left unfinished long ago. The walls of their rooms were crosshatched with wooden cases for their hundreds of bootlegged Grateful Dead cassettes—illustrated, usually when high, with colored-pencil spirals, bears, and dancing skeletons. The buddies' speech was slowed and their hair often unwashed, and they wore thin-wale Levi's corduroys that were allowed to droop off their hips and pool atop their Birkenstocks. These were sported year-round, so that the true buddies arrived in Chapel just as the last of the bells were sounding eight o'clock, and raced, their twiggy corduroy thighs rasping like crickets, up the aisle, dropping snow from the tops of their bare toes.

Contrast these with the *zees,* short for *buzzards,* boys who listened to acid rock, played hockey, and kept wads of chewing tobacco deep in their bottom lips so that they could punctuate their episodic bursts of sardonic conversation with a comet of hot spit aimed at a sawed-off Coke can beside their chair.

Also *frelks,* a coed set who were just weirdos of a particularly energetic sort (a *frelking* incident looked like a friendly possession); and *tools,* who tried too hard; and exchange students, who smiled a lot; and black students, who had more sense than to engage in any of this shit. Also local kids from Concord, a few Latino and Latina students, several Chinese-American children of Hong Kong–based traders who went home once a year. Plenty of bog-standard Wasps, freckled boys and horsey girls. A few precious show-ponies, like my New York and D.C. friends, overindulged and perennially jetlagged. Among them all, there were some really nice kids. I'd met several, but for whatever reason, I hadn't tried hard enough to talk to them and meet up with them again.

Leighton Huhne turned as our black car passed, and held up a giant paw of a hand in hello. He couldn't have seen who was inside. It didn't matter. I'd gotten my answer.

"Leighton Huhne!" I called out, in the slowing car.

"Cool," said Gaby. "That's a good one. You're going to have a chill term."

This was by far the nicest thing I ever heard her say.

Other Paulie slang that might prove useful: as I've noted, the physical exertions between two students were called *scrumping.* This was the general term, and it functioned exactly like, say, *snacking,* in that it implied no specificity beyond satisfying a moderate desire. Guys who *hooked up* with a girl *scored,* or occasionally (going all the way) *railed* or (with particular vigor) *boned.* If they succeeded in doing this, they might think to use a *domer* to prevent pregnancy. When the subject was a male, the verb was active and transitive: Henry *boned* Alexa. When the subject was a female, the verb was passive: Alexa *was* scored or *got* railed or *got* boned. I heard *bone* as an active verb in the female context only once: at the end of our fourth-form year, when my friend Brooke was given the choice between two fifth formers who wanted to date her. Her older brother, a graduating sixth former, had talked with them both. One of them, Trevor, was handsomer, but he had asked Brooke's brother, evaluating her, "Does she bone?" We repeated this question among ourselves after Brooke reported it, jarring not least for the intransitive form of *bone*. As in, does that chicken lay?

Indeed, Brooke did bone, but not, she decided, with him.

If a girl had scrumped, etc., with a boy who was not held in high regard by other boys, she might well be tainted by the liaison. In that case, she was referred to as *sloppy seconds,* and other boys might not be interested in the sloppy seconds of certain classmates.

This taint was not known to work the other way around. No boy was some girl's *sloppy seconds.* Only girls, therefore, could be socially contaminated by their partners. They were both target and vector.

Boys did not scrump with or rail or score or bone other boys. Nor girls with other girls. It just didn't come up. If two male athletes, for example, pushed their beds together and hung out in just their boxer shorts in the dark after check-in, they must have had something else in mind.

All third and fourth formers were required to participate in three sports a year. ("This is to wear you all out so they can keep you in line," observed my mother.) I'd played soccer in the fall, and after I recovered from my initial disappointment at failing to make the varsity squad, I'd discovered that the skills I'd learned at my father's insistence all the years he had coached my rec team earned me a starting spot on JV defense, right where I liked to be. The wind in the grass was familiar. Shin guards and shivering were familiar. If I blocked out the hilly horizon and the varsity football crowd over on the prime field, I could pretend I was back at home in Illinois. I almost expected the train to come through. I imagined Dad on the sidelines so clearly I stopped missing home. What a gift he'd given me, with soccer. I knew this game, I knew my team, and if the ball came my way, I'd know what to do.

In the winter months, my choice was not as clear. Tennis was my strongest sport—another reason I couldn't wait for spring—and I didn't want to try squash because kids swore it was hell on your tennis game. I couldn't get a basketball as high as the net nor a volleyball over one. In those years, St. Paul's had no pool. This left ice hockey.

And ice hockey was gospel.

As I've said, and as they told us regularly, the first proto-hockey had been played on the Lower School Pond, at the heart of our two thousand acres, in 1856. St. Paul's had turned out stars for a hundred years afterward—even in my time students in every year saw paths to the NHL. I wouldn't have dared to claim my part of such self-satisfied glory, but when I was at St. Paul's, girls' ice hockey was still young in the world. Women did not yet have an Olympic team, though one of my classmates, Sarah Devens, was a prodigy who spent summers training with the group that would form the first Olympic squad.

I'd grown up skating, like so many other kids in my town part of a frigid pack that met up winter afternoons after school. The rink was arctic, unloved. But its high hissing lights blazed by four-thirty, erasing the dead winter sky and giving us wild shadows, and every other hour the maintenance crew shooed us off to bring out the Zamboni. It took forever; our hands froze; the machine laid down ice like pooling cream. We clung to the boards to wait for the first fresh steps.

When I was ten or so I'd asked my father for hockey skates, not caring for the fiddly picks on the front of figure skates' blades or the million dainty little hooks required by their laces. I thought I'd seen pride in his face when I asked, pride in the way he took me to the sports shop as soon as a weekend rolled round.

Nothing at St. Paul's came easily to me. Nothing felt like my natural due. But I'd been on hockey skates for years. I showed up for tryouts and made JV.

Because I could skate backward, I got to play defense (in theory, to block an incoming forward). I could deliver a good Iron Cross: front-stop, back-stop, side-stop, side-stop, over and over, until our sides knotted and we'd cut deep crosses into the ice, leaving piles of shavings all around. Our games were a circus, because so few of us knew what we were doing or where we were supposed to be (I certainly did not). It could take a good twenty-five minutes in the locker room just to figure out how all the pads were strapped on. But there was solidarity there, and there was a place for me.

The hierarchy of hockey teams went like this: boys' varsity, boys' junior varsity, girls' varsity, girls' junior varsity. We ponytailed scrubs were relegated to practice at 6 a.m. I'd troop across campus from Warren House, heading toward the first peach light in the sky, making a left at the library, and taking a shortcut through Kittredge House to where Gordon Rink was set back in the tall pines. Kittredge was ugly, with lousy light even on the brightest day. I'd still be waiting on the January dawn when I pulled open the heavy door. But several girls from my team lived in Kittredge, and they'd come pouring out of their house into the main hall, and in this way hockey delivered to me—finally, I felt—my true friends.

The hockey girls, six of them, were familiar faces. Two had played on my soccer team. Others I'd met in the halls. We met up in their dorm, exited into a wall of cold, crossed a footbridge toward unlit woods, and barreled through the door into the thrumming rink.

Our locker room was an unheated trailer. At 6 a.m. on a winter morning the wooden benches sang if clipped by a skate. We stripped to shorts and T-shirts to suit up, peered through clouds of breath to find where the Velcro of our pads snagged our tube socks, and tugged those socks up over skin goose-bumped so tightly it hurt. We dressed miserably, anxious, trying to take courage from the rancid plastic padding, our coughing and hacking, our halitosis.

One morning Brooke, a fourth former from California, could not find one of her kneepads. She'd asked a few times, but nobody replied. Finally she sat and opened her mouth and bellowed, "I NEED MY KNEEPAD," in a monotone that went on and on until we all stopped to look at her because the sound she was making was so unsettling. When we were all quiet, she said, "Thanks. Can you help?" And we all laughed, and tossed our bags around until it was found. She'd been so rude, but everything about hockey was rude: the cold, the smell of unwashed pads, the hot morning spit in your mouth guard as you heaved after sprints. It felt delightful to be aggressive, to be a girl especially who could be crass and cranky and cold. After Brooke did this, we were easier with each other. On the ice we scrambled about like bears. And it might not have been pretty, but we were part of the hockey tradition at St. Paul's School.

The passage through Kittredge to the rink became my normal route, and after practice I'd just head back to my friends' dorm and stay. Brooke lived there. She had curly hair that was buzzed on the sides and earrings all up the edge of one ear, and a scratch confidence I could not chalk up entirely to the fact that her older brother was a much-admired sixth former (who would, by year's end, be helping her select her next boyfriend). Her roommate, Maddy, was an Ohio brunette with green eyes, a dimple, and enormous, lovely breasts that the sixth-form boys had nicknamed *the big guns.* We all knew this—even Maddy, giggling, told us about it, her eyes wide with slight alarm—and instinctively protected her. She was exuberant and often imprecise, which endeared her to those of us who were so afraid of making mistakes. Hearing an excellent story, Maddy would mourn not having been "a spy on the wall." Returning to a tiresome topic, she'd say, "Guys, not to kick a dead cow, but..." We all kicked dead cows thereafter, aware of the way Maddy might be caricatured at school (given those big guns) and unwilling to participate. Though we did not have words for this yet.

Next door to Brooke and Maddy were Linley, from Colorado, a pretty blonde whose dirty sense of humor lent power to her claim that St. Paul's boys were coarse and lame, and Elise, a lanky artist from Kentucky with sultry, half-open eyes who had a serious boyfriend in the form above us. Elise's refusal to say much about her beau seemed to me testament to her love's maturity, and I was fascinated by the quiet steadiness of their relationship. Next door to Linley and Elise were Boston-bred

Caroline, tall and elegant, with porcelain skin and a grown woman's smile, and petite Samantha, who was the youngest of eight and hated being "cute." She insisted on *Samantha* or *Sam* but never *Sammy,* but this didn't help, because she brushed her bangs out of her face with a toddler's open palm and wore her too-big sweaters with their sleeves tucked into her fists. On icy paths her backpack threatened to turtle her. It would take her Harvard and fifteen years to find the calling we saw for her already: helming the second-grade classroom that had been hers when she was seven.

These girls called me "Lace" and patted their beds to invite me to sit. Shivery with hope and envy, I pressed my palms into their quilts. They were new students too, and their attentions allowed me to imagine a benevolent map of the school, beginning with this dorm and the tremendous luck of the room draw that had put them on the same hall. My exclusion was awful but thrilling: these girls were here together, I figured, because of some virtue mysteriously apparent before they'd even arrived on campus. I felt I belonged with them. The school had not. I could not work out the mix of luck, legacy, and smart manipulation that allowed students to flourish or doomed them to fail through the school's opaque administration. But I had no doubt that everything was coded. Everything offered tells, if only you knew where to look.

Take my big-city friends, New York and Washington. Was it coincidence they ended up assigned to the same room, where they could stay up all night swapping couture blazers and plotting trips to islands? I tested this theory with the Kittredge girls, who thought these two were bitchy and strange but were fascinated to learn the tips I'd received, like how to give a hand job in a yellow taxicab or which debutante balls were not worth bothering with. In quieter tones I revealed to them rare moments of vulnerability. I lowered my voice almost to a whisper when I told them about the late night back in October when the senior girls on the third floor had come into my big-city friends' room to do facials. This was the invitation New York and D.C. had been waiting for. The seniors in Simpson House were glamorous and highly styled. They came in fully equipped and took the new girls' faces in their hands. They steamed their cheeks with warm towels and covered their eyes with lavender-scented muslins from the most luxurious cosmetics lines. They tipped my friends' heads back into their laps, massaged their soft skin, said it was time for the world's most nourishing mask, and lovingly applied plaster of paris instead.

The Kittredge girls could not speak when I told them this. Cruelty was electric. Its proximity enlivened us and drove us closer together.

I remember one evening in this first winter, when the Lower School Pond had frozen over sufficiently that the crew had set up hockey boards so we could play outside. Saturday night there were lights, and long card tables propped on the frozen grass to hold tankards of hot cocoa and red paper cups. Some of the theater kids dragged out stereo equipment. I met the Kittredge girls at the edge of the pond to lace up. Skating without pads or a helmet, in jeans and a jacket and soft red gloves, made me feel like a passenger who got to shake off the jet and just soar. The ice was knotted, and in the spotlights it was impossible to work out depth of field. We skittered and zoomed. Above us towered the illuminated steeple of the chapel, whose bells marked our hours. For a while we batted around some pucks. Brooke and Maddy, who were the best of us, joined the boys for a bit. But eventually we set all that down and just skated. The pond was frozen across to the far woods, but away from the lights the ice seemed to disappear. We giggled and called to one another. Sometimes we lost sight of a friend, who'd then return, squealing, racing in from the dark distance. I remember feeling that my friendships had come to life. I remember going very fast, closing my eyes, and imagining the deep water beneath me completely still.

In the wintertime, Seated Meal dropped to two nights a week, on the theory that it was too dark and cold for us to have to dress up after sports every evening. Nights we did not have Seated, we could shuffle up to the dining halls and choose our spot among the two rooms set aside for cafeteria dining—they were called Middle and Lower. Middle was brighter and larger than Lower, though still, on winter evenings, almost industrial in the way the black windows glowered at us. Lower, with its accordingly low ceiling, was positively denlike. Overflow panels of alumni names were pegged along two of the walls here and downlit, creating a spectacle of departed alumni. These belonged to far more recent classes, including some older brothers and even sisters of kids we knew (it took a lot of hallway before female names began to show up). By unspoken compact, Lower was a fifth- and sixth-form haunt, but my friend Brooke thought this was bunk.

"Why not?" she asked, tray in hand, loaded with fruit and whatever protein was identifiable, and she headed down the long, forbidden hall.

We followed her past the tanks of milk and the toasters, which were always running (toast was a reliable source of basic sustenance), and into the oddly lit room. The walls were bright, the center dark, and your eyes seemed never to adjust. This was probably why the older kids liked it—there was room for uncertainty, like hanging out in the shadows or at the back of the bus. As we came in, heads turned, mostly male. Caroline in particular could send a flare of attention through a group of boys. Sam drafted her, staying small. Elise cradled her tea mug: most of the time, she did not find food interesting enough to bother. I'd have been toting my third PB&J of the day and two glasses of chocolate milk.

"Oh my God," Maddy said, "there's Brophy." The fifth-form hockey player she loved was everywhere, I thought, but seeing him was always a shock to her.

Beside Declan Brophy sat the famous grandson of a famous actor, self-satisfied and, if you were into cherubic looks, devastating, with blond curls at his temples. He was the Luke Skywalker to Knox Courtland's Han Solo, and we were split over which was the hotter guy. Both played in bands—the famous grandson, who was also in choir with me, singing lead vocals and Knox, silent and brooding, on guitar.

"What about you, Lacy-o?" asked Caroline softly. "If you could have anyone."

I looked around. It was delicious to picture these boys singing or playing the guitar to me. It was also silly, a fairy tale, and not only because I would not have risen to their attention. I did not yet know even how to imagine a relationship with a boy. I didn't consider them individuals who had things to offer that I might share—conversation, say, or experiences we might have in common. I could think only of transactions: what it would feel like to be adored by one of them, and how that would elevate me at the school and keep me safe. Also what they would expect from me in return. The crushes I nursed were dalliances of fantasy that left untouched my real fear of intimacy, in whatever forms it would eventually take.

"I just don't want my name to end up in here," I told my friends, pointing at the name panels along the walls. "It's depressing. I just really don't want to spend eternity in Lower."

I was spared further questions by the sight of a third former who had come in to eat alone. Amelia was known as *cocky,* which meant she was not sufficiently obsequious for a freshman girl. Not only was she willing to eat alone, for example, but she would do so, as a third former, in *Lower.* She was a knockout. She could barely close her full lips over her white smile, and she flashed that thing at everyone, boys and girls, losers and stars. We watched in silence as Amelia set her tray down, picked up an orange, peeled it with her long fingers, held it at the end of her slender arm, and then commenced to eat it like an apple. Juice ran down her arm and chin. The whole room had fallen silent.

We didn't know it then, but she'd be Famous Grandson's girlfriend before long.

"Pardon me while I make my banana into a dick," said Brooke, holding up her own dessert, and then, with us red-faced and bursting, she did just that.

What I mean to suggest is a kind of hierarchy of attraction that mirrored, in its forms, the ranked dining halls, the successive libraries (old and new) and successive chapels (old and new), the striations of value both earned and unearned that made a star hockey player more important than a star wrestler and a legacy girl more desirable than a girl from town. You could have lined us up on two sides of a dance hall, boys here, girls there, and, after ten good minutes of inspection, predicted most of the couples that formed. (You might have kept some couples separate, thinking they were siblings.) Though increasingly I felt that I would be the last girl on campus ever to have a boyfriend, it was not love that troubled me. I was fascinated by hate. The forms it took at St. Paul's seemed to offer lessons I imagined were crucial. I did not dare look away. I watched as a black girl, unassimilated and beautiful, walked through the common room to a meal. The uneven pigmentation on her face was striking, but so were her eyes, and altogether she had a calico appearance I found arresting. A white boy her year called out to her from a clutch of boys: "Hey, Sarai!" And she turned, face open to them, to hear him say, "Two-tone went out in the seventies!"

We all—boys and girls—saw that Sarai was gorgeous. If she'd been courted by a different white boy, we might be able to say that the community had its off individuals, as communities do. But of course this did not happen.

If my fear made me cynical, it also made me cold. I looked at a third former eating an orange like it was a burlesque show and made up my mind. That she might have been an artist or a goofball or a kid with this funny old habit with navel oranges, far from home, just fourteen? Never occurred to me.

The name panels on all the walls were of particular interest because I was not entirely sure what my name would say, if and when it ended up on one.

I had been christened Lacy Cahill Crawford. The first name was my great-grandfather's, and *Cahill* also was from my father's side.

But when we'd filled out my formal paperwork for my enrollment at St. Paul's School, the summer before fourth form, Mom did a curious thing.

"Let's give you another name," she said.

I understood that she meant an *additional* name. Her pen hovered over the lines on the form, red on thick white stock.

"Um, okay."

"What's this?" Dad came close. He was eating from a bag of pretzels, and he stood over the table crunching. Mom was seated and held her pen in two fingers in the air, like the former smoker she was, while she thought.

Paperwork, in my family, was always a bit performative. Mom's handwriting grew large and rounded, almost Gothic. She avoided common abbreviations, even if this meant spelling birth dates into the margins, and pressed hard enough that the pen made a sound. After her ordination, she started adding a little plus sign at the end of her signature, which I didn't understand at the time was a common habit among priests and meant to suggest a blessing being given, as a little cross. On the medical forms she completed for her children, she'd enter our full names and then, on the blank line following *Sex,* rather than *Male* or *Female,* Mom would sometimes write *No.*

"How about *de Menil?*" Mom offered. I had never heard the name before, and couldn't picture its letters.

"What's that?" asked Dad.

"De Menil," she said. "You know, the art collection in Houston? Way back on Pete's side of the family we're related."

Dad ate another pretzel. "Huh. I hadn't known that."

"Yes," said Mom. She explained that her beloved grand-mother, who had died several years before, used to talk about a great-great-uncle who had come up with his siblings through New Orleans. I'd heard this story. Almost everything from that particular family line had been stolen in a home invasion in St. Louis ages before, but the robbers had missed a ladies' fan, ornate silk and paper, that someone's great-great-great-great-grandmother had brought from France and waved in front of her face during the steamboat voyage up the buggy Mississippi. One of these relatives had stayed behind in New Orleans. I liked this ghost, the man who had stayed—there was a suggestion of booze, cards, some fallenness. I imagined him putting the rest of them on the boat with their petticoats and silk fans and disappearing into the city streets. He'd escaped us all that way. Nobody alive even knew his name.

Mom wrote, in her distinctive hand, *Lacy Cahill de Menil Crawford*.

Dad didn't protest this change, and I, standing barefoot in our kitchen, didn't understand it. Why did I need another name? What would this give me that I didn't already have? Now that I had it, would I be okay?

I didn't think of the word *impostor*. It would have been useful to have this word to describe the way I felt in the world every day, given how much my smallest mistakes burned me, and how I figured they marked me as not belonging, but I didn't try to describe that feeling even to myself. The word for my mother's adding a new name was *wish*. I thought I understood the spirit of it, and how it was consonant with the school itself. When we had toured St. Paul's, I'd been so struck by the school's beauty that it had seemed all pretend. It looked like what a child might dream before ever having seen an actual school: in bright red crayon, a schoolhouse here, with a tower, for learning; and an enormous red chapel like a cathedral here, for singing; and here a gray library rising out of the pond, and here and here long stone footbridges for zooming across; and here and here, gray and white manors where the kids will sleep. There'd be a flagpole and woods to run in and a white egret fishing beneath a waterfall. There'd even be a dorm hidden high on a hill in the woods, like a castle, and stained glass, and an ice rink, and a boathouse . . .

So why not get a little imaginative ourselves? Why not make me into anyone we wanted me to be?

Almost twenty years later, I met a man at a dinner in London whose name really was de Menil.

"Oh," I said. "That's my middle name."

He said, "No, it's not."

"Actually, it is. One of my middle names."

"No, it's not."

"Oh, okay, well—"

"It can't be."

"Ah," I said lightly, intrigued. How could this stranger deny me my name, *any* name? "Well, it is."

"The *de Menil* name was conferred in title by Napoleon," said this man, "and we have traced every single person who possesses it. You cannot."

My mother may have gotten her genealogy wrong, but if she had intended to give me a boost into a world of holdings and pride, her aim, it seemed, could not have been better.

By the middle of fourth-form year I'd sort of gotten used

to seeing my name written this way or, as it often was, abbreviated on a computer form as *Lacy Cahill deM.* The school used complete names wherever possible, and especially if you were honored to have your name read in Chapel. The sole exception to this was when the rector, at the end of the day's news and just before the hymn, would announce a disciplinary action, and in this case it was one's familiar name and nothing more:

"Benjamin McKenna has been suspended for violating the expectations of intervisitation."

"Lucretia Turner has withdrawn from the school."

Then the organ pipes would explode above the noise of our whispering, and the faculty, seated all along the walls looking in, would stare at each of us to ensure we sang.

I wondered how they'd fit my whole new name on the boards at St. Paul's once I graduated. Some of the longer names had to be abbreviated, and their capitals, periods, and Roman numerals ended up looking silly. Maybe, in victory, I'd drop the *de Menil* when I left.

For now it was a secret Mom and I shared, an extra name like a good-luck charm she'd tucked in my pocket that was also, happily, a little joke on the school. You want heritage? We'll give you heritage. *Render unto Caesar that which is Caesar's,* she'd have said.

So, *Lacy Cahill de Menil Crawford.*

In February of my fourth-form year, I heard it read aloud.

I hadn't been paying much attention in Chapel. The rector had begun intoning the full names of classmates, and before I figured out why this was happening, he came to mine.

In the carved chapel seats opposite me, my adviser's face lit up.

More names followed, beautiful words I thought evoked places, not people: *Heath. Pell. Gallatin. Troy.* This last name I recognized as my friend from soccer, who went by *Robin* and was already writing novels in her room after supper. After a moment, I worked it out: we were the fourth-form nominees for the Ferguson Scholarship, the highest academic prize offered to underformers. It was named for the celebrated nineteenth-century alumnus Henry Ferguson, and it aimed to confer the gravitas of decades and of his particular genius. Candidates were nominated by their teachers in a process wholly opaque to us. In a few months' time the nominees would be pulled out of class to sit for a series of personalized exams in each of four subjects. The Ferguson was qualitative in the extreme, forbidding and admired, a test of the individual.

And I, without any anticipation at all, had been nominated.

My mind wheeled. My teachers—Ms. Conklin in English, Ms. Clunie in French, Ms. Zia in math—did they really think I was bright? Was I really doing well? I knew my grades were good, but whose weren't? We were all accomplished. We'd gotten the small-fish-in-a-big-pond lecture a dozen times as we'd tried to acclimate to this new school. There was nothing special about me.

Outside Chapel, my friends clustered around me with congratulations. Caroline hugged me. Sam gave me a fake Groucho: "I bet you think you're pretty shmaaht." Brooke said, "Wow, man!" They were genuinely proud, and their kindness gave me space to savor this honor. I walked the path to the Schoolhouse in the heart of their banter.

• • •

Ducking among bodies between classes, working my way up-stream to French, at the end of a long Schoolhouse hall, I bumped into someone. "Sorry," I said, and tried to go around, but the someone moved left to counter me.

I looked up. Khaki pants, blue jacket, rabbit smile half-open on his face: it was Shep. Library Shep. Well, Not-Library Shep. Whatever had happened with Shyla and her blue lingerie, I didn't know. I hadn't bothered to keep track.

"Hey," he said, looking down at me. "Congratulations."

"Oh. Thanks."

"I've been meaning to tell you."

It had been only about an hour, but I didn't point this out.

"It's pretty cool," he said.

"Yeah. I'm surprised."

"Well, I'm not," said Shep. "You're like a Doogie Howser, aren't you? Are you even fifteen?"

"Last week."

"Happy birthday."

"Yeah, thanks."

The second bell was about to ring; our bodies were tense with the anticipation of it. The halls had emptied. His smile opened up, and I thought, *Gosh*.

"Well, cool," he said.

I nodded. Had there ever been a day this cool?

"Hey," said Shep. "See you around."

"Yeah. See you."

Then he was in the common room on the way to lunch.

"What's up?" he said. I raised a hand. He'd been waiting for me, and now that I was there, he drifted off with his friends and I with mine. We fell into line with our trays.

"What was *that?*" asked Caroline.

"Um, Shep."

"I know who he is."

I hadn't told them about the whole blue bra thing. I wasn't sure whom I was protecting, but it had never seemed germane. "He's being really nice to me about the Ferguson nomination," I said.

"Yeah, I'm sure that's what it's about," said Brooke, behind us.

I turned. "Why? What?"

"Just saying."

"Come on, Lace," said Caroline.

I had gone from invisible to obviously appealing in one morning? "Come on, what?"

"He's not seeing anyone," reported Brooke.

"He will be soon," said Sam.

"What? What?" I felt panicky. This mix of excitement and concern was entirely new.

"Oh, come off it," said Brooke. "That boy wants you."

"I think he's cute," offered Maddy.

Sam said, "Totally."

I looked for him as we ate, but he was in Lower with his friends, and today we were eating in Middle, as we were supposed to do. My friends got in line at the salad bar. The dance instructor was there, as usual, watching his dancers make their choices. My friends weren't dancers, but they brought back plates piled with iceberg and watery cherry tomatoes.

I choked down half of my PB&J. I had no appetite. How wonderful that was, to have no appetite: for once, not to feel

I needed something I did not have. Why eat at all? Why ruin this beautiful run of fortune with consumption? I sat. I waited. I didn't dare to smile.

Spring break spanned almost the entire month of March. My parents took my brother and me skiing in Vail. This was a triumphant and sentimental return for my father. As a boy in the 1950s, Dad had piled with his brothers into the back of the family station wagon for the drive from St. Louis to Colorado in the first years of the big ski resorts. Dad told us about the car full of sleeping bags and comic books, how happy his father had been on skis. My grandfather called the mountains God's country. When we arrived in Vail some forty years later and checked into the time share Dad had found, he stepped out on the balcony and gulped mountain air, holding his face toward the sky. I quit the little apartment and found my friend Linley, one of the Kittredge girls, whose family had a house a stone's throw from the gondola.

I didn't really understand why my parents gaped when I described drifting down from her door to the back of the lift line. At school, Linley seemed a lot like me, I thought, with one brother and a dog and similar tastes in music, and I'd imagined our circumstances comparable. I was just privileged enough to assume that my family was about as well-off as other kids' families, except of course for the flagrant consumers, like my city friends with their Chanel suits, or the son of the scion in his limousine. Everyone knew about them and everyone rolled their eyes. I did not understand that wealth was shifty and could be shy. Off campus, the small grandiosities I observed among my friends in the dorms bloomed into full occupation of their impossible lives. Linley put her skis on at her own back door, stepped off into the snow, and floated over everything in her path, her blond braid barely lifting off the back of her parka. I was terrible, tripping and shivering behind her, but I'd been on skis only a few times before, and by now I was used to this feeling of forever failing at what my peers had mastered. I did not question that it should happen not only on campus but in the world too.

At dinner the first night, my father cut me off mid-sentence: "I do *not* want to hear how good Linley is anymore." I was stunned. We were champions of excellence. We always admired performance. I thought he'd be as proud of Linley as I was. How could he not love that I was hanging with someone whose bedroom was basically a stop on the gondola? This was what they had wanted, I thought. Or had I now, with the convert's zeal, fallen too far into my adoration? Where precisely on this wild chain of privilege did my father wish me to be?

The next night I followed Linley home to a party at another house, a *chalet*. We arrived there on skis, aimed at an elevated slate platform by the back door, and continued until our ski tips slid into the gutter-sized gap between the bottom of the platform and the snow. It was dark under there so I couldn't see, but once I had wedged my rental skis in all the way to my boots, as Linley and her friends had, they instructed me to kick out of my boots and step up onto the slate. In my socks? Yes; the stone was heated. My skis disappeared. There was someone in a room down there who had pulled them in, to be sharpened and re-waxed for later.

Inside, teenagers filled a home movie theater. I couldn't see anyone because the captain's seats were huge. Names were thrown out—Oggie, Tyler, Tad. They were drinking beers as though this were a bar. Linley and I watched for a bit. We padded around the mansion in our warm socks. I don't remember collecting my skis to return, but I felt guilty that the house crew had had to sharpen and wax rentals, as though unowned equipment was somehow beneath their efforts.

I knew better than to tell my dad about this even bigger house. By day, Mom and I met up with Linley and her mom. Our mothers hit it off. Linley's mom was divorced from her father, but folks referred to him happily as "The Wallet." Mom thought this was hilarious. Linley didn't seem to care. Everyone was beautiful, and there was fresh powder on the mountain, and the air was delicious with the smell of burning pine. I was trying to work out how much of my new moneyed world I was supposed to inhabit—when was I adding to my family's sense of stature, and when was I not?

My dad was a spectacular skier, so good that when he wore a blue ski suit, he'd have snake lines of skiers following him, thinking he was an instructor. And my grandfather had thought God lived in those mountains. Though I was clumsy and cold in Vail, I let my time on the mountain feel like the closing of a gap. *I'm still learning,* I reminded myself. *I'm not very good yet.* I'd stand up on my skis, lay them parallel, inhale deeply, and push myself down the fall line. One good stretch of balance would lead to a turn I couldn't make. How quickly I lost control. I'd catch an edge, get catapulted sideways, and spread all of my limbs out in an effort to stop myself, losing equipment all over the mountain. It took long moments of stillness to inventory my body and make sure nothing hurt too badly. Snow up my sleeves, snow down my back, ice in my hair. Then, blinking, I'd hike back up for my missing ski or poles and try again. Linley and her friends waited for me but made no effort to help me down these treacherous patches. I was grateful. I'd have been embarrassed to be seen, and they'd have been embarrassed to see me. What I appreciated most of all was the assumption—which I inferred from their absence and my solitude on these double-diamond slopes—that I could handle myself just fine. I had no business being up there, but I'd sooner break a bone than admit that the gentler slopes were where I belonged.

We returned to a cold campus, but by the end of March you could feel the sunlight on your skin, and at night the ponds failed to freeze. Slush gave way to open water. The light of our street lamps reappeared on its surface. Before Seated Meal, Shep stopped right in front of me, made his rabbit grin, and asked, "Hey, you want to hang out tonight?"

I'd been practicing for this. I might even have made a little shrug.

"Cool," he said.

The great doors opened, and people streamed by. Somebody thumped Shep hard to heave him forward into me, and by the way he smiled when we tangled I thought I could tell that he didn't mind at all. I loved this far more than I loved the feel of his body.

"How about you come up to Wing?" he asked. I'd never been in that boys' dorm. I had never been invited.

"Okay."

"Because you have a roommate..."

He was right—she would have ruined conversation. I smiled.

He suggested 8 p.m. We separated to report to our assigned

tables—like our seats in Chapel, seating at formal supper was always assigned. Twice a day the school wanted us precisely where they had placed us. ("That's so they know you haven't disappeared," said Mom. There was a famous story about two students at Groton who failed to appear in Chapel because they were at Logan Airport on their way to the Bahamas. They spent three days on the beach and were expelled upon their return. Mom loved this story.)

I did not eat. I sat in that grand candlelit hall and looked down at the front of my dress in case I might catch myself becoming the sort of young woman who went to a senior's room to hang out. I could not. My flowered dress was tied with a bow.

After supper I found my library sofa, occupied it as regally as a duchess until time ran short, and just before eight returned to my room to drop off my books and change clothes. I chose jeans and a turtleneck beneath a wool fisherman's sweater, blue with a white patterned band across the chest. Over that I zipped my parka to my chin and added a scarf for my ears. I stepped into my trusty duck boots and tucked my gloved hands into my pockets. Shep's dorm was a seven-minute walk via a shortcut up a lamp-lit, leaf-covered path. The leaves were soft and smelled of earth. I looked like I was going to set lobster traps in the North Atlantic.

"Warm enough?" asked Shep's hallmate, eyeing me on the stairs.

The boys had their doors propped open with cinder blocks to try to cool their rooms. The campus of St. Paul's School was heated by an enormous boiler system, housed in what we called "the power plant," which was forever churning in a dense pocket of trees at one edge of campus. The heat was never turned on before October 1, no matter how chilly the September nights, but from that day, each room's radiator sounded a whole kitchen's worth of pots and pans. They hissed and shrieked. We fiddled with knobs and got scalded, or ended up with a dud and had to sleep in a parka. No matter where you were on the school grounds, flung as it was across ponds and fields, the pressure of those boiler pipes ran beneath and around you. It kept us alive in the winter; it was also, in its strange animation, vaguely sinister. After a freeze you could make out where the pipes were buried because green strips of grass persisted, lush as July, shrugging off snow.

Someone on Shep's hall had raised the window at the far end of their corridor as high as it would go. There was no screen. This was the third floor of a building atop a hill. If I started from a run, I could have launched myself halfway across campus. The open window did not seem legal. Condensation dripped onto the sill.

"I'm fine," I said.

Shep, appearing in his doorway, laughed. "Come in."

Other friends were in his room: one boy was on the sofa, and one sat astride a desk chair. I recognized the student named Juan, a baseball player. I did not know the other boy at all. Shep said, "Have a seat."

It was either the bed or the sofa, next to the boy I didn't know. Hands still in pockets, parka still zipped, I perched on the open end of the couch. Shep leaned against his desk, his legs crossed at the ankles in front of him. He had a habit of bending together paper clips and twining them with his fingers, and he did this while we talked.

What did we talk about? I have no idea. I was working too hard to understand the shape of this setup: three boys, one girl; three seniors, one fourth former. I had been to boys' rooms before, but only those of classmates (for study projects or in a group to see guys who dated my friends), and in each case I'd known my role: either be smart and useful or unobtrusive and friendly. I'd let my eyes drift over the boys' spaces. I studied their foul nests of school-issue sheeting, the absurdly sophisticated components of their competitive stereo systems stacked like the instrument panels of commercial airliners, their posters of Neil Young and Cindy Crawford. I'd tell my little story about the Crawford family reunion in downstate Illinois somewhere, which my dad had been excited about for a while, and how Cindy hadn't shown up but had been on the list, which meant that she was my cousin, kind of.

Maybe I told this story again to the seniors. I would have wanted to offer them something, and I was anxious not knowing what I was expected to produce. Was I auditioning? Had Shep changed his mind and asked me up so they could make fun of me? But to be alone with Shep would have caused me a different sort of fear.

On this evening, it was simple goodwill that surprised me. These boys, with their open faces and curious grins, their teams and classes and work and college plans, proved to be normal, friendly, bright young men who seemed to occupy the school more honestly than I did, as though I had climbed a flight of stairs and come upon the real students, the ones who knew a St. Paul's I had not found.

After an hour or so Shep accompanied me back down the hall. We'd left plenty of time for me to walk alone back to my dorm before check-in. The open window sucked cold from the night like a flue. At the bottom of the stairs, he leaned down and kissed me. I felt the hair at my temples dancing, which was from my smiling, or from a breeze. This was no more or less strange than anything else. Benediction could appear out of nowhere at school. It was less common than cruelty, I thought, but every bit as mysterious, and all the sweeter for this.

The only person I told at first was my friend Caroline.

We were all a little bit in love with Caroline, the whole school was. Not just for the heavily lashed blue eyes, tall thin body, and high cheekbones—there was a lot of that at St. Paul's. Caroline was unassuming and quick to smile, an artist and a Joni Mitchell lover, fond of candles and horoscopes and swishy, colorful, handmade clothes. Then she'd put on black heels for Seated Meal and senior boys would groan when she passed. She wrote her friends casual notes illustrated with cartoons of our latest mild anguish—a physics exam, a slip on the way to Chapel—and in her rendering would be a sympathy that we could borrow for our own. She was the friend who reached for a piece of hair that had fallen into your eyes. She noticed when you were coming down with a cold. As we'd grown to know each other as fourth formers, I'd wanted to be able to offer something like what she offered me, but I couldn't think what I had to give. I'd suspected I could find her in the art studio, stealing an afternoon for her work. She was at her easel with her back to the door.

"Sooo," Caroline prodded, "how was it?"

"Just a kiss," I said.

She replied, *"Delicious."*

Telling her, the kiss became even better than it had been.

I'd never been in the advanced art studio before, because I'd taken only the standard survey art course, Visual Design (or Vis Des), taught by grumpy Mr. Atterbury, whose breath was so redolent of booze that when we came to the welding unit we joked he'd ignite. One of my tasks in Vis Des was to recast a photograph of the chapel in a new color palette by affixing cutout swatches of complementary colored paper. This was an exercise I abhorred. Snipping and pasting when I could have been reading, or napping, or getting ahead in math?

Caroline was holding an actual palette in her hand, arrayed with gobs of pigment. I wanted to press my fingers into it.

"Did he use tongue?" she asked.

"Not much." Just right, I thought.

"Bad breath?"

"Good, actually."

"Hands?"

"No, nothing."

Caroline beamed. "Lacy-o! I like this guy!"

She was working in oils, which we lowly Vis Des students never got to do, and she stood back from her easel so that I finally noticed what she'd been working on. It was a portrait of a woman. Caroline had completed the contouring of her subject's cheeks and mouth and was bringing forward the eyes, but the hair was still a suggestion and the background untouched. The work was dynamic, as though this woman, whoever she was, was quite literally coming into existence on the canvas. My friend had pencils behind each ear and paint all over her arms.

"My God," I said, staring at her work. "That's amazing. Who is that?"

"Oh, I don't know."

"You're *making this up?*"

She tipped her head at her woman. "I think I'm more letting her out."

Of course. Caroline could put color on white and make you think, *That's a person.* Whereas I had no idea what was in front of me.

Behind her easel a form-mate of ours was working on his own canvas. I hadn't noticed him before, but he'd allowed us our privacy while I was gushing about Shep. I didn't know Pete Walters well. He was neither buddy nor jock, a self-contained blond guy who was handsomer than his social standing would suggest, but also more aloof than you wished him to be. He had a brother in the sixth form who was a redhead, and once, looking at him in Chapel, I had wondered what it might have been like to have my own brother at St. Paul's. But my brother was five years younger, so we couldn't have overlapped anyway.

Pete's painting was a hyperrealist depiction of a row of telephone poles along the edge of a desolate road. The earth was yellow and the sky blue, the road gray, and on each telephone pole's outstretched arms was a Jesus nailed as on the cross. It was one hell of a Jesus he'd painted: head bowed in death, blood weeping from the gash in his side, over and over and over, growing smaller and smaller toward an empty horizon. It was impressive and horrible. As for what it meant, I figured there was a compelling message in there somewhere, maybe about manifest destiny or the rape of the earth, and I'd think about it later.

"Holy cow, Pete," I said.

He smiled. "Yeah?"

"No, really."

Caroline stepped out from her own easel. "I know, isn't Pete doing cool stuff?"

The three of us stared. I counted six Jesuses. I remembered that my mother had once told me that her father, my grandfather, was not a part of her life because he had decided to go work for the telephone company when they were first stringing lines across the West, and my great-grandmother had said that no son-in-law of hers would work for the utilities. "He just wanted to climb telephone poles," my mother had told me, disgusted, and I remembered wondering what was wrong with that. It must have been obvious, though, because he'd vanished when my mom was an infant and never returned. I did not even know his name.

"My grandfather worked for the telephone company, stringing wires across the West," I said. More and more at St. Paul's I found myself saying things that sounded like a script I'd been working on almost long enough to pull off.

"Really?" Pete asked.

"Yeah. He loved it. The freedom. Climbing the poles." This must have been true, if he'd left his wife and baby daughter to do it.

"Gosh," said Caroline. "I had no idea, Lace. That's really cool."

Pete made big eyes at her. "It's *very* cool."

If it weren't for the verisimilitude of the dead Jesuses, I'd have guessed Pete might be in the painting studio solely to be close to Caroline. But he had talent. And some serious angst, too, from the look of his work. He puffed his hair off his forehead and squinted. "I don't know," he said. "Something's not quite speaking to me."

There was a long pause. We heard the stream rushing behind the art building. Pete stood sweetly, his apron doubled at his waist. His painting was accomplished and grotesque. It was a very St. Paul's project: more intention than meaning and more striving than intention. We three kids cocked our heads at the Jesuses and tried to come up with the right thing to say.

Pete began to laugh. He said, "Maybe it's a little too..."

Caroline laughed with him. "Determined..."

Pete said, "Naked..."

I added, "Ambiguous..."

"A bit too, what-in-the-heavenly-fuck?"

I was thinking about my grandfather climbing telephone poles. I was interested for the first time in how a family with a baby might fall apart. For ambition? Adventure? For a job?

Thirty years later, after my grandmother died and I inherited her journals, I learned more. The marriage was collapsing by the time my mother was due to be born. Someone else took my grandmother to the hospital. My grandfather stopped by Maternity to leave a box of caramel candies and a message: if the baby was a boy, he said, he would contest the divorce. This was in 1950. The baby was a girl.

Caroline sobered us up. "I don't know what it's about, Pete, but I can tell your heart is in it."

He gazed at her, smiling wide. My friend had said the perfect thing in the moment, and had also hit on what I most wanted. I wanted to feel my heart, to feel it moving toward something that was not me. Seeing my peers with their bright canvases made me ache. I had no art, no imagination or devotion. Convention seemed to suggest a boyfriend was the solution. I thought about Shep and figured I'd give that a try.

A few weeks later, Caroline, pushing too hard to recover from knee surgery (a hockey crash had torn her ACL) and rehabilitate while rowing crew, fell into exhaustion. She had discovered that she was, pound for pound, a rowing power-house. Her bones were light and her stroke long, and now she was not just a beauty but a known athlete too. Colleges were paying attention. But she couldn't eat enough to keep weight on. Her blond hair fell limp to her shoulders and never grew much longer. I noticed her looking thinner than usual, and when she held her tea at breakfast she shivered, even though the windows were open to the sun.

We walked together to Chapel, slowly—she was still in a brace. "I think I just need a nap," she said. "But I can't get any rest in Kitt." Her dorm was my dream—awash in friends—but to her it was a zoo. "I just need some space. You're so lucky to be in Warren, Lacy-o. You can just disappear."

If only I could have borrowed her perspective on my own life.

"Come to my room after lunch," I told her. My roommate would be away with her team, and I'd be at tennis practice. "You can have it all afternoon."

When morning classes ended, I raced back to Warren House. I made my bed, brushing grit off the sheets, folding back the top coverlet, and tucking it all in tight. The flowered duvet matched the flowered pillow sham, and my mother had included a little flowered pillow in a complementary bloom. I pounded them all to expel stale air and make them look fresh. I lined up my shoes at the base of my closet and shut the door. Behind my bed was the window, at this time of year filled with new green. Finally, I tore a square from a notebook and wrote, *Sweet dreams,* and set this atop the pillows.

When I finished tennis practice, the day was withdrawing its warmth. It was still early in the season for New Hampshire, and as the sun lowered, the cold came back fast. I ran from the courts and sprinted up the stairs, legs goose-bumped. My room was dark, the light having moved. The bed was remade, and a new note read:

Best nap I've ever had. Thank you, kind friend.

I saved it, so I could remember how it felt to take care of someone I loved.

Shep's lean top lip was deft, perfectly precise. I hadn't had much practice kissing before, but where, in the preteen fumblings of my ninth-grade classmates, a boy had sensed an opening and pushed forward, tongue out like a hunting lizard, Shep understood that distance was sweet. He'd retreat the tiniest bit. We could make out against the stacks in the library and my back didn't hurt from arching away from him. He held me upright and tight in his arms. I wanted more. He kept it this way. He was fastidious and his breath always smelled of mint. It got so I'd walk the paths back to my dorm with him—I, as an underformer, had earlier check-in, so he would drop me off— and I'd breathe as deeply as I could to catch the mint mixed in with the scent of thawing earth. What a blessing it was that Warren House was way off in the farthest corner of campus! It took forever to wander those paths. Beneath lamps, he'd stop me and lift my chin, and not care who saw us kissing right there in the dusk.

A decade or so later, when I was in graduate school in Chicago, I came across a feature about Shep in the non-celebrity pages of *People* magazine's "Sexiest Man Alive" issue. The rabbit smile was come-hither now, as I'd known it would be, and he had grown into his shoulders. *People* wrote about his family, his skiing, his Ivy League degree, and his work ethic. They wrote that he was a catch for any woman. I thought, *You don't know the half of it.*

After a few good-night kisses, that spring when I was fifteen, I felt brave enough to ask Shep about the blue satin bra and our missed meeting in the old library. We were sitting on the low-slung sofa in his room, alone this time, trying to find things to talk about. I asked about Shyla to get him talking, but I wasn't sure I wanted the answer.

"So whatever happened with, you know...?" I said.

He pressed that fine lip even finer and gave a left-handed shrug. "Yeah. That just wasn't going to work out."

I waited.

"It was just way too..." he said. He looked off across the room, toward his bed. I was imagining a lusty heartbreak. I was thinking I hadn't seen her in a while and maybe she'd been devastated and had to go home. Shep looked back at me, some mischievous light in his eyes, and then he reached his arm around my shoulders and across my chest, above my breasts, hooking me into him. With a turn of his free arm at my back he twisted me facedown onto the sofa. I didn't resist, so he guided me there, to the cushion, and then unwound his arms.

I wasn't afraid. He had never tried anything with me before, never taken me by surprise; if anything, I wondered if he would ever try to touch me beyond holding hands and kisses. I took a full breath of rancid air from his sofa, utterly baffled, waiting to see what he'd do next.

"That's a wrestling move," he told me, as I sat up. "I just pinned you."

He was a varsity wrestler, and a pretty good one. I'd tried to watch a meet once but had been too embarrassed by the sight of him in his singlet and padded-ear helmet. I hadn't even told him I'd been in the stands.

"Cool," I said. I smoothed down my shirt.

"There's pretty much nothing you can do to get out of that," he said. "That one's a killer."

"I can imagine."

"I can show you others," he said.

"That's okay."

He nodded. Poor guy, he was more frightened by Shyla and the promise of her shiny bra than I was. All the kissing? It wasn't prelude—it was, quite simply, where he was. It would have been hell for him not to be boning and scrumping all over the place. He was a sixth former and an athlete. I knew what other guys would expect of him. My chest was tingling from where he'd held me with his forearm. My breasts were untouched. He smiled, and his top teeth stuck out.

"Okay," I said. "Show me another good move."

He hopped to his feet. "Come on!" He helped me up, hand wrapped around my wrist, and stood me in front of him, showing me how to widen my stance, how to get moving and stay light. We grappled. His arms were alarmingly strong, but his focus, which was not on me, left me puzzled. It took me a long moment of watching him hop around, arms ready, to recognize this feeling I had, a deeply familiar mix of tenderness and condescension, for what it was: sisterly. Shep might have been my little brother. We might have been at home roughhousing, ages ten and five.

We were dancing around the little space between his bed and his sofa. I waited for him to make his move.

"I kept your note, though," he told me, grinning, and then he gently threw me to the ground.

That April, Shep was admitted to Cornell. Tennis season had started. I was going to sign up for the housing lottery with the Kittredge girls so we could all live together as fifth formers. Shep would be off to college, where he could start over again as the fully fledged heir come into his own instead of the scrawny boy with the rabbit grin and the cooler, bigger friends. We were united in our potential, but our ambitions depended on one day getting away from each other.

But we kept dating for another few weeks. Why not? To leave the common room after Seated Meal and see someone attractive waiting for you? To walk with that person down the long chilly hall and out into the spring night? Why quibble about things like love or a fetish for wrestling throws?

On his way out of St. Paul's, Shep was helpful to me in decoding the place—I had the sense he was preparing himself to leave by parceling out his experience for my naive ears. One night, walking back to my room, we worked through the problem of the tennis team. I'd been frustrated by my inability to advance. Spots on the varsity and junior varsity squads were managed via a ladder, with players ranked 1 through 14, the top six forming the varsity singles team. Every week, during Thursday practice, we'd play a challenge match against the teammate one rung above or one rung below us. This was to ensure that our ladder was as accurate as possible, and to keep us in fighting form. I had beaten every girl on the bottom half of the ladder, and then I'd beaten the fifth former in seat No. 7, earning me her place and a shot at varsity. But the coach would not let me challenge the girl at No. 6. Every week I again played the girl I'd already beaten. She was given the chance to unseat me, but I could not advance.

When I asked, the coach explained that as a fourth former I had plenty of time to shine, and that I ought to focus on my game and let her worry about the rankings. This stung. Winning made me uncomfortable, just as the Ferguson nomination had made me feel painfully visible. Was I behaving inappropriately by wanting to challenge up, being ungracious or arrogant? I knew I was a stronger player than at least a few of those girls above me. Was it wrong to want to prove it?

"Oh, good Lord," said Shep, his arm around my waist. I felt through my leather flats how the earth was soft now. Even the shadowed edges of the ponds were iceless. The buddies had ditched their Levi's cords for cargo shorts, and my urban friends, whom I didn't see much of anymore, had debuted in class a series of miniskirts that made our tennis skirts look like kilts.

"What?" I asked.

"Just think about it. Think who's number six."

"Fiona?" A fifth former who was unfailingly friendly and kind.

"Precisely."

"She's a sweetheart."

"Of course she is."

"So I'm not allowed to beat her?"

Shep was smiling. "Not as long as you're playing on those courts, you're not."

I pictured our shiny indoor courts. The facility had not been open long and still smelled of rubber and lemon cleaner. I loved playing there. It was loud and thrilling, the surface fast, no rude New England gusts to shove a ball off course. I puzzled until I realized: the courts bore Fiona's last name. On every map, on the transom, in our athletic calendar. We played on Fiona's courts. I remember the shape of the woods around us as Shep and I turned up the lit hill toward Warren House. I found at once that he was absolutely right about why I was stuck on the tennis ladder, and that I did not care. I loved Fiona. I didn't want to kick her off the courts named for her family. This was just how things were at the school. The labyrinth was mine. I was in it. With the Ferguson nomination, with the arrival of spring, with Shep, the place had committed to me, and I would be faithful in return.

"Next year there'll be more spaces on varsity," Shep said. "Then you can kick her ass and it'll be okay."

I wished he'd come back and watch.

I told Shep about the Ferguson exams. "That sounds horrendous," he said, laughing. But I'd loved the essay questions my teachers had drawn up. I wrote about Willa Cather and *Manon Lescaut*. I worked precalculus problems with the galloping pleasure of new confidence. "You're a total nerd," Shep teased.

"Absolutely."

Shep came up to the third floor to hang out with me until intervis hours were over. My roommate had found friends on the opposite side of campus and was home as little as possible. Shep was careful and anxious, like me. Usually when we were in my room, I sat on my bed with my back to the wall and he sat in my desk chair, alternately chatting with me and making fun of my photographs from home. But this night he sat next to me on my bed, both of us upright. No feet were on the floor, but we dangled them in parallel over the edge of my flowered comforter.

"Maybe you could come visit at Cornell," he said.

We both knew I wouldn't. I kissed him. Mint, the feel of his smile on my own mouth.

"Maybe you can come back and visit me here," I said.

"You'll have moved on to someone else."

"And you'll be dating some college babe."

"I sure as hell hope so."

I tried to throw him, using one of the moves he'd taught me. He let me wrestle him down. "Excellent," he said, patronizing. I was on top of him now, pinning him, and I wasn't thinking of anything except that at that moment his hand was undoing the sash at the back of my dress, and then I felt his hand on my skin, under my dress—modestly, because he kept my skirt down, reaching his arm up past my waist toward my breasts, as best he could figure out how.

"Do you know this move?" he whispered.

I shook my head no.

His arm was trapped between my skin and my drop-yoked dress, which suited both of us just fine—it was electric but it was limited, a hot wire of touch, just exactly right.

He kissed me again. And at that moment, the door to my room swung open and my adviser, Ms. Shay, was standing there.

We scrambled. Shep jumped to his feet. I gathered my skirt under me.

"I promise we weren't," I stuttered. "It wasn't." All of the lights were on. We were fully dressed. Already I was forming my defense, and in spite of myself I was beginning to cry.

Ms. Shay looked to Shep. He ducked his head. She said, "You may go."

Without a word to me, he left.

"You can come talk to me about this when you're ready," she told me, and closed the door.

I marched downstairs in a tumble of indignation and terror. My urban friends signed out for weekends to the Cape to have sex all night long! Shyla delivered lingerie at lunchtime mail drop! Everyone knew who was boning whom in the library, the choir stalls, the lower-school woods. And Shep hadn't even *done* anything to me! He only ever taught me stupid wrestling throws!

Ms. Shay, my mother said, looked like a Botticelli. Tall and graceful, with a heart-shaped face, a cherub's red lips, and dark curls held in a loose clip at the nape of her neck. She was married to a novelist we glimpsed only occasionally. Their marriage was foundering, and we intuited this instability from her wide eyes and soft attentions. She fixed me with a look far too forgiving to provide fuel for my self-important defense. I crumpled before her at the door to her apartment.

"I'm sorry," I said.

She was quiet.

"I promise you I have never done anything inappropriate. We have only kissed."

She nodded.

"He likes to make me do these wrestling moves."

Her eyebrows went up.

"It's sort of annoying, actually."

Now she smiled.

"Lacy," she said, and I shivered. I hated to hear my name like this. Ms. Shay was the one Dr. Miller had written to about my Prozac. Ms. Shay was the one who monitored how often I walked across the dark road to call home and cry from the pay phone by the gym. She knew how sad and lonely I'd been, how needy I was, and I felt deeply betrayed by a world in which she was the one to catch me when I was finally not desperate, to catch me almost doing something that was nothing compared to what everyone else was up to, but that was everything to me. I felt trapped by my own reckless feelings: too much sadness on the one hand and too much happiness on the other. Either way, it seemed, I was going to have to be reined in by an adult who would look at me this way—head tipped, mouth pursed, arms crossed over her long, lovely sweater.

"It's almost the end of the year," she said. I understood exactly. *Don't fuck this up now.* She was going to let me go.

"I know."

"Good." She looked at the clock. It was a while until ten. "I trust you're in for the night?"

"I'm in."

The Kittredge girls and I were down at the Lower School boat docks, working up the courage to strip down to our swimsuits.

Brooke's boyfriend, Andrew, had been new as a third former, and as a veteran he introduced us to spring swimming at the docks. It was possible only on the rarest of hot days, after the sports season had ended but before the final commitments of the year.

The pond was murky and cold, not terribly deep. Grasses pushed up from the mud all along the shore, and we were a short reedy curve away from where just four months earlier we'd laced up skates. I studied the spot where the hot chocolate tables had stood. How could the earth change so utterly? How could I?

With the arrival of exams, the sixth formers were readying themselves to graduate, and the school's intricate scheduling came apart. It was a release, a loosening of the daily corset around our attention. My friends were gleeful. I imagined something more like a breakdown, as if these gaps between commitments at the end of the year signified a great beast stumbling in its gait, falling to its knees. I couldn't believe I'd done it. Survived the work. Found these friends—these friends! Giggling and sidestepping around the old wooden boards, dipping their fingers in the water to exclaim how cold it was.

"Oh, for God's sake, just do it," said Brooke, already in a black two-piece. Andrew lay back shirtless beside her, one hand calmly on her belly. A few of his friends had joined us too—Kent and Mike and Clem, all fourth formers like us. These were boys who talked about things, who did not regard conversation as a sniper's convention and who seemed to have thoughts beyond our bodies (and theirs). Kent sang in the choirs and a band. Mike practiced piano in the music building every day. Clem had been dubbed "Nuprin" by the older boys in his dorm after the popular advertising slogan of the painkiller—"Little, Yellow, Different, Better"—because he hadn't hit his growth spurt yet, was quite tawny-skinned for a white kid, and sometimes had a weird sense of humor, but everyone liked him. He wore his nickname with good cheer.

Together we all offered encouragement to Maddy, who was quivering like a waterbird, her arms crossed, hems of her shirt in her fingertips, paralyzed by the presence of Brophy farther up the bank on the grass.

"He's with a million other guys," said Brooke.

"That doesn't help!"

"He's not watching you."

But we were all watching Maddy. The big guns were about to be revealed. I'd seen her changing, of course, casually, as girls did—in the locker rooms and before Seated Meal. But her breasts in a swimsuit would be a revelation even to those of us who knew her well. Anyone's body, held plainly in the daylight, was a revelation then, my own included.

Andrew sat up. "Maddy, honey, you're beautiful. Don't worry about it."

"You're all beautiful," said Clem.

"Ditto," said Kent.

A light breeze moved over the water. I felt I was moving too. In the late May sun, the chapel tower was as saturated with color as the dumb cutouts I'd had to make back in the winter.

Maddy pulled off her shirt. She shook out her hair and sat down. Nothing happened. We all laughed.

I was self-conscious too, but I didn't say anything about it, and nobody noticed. I pulled off my shirt and dropped my shorts and lay down quickly on my towel in my one-piece swimsuit. The sun blanketed me. I thought of Mom, how soon I'd be going home.

"All right!" said Brooke. "Who's going in?"

They did, one by one—the girls diving and the boys tucking into cannonballs that swamped the old wood and our towels. Still on the dock, Sam and I shrieked.

Then she narrowed her small face at me. "Last one in!"

We let the others pull themselves up and out before taking our places at the end of the dock. I waited after Sam dived. She surfaced, gasping and smiling. I waited so long that the moment passed, and I felt chilly and wanted to change my mind.

"Come on! It feels awesome!"

Sam was climbing out. My friends were dripping and hopping, shoving and hooting on the docks, shining like fish. I dived in.

The water felt gorgeous. An envelope of cool that opened around me and closed me in. I arced up gracefully, imagining myself doing so. Just before my head broke the surface, I felt a sharp drag on my right thigh, and my leg began to burn.

"Jesus!" I sputtered, coming up.

Nobody heard.

I paddled a bit, looking down. I couldn't see anything, but my leg was searing.

Leeches? Weeds? What lived in New Hampshire ponds?

Legs dragging, I pulled myself to the dock with my arms and hoisted myself up. As I left the water, blood poured off my right thigh. Something had sliced me from high up, near my crotch, all the way down to above my knee, forming a long, thin C. The combination of the injury and the scummy pond water made my body look greased with blood. There were screams, but not from me. I was just breathing. I worried about getting blood on everyone's towels.

"Hang on," I heard myself saying. "Hang on."

I sat back down and cupped water out of the pond and poured it onto my leg. The moment the blood was washed away, the slice re-illuminated itself.

"Holy fuck," said Brooke.

"What the hell?" asked Kent.

Andrew said, "Oh my God, Lacy. Just wait. Just hold still."

There were shouts up the docks and onto the lawn, where the fifth formers—now almost sixth formers—were lying about, as though they'd been blown there. Someone's boom box was playing, and a few guys were tossing a lacrosse ball back and forth with tasseled sticks. Turning back to the water, I saw, as the surface settled, what I had hit: a bicycle on the bottom, its rims glinting. I'd managed to dive toward it and turn up to the surface so that my thigh ran across the rusty derailleur like a ham through a meat slicer. In a million years it would have been impossible to repeat.

"But nobody saw that!" said Brooke, pointing. "Nobody ever saw that!"

"Christ," said Kent. He squinted at the water. "That thing's probably thirty years old."

I got up and started limping toward the shore. The dock was short but splintery and uneven. I was starting to feel faint but knew I was fine. I would be fine. It was just startling, and it stung.

I was aware of people pounding up around me, and others

117

coming down to meet us at the shore. Someone very tall wrapped a towel around my shoulders and then scooped me up like I was a child.

"Got her," he said.

"Take her to the infirmary."

"Take her quick."

I didn't need to be carried, but it wasn't a bad idea. I closed my eyes. My leg really was burning. Behind me I heard the boys strategizing how they would hoist the bike from the bottom.

"The thing was rusty," someone said.

"It's not safe."

"Go get Security."

"Go get her adviser."

"Does she need an ambulance?"

The infirmary happened to be just up the hill from the shore where we'd been swimming. The student carrying me was huffing hard as he carried me over the grass and onto the short stretch of road to the infirmary door. Someone else had gone ahead, so a nurse met us there.

"Thank you," she said. I was set down, and she guided my arm across her shoulders. "Come on in now. Thank you, all of you. Thank you."

My towel was soaked with blood. She gathered up new towels for me to sit on, and pressed another on my leg. In a few moments the bleeding slowed.

"You could take a stitch or two here," she said, pointing to the top of my thigh, "but it's not necessary. How do you feel about just waiting?"

I didn't want someone stitching me in the place where she

pointed. I shivered. My suit was puckering, and I smelled the froggy musk of the pond on my skin and in my hair. "I'd just like to get clean and dressed."

The nurse had me lie back with gauze pressed to my thigh, and she covered me with a blanket. I watched the ceiling: white, tacky. I considered how it was only ever observed by sick people, and wondered if surfaces absorbed the aches of those who studied them. This ceiling deserved some sun. *I* deserved some sun.

A doctor came in and lifted the blanket, dabbing gauze along the length of the cut.

"Found something special, did you?"

I didn't answer this.

He'd checked my health file. My tetanus shot was up to date. The bleeding was slowing. "I think you're going to be just fine."

I thanked him.

I wondered where Shep was, whether he would have helped me up to the infirmary and then back to my room. I was in a swimsuit, after all. How would that feel? What would he think?

But he was with his fellow sixth formers somewhere, and my friends appeared in a cluster at the door—wet-haired and eager—asking after me, peering around the room.

It was a fearsome bandage I sported for the last week or so of fourth-form year. Everyone heard about the bicycle. I was congratulated for hitting the jackpot, mocked for aiming for underwater hardware. I was secretly proud. A visible wound counted for something.

I raised twin singeing currents down the tops of my thighs

by replaying in my head the swan dive, the graceful arc, the slice. I remembered how I'd stood, in my bathing suit, alone on the end of the dock like it was a ship, with all of those students behind me and the pond and the forests in front of me, and gone off those boards with summer on my shoulders and pride in my chest.

I did nothing I hadn't seen or known a zillion other students to do. As I had with Shep, when Ms. Shay came through the door. I was straining to burst into this place, into life at St. Paul's. Look at how sophisticated and bright and beautiful they all were, we all were. How lucky. How fated. How good! I felt I measured each leap and made it fairly.

Not you, replied the school. *Not you.*

I did not win the Ferguson Scholarship. After Ms. Shay caught us, Shep never kissed me again. I watched him walk with his class down the chapel lawn to graduate. In the hugging, tearful scrum that followed, he embraced me, and I held very still so I could hear and feel the extra attention I hoped he'd pay me. But he released me and moved on. I haven't seen him since.

Why would I? We had not belonged to each other, we'd belonged to the school. There was majesty in the chapel soaring over us, in the valediction of the departing class. Majesty on the green June lawns. Majesty in rising up to the next year. This was both the glory and the slap of the place: take it or leave it—the school, like time, did not care. It continued on. Yours to decide what to love, or if, or how.

5

Summer 1990

My father insisted that I learn to drive on a *manual transmission automobile*. That's how he said it, and not *stick shift*. He said it was important for safety reasons, because what if someone needed to be taken to a hospital, and the only car around was a manual?

Mom said, "Yes, or if her date is too drunk to take her home."

"Right." Dad turned to me. "Then you just take the wheel."

When they spoke like this, I tried to imagine the shared history that informed their dire scenarios. *Who'd been drunk? Who needed a hospital?* They'd met when they were seventeen and twenty-one and married at nineteen and twenty-three. Their wedding portrait, silver-framed on the bookshelf, showed an impossibly young Mom, her bashful eyes downcast. Five years into their marriage I was born, and after another five years my brother arrived and was given the same name as our father, grandfather, and great-grandfather. Neither of my parents drank much. Dad went to work. Mom wrote sermons and baptized babies. Our toy spaniels had asthma, and bows in their ears.

So this left me, my life, to provide crisis. I wondered when it would begin.

"Absolutely," said Mom. "Your great-grandmother Petey

always told me to keep what she called *mad money* in my shoe."

"Who was mad?"

"She just called it *mad money,* is all. Shisha, she'd say, be sure you tuck your mad money away before you leave that door, because you just can't trust a young man."

Dad nodded. "I'd agree with that."

Dad owned a used BMW that was by then ten years old, and the summer I was fifteen he drove me and my new learner's permit in this car out to the empty parking lot by the middle school in what we called West Lake Forest. Weekend mornings the lot was abandoned. The soccer fields I'd played on when I was little spread out beyond—you could roll a car ten times and never hit anything taller than Queen Anne's lace. Past the train tracks began rows of corn that did not end until the foothills of the Rocky Mountains. It's all built up now, but back then, in the early light, this pavement marked the edge of the map. The school was dark, energy-efficient, dun brick and black glass. I had never been inside.

I got behind the wheel. Dad explained to me how a car's transmission works, forking his fingers to demonstrate cogs engaging. He told me that a good driver knows by the sound of the engine how fast it is spinning, and that I should down-shift to decelerate so the engine took as much of the work of braking as possible. The car shuddered all over. Our backs ached from jolts. But I thought nothing on earth could make him happier than my easing out the clutch and, using sound alone, determining exactly the right moment to send the car smoothly into second, and then third, and then—along the long exit lane to the road—fourth. "It's a two-step," he said. "It's a dance."

After a few weeks Dad upped the ante. "What you need to learn now is how to skid. And that means rain."

While we waited, he cleared his intentions with the local police department. There was an officer who sang in our church choir and liked to stop by our house on his motorcycle just to check up on things. We suspected he had a crush on Mom. Dad sold his skidding plans as student-driver education, which wasn't untrue.

Finally in July came a dripping mist. Saturday morning, lights on and wipers slow, Dad and I drove out to the middle school before 7 a.m.

"What driving is really about is mastering what you can't anticipate," he told me, getting out of the car and motioning that I should join him. As I passed him, swapping seats, he handed me the key. "Now, go straight, and go fast."

The school loomed darkly. The windshield was steaming up, and droplets streaked across the glass at my side. First, second, third. "Okay..." said Dad, and then he reached his left arm over and yanked the wheel hard—"Now!"—sending us into a right-hand skid. He braced his arms on the dash (no air bags in this old sedan) and waited for me to stop flailing and steer into the swerve, allowing the car to catch and shoot out, like a swimmer exiting a riptide. It was a sharp turn, but the tires found the ground. My heart was wild. I stopped the car, forgetting the clutch, and the engine stalled.

"That's okay!" he said, exuberant. "That's it! Did you feel that? How we were hydroplaning, and then you got the tires back under the car and regained traction?"

Yes, if that's what you called that, then yes, I felt it.

"Terrific," said Dad. "Let's do it again."

He threw other things my way. He pulled the wheel right or left, turned dials, switched off the ignition. I learned to work with panic: just a healthy physiological reaction to going faster than I wanted to go. A skid? Just misguided momentum. A shudder was the engine begging for gas. The car shrieked and smelled. "That's okay!" said Dad again. "That's a car doing what it's built to do."

When it was over I imagined the steel panting, like I was, bowed over its tires. Then Dad drove us home through the cool rain, the trees bending low and green.

Where I feel defensive in telling this story is, I sense, exactly where I need to steer. This means going where I'd rather not go. Physics dictates that your only choice for regaining control in a skid is to head in this new direction. It's the first thing that happens in a sexual assault: somebody grabs the wheel and shit starts turning, fast. Next thing you know, you can't find the ground. You're on a mattress, say, pushed up beneath a window. The entire time I was in the boys' room, my feet never touched the floor.

I have a friend whose vocation is supporting Native American-led institutions on tribal reservations. These institutions serve indigenous women, children, addicts, the grieving. Andrea is a skilled navigator of predatory power structures, and because she's been my friend since I was in grade school, she knows what happened at St. Paul's. Recently I found myself telling her, again, about the bind I found myself in once I landed on the boys' bed. The faculty adviser lived right through the wall, I explained, pointing severely, as they had done, as if across a room. (Andrea did not go to boarding school.) "I got it," she said. I continued: "His name was Mr. Belden. He taught computer science and did not know me from Eve. He'd have come in and found me, a fifth former, out of my dorm after check-in on a raft of mattresses with two sixth-form boys *in their underwear.* Can you imagine what he'd have thought of me?"

"Yeah," said Andrea, "I think I can."

I opened my mouth to continue, but then she said the opposite of what I thought she was thinking.

"Any mature, boundaried adult would have seen a fully clothed girl with two naked men and said, 'One, why is she here? And two, why are you not wearing clothes?'"

I was in my fifth decade of life when my friend said this to me. Her construction alone was boggling: the accused *you* would have been them. And I got to be simply *she.*

It had never once occurred to me that Mr. Belden, storming in and flipping on those dentist-office lights, might not have blamed me.

Why?

So here's what I don't want to write about.

In between driving sessions, my family hosted the Lane family for a weekend "in the country," meaning our suburban town. I'd forgotten the promise that Jed Lane had made a year before to fly to New Hampshire and see me; deep in my new world at St. Paul's, I'd forgotten about the Lanes entirely. They drove up from the city with gifts and a bottle of wine. Mr. and Mrs. Lane were given the guest room that was next to my parents' room, at the end of the upstairs hall. Morgan, their little boy, was billeted in my brother's room, and Lilibet, younger than I was by several years, shared my room at the top of the stairs. My family had never had guests like this before, and our house was as festive as Christmas. The dogs swirled around Mrs. Lane's feet. Jed—Mr. Lane—cut back and forth across our kitchen, mixing drinks. Their children had inherited his grin. They were bold, adored. The locusts were loud in the oaks and my mother's roses were in bloom. She opened the French doors. Everything my parents wanted for me, for us, was on the hoof.

That night, though, I couldn't sleep. As a fifteen-year-old I found sleep cagey, receding when it was intended and swamping me in the day. I woke up too hot in my sheets, everything all wrong. I'd go downstairs in my nightgown to watch television. We had an old set in my dad's office, where the bookshelves were, and down there, nobody in the sleeping house would be awakened by the sound. This was the first year we had cable. I flipped idly through the stations: nothing, something, nothing. I was sitting on the floor, right up close to the set, so I could keep the volume low.

Was it eleven or eleven-thirty or twelve when Mr. Lane appeared in the doorway?

I turned. His grin first, Cheshire cat, as my eyes adjusted to the hallway where he stood. He was in boxer shorts and a white undershirt, and he held a silver flask in his hand.

I hopped up, conscious of my knee-length nightgown, conscious of not having a bra on underneath it.

He said, "Can't sleep?"

"I was just going to bed," I said. "Just now."

But this meant switching off the set, which would leave us

in darkness, and getting past him to get to the stairs. I looked directly at him to keep his eyes off my body.

"If you say so," said Mr. Lane.

He had a little tummy under his shirt. I hated its softness. I'd have hated a well-built body, too, though differently.

He turned and retreated into the hall.

Prickling with nerves, I waited a few long minutes, and then, when I heard nothing, I scooted down the hall to the bottom of the stairs.

He was there, a few steps up. The grin again.

"I'm just going up," I said.

"Not without giving me a good-night kiss."

"No."

"You have to give me a good-night kiss."

The kitchen on one side was dark, the hall on the other side was dark. Our only light fell through the hall window, from the street lamp at the foot of the driveway. I took a step up onto the staircase. Jed Lane was two stairs above me, where there was a slight curve and the steps narrowed.

"Come on. Just right here." He pointed to his cheek.

I darted into the air alongside his face, pantomiming his silly European air-kiss, and he reached his hand behind my head and caught me. He smashed his mouth on mine and stuck his tongue inside. Liquor.

I remember being disgusted but not alarmed. I pushed him off and ducked under his arm up the stairs to my room directly at the top. I closed the door quietly and then leaned against it, half in case he tried the knob and half because that seemed like what you should do in a situation like this, when you were fleeing up the stairs at night. I was playing snippets of other lives, other dramas, in my head because I did not want to think about what had happened just now.

His little girl was asleep in my room, honey hair on the pillow. I couldn't get to my parents at the end of the hall without encountering him again, so I pulled on shorts and a T-shirt and sneakers and climbed out my window. From there it was an easy gutter-hang to the driveway. I was careful to latch the screen behind me so Lilibet wouldn't wake up alone in a strange house and be in danger of climbing out too.

I ran to my grade-school friend Casey's house half a mile or so east and threw stones at his window, but he didn't appear. So I continued east to the beach and sat in the sand until the sun rose over Lake Michigan.

Was I sad? I remember being frightened, though not of Mr. Lane. I was frightened that some other man might find me there at the public beach, in the park, and take me. I didn't imagine what he'd do next, but I kept remembering Jed Lane's hand on the back of my head, the way I'd had to use even the strength of my neck to push myself away. I turned often to peek over my shoulders. The bluffs were still.

When I came back in through the back door, Mom was making coffee. The Lanes were not down yet, but I heard feet thumping around upstairs.

"Where were you?" she asked.

"Out on a run."

"Okay. Where were you?"

"I just had to go for a walk."

"Why are you not telling me the truth?"

I held her eyes to show her I was lying but not hiding.

"I just had to get out."

She watched me, and I saw her shoulders rise and fall. She dropped her eyes to the cabinets, blankly, and then raised them again. She had a dish towel in her hand and she balled it up before speaking, like she was packing a snowball. "Lacy." Her voice was low. "Did something happen with Jed last night?"

That she somehow already knew struck me as no more or less shocking than the thing he had done. I gathered that I was newly arrived to where my mother was, in this world of downstairs men at night, where I supposed all women lived. I didn't like it, but she wasn't surprised to find me here, so what choice did I have but to be here too? Jed Lane's name was on my father's business cards and frosted on the executive glass in his skyscraper door.

I nodded.

Mom exhaled hard. "Okay. Tell me everything."

Her hand on her coffee mug was as white as the ceramic as I talked.

"That's all?"

"That's all."

"He tried nothing more?"

"Nothing."

She ran her finger around the top of her mug while she thought. I had no idea where she would come down, where her intention would drop. Finally, she said, "Oh, man, this would create a big stink."

Around town, she meant. I didn't disagree. Everyone knew the Lanes; at least, everyone who mattered to my parents did. "It's okay," I said. The gossip would have been horrible. Already my memory of what he'd done felt intrusive and embarrassing. I watched Mom calculating. My father came down, said,

"Good morning, Say-see," which is what I had called myself when I was small. "You're up early. How'd you sleep?"

I looked to Mom. She was still unsure. Dad unfolded the papers, poured OJ, headed back out for something else.

"Is it okay if I tell your father?"

"Yes," I said.

She nodded. "Later."

I agreed. The Lanes would be with us all day. We'd drive to the country club for lunch on the patio, overlooking the greens. I'd offer to take his children to the pool. The trick would be to get into the water without being seen in my swimsuit, to stay submerged until he left for another Scotch and soda.

At some point Mom talked to Dad. I wasn't there when she did. It was decided that nothing should be done about Jed Lane's little bit of *droit du seigneur,* and the less said, the better. We'd just not have them stay the night anymore. And no more lunches downtown. This stuff happens. It's infuriating, said Dad, but it does.

So that was that.

I turned it over and over. I was proud to have passed muster. I'd met an upheaval with nonchalance (my father's daughter). I'd escaped my home without disturbing the honored guests (my mother's daughter). In the churn of my thoughts I had the sense of both ascending and descending, as in the cartoon of two escalators crossing and the principals, heading in opposite directions, meeting in the middle. That July, that August, I was both rising to an adult comprehension of the fallibility of appearances and sinking toward an awareness of the ugly contortions of discretion. Maturity: people lie, or at least deny, and you must too. Maturity: this means you can do things you are not supposed to do.

It seemed fitting that it all went down on a staircase at night. Staircases are for lovers and getaway artists, the in-between of floors and ages. I replayed the scene in my head and tried to imagine what I should have done. Mr. Lane had never been interesting to me as a person—just an adult man, opaque and mustachioed, whose jokes I did not understand and whose desires were not my concern, so he was not a character worth wasting time on. When I imagined alternate outcomes of that night, I never animated him. I imagined myself bigger, bolder, cleverer. In my mind I'd humiliate him, or punch out his gleaming teeth, or trip him down the stairs so his flask spilled all over our floor. In my mind I wasn't a girl in a nightgown, so I could do these things.

I understood my parents' silence to be protective. They were right: the story of what happened would have attached to me, the high school sophomore out of bed in the small hours.

Even there—do I write *the story of what happened* or *the story of what he did?*

Trying again: the story of what he did would have attached to me, the high school sophomore out of bed in the small hours, like a cursed baton he'd passed to me on the stairs while my parents and his wife and his children and my brother slept.

Why invite all of that? I imagined my family's concern and understood it, and I took it in stride.

But this is not the whole of what I'm afraid of writing about. It is the easier part, the bit that came first, when I was vulnerable.

Jed Lane smash-mouthed a lot of girls. His hands went up and down the backs of daughters at holiday balls, his shoulders blocked doorways all over. We young women worked this out in our twenties, as we met one another either for the first time or finally in a position to talk. We sighed and shook our heads and laughed a bit. The man was a fender bender, a rite of passage. Eventually, his marriage fell apart. He left town.

But later that summer, when I was fifteen and Jed Lane was still a part of the firmament, I went to a party and took a boy's penis out of his pants.

I had been invited to the party by Steph, a local girl I knew from tennis. She was a few years older, with a driver's license and a little cabriolet I coveted, and because our parents were friends she was the perfect person in the perfect vehicle to take me to what was essentially the first teenage party I ever attended. My sense of such events was largely formed by the canon of John Hughes, which, even if it hadn't enchanted me—and it did; I was nine when *Sixteen Candles* came out and ten when *The Breakfast Club* appeared—was visited upon me by peers who could not see an academically capable but naive redhead and not invoke Molly Ringwald. (I was also haunted by some eponymous doppelgänger named Lacey Underall, from *Caddyshack,* but *Caddyshack* was rated R so my parents hadn't let me see it.) I tried to learn from Molly Ringwald to feel stymied but not hopeless, to pout my lips and wait to be discovered for the perfection of my quirkiness and the dignity with which I bore my awkward self. In particular, other kids always asked if I could apply lipstick by securing the tube between my breasts. This was not an option that summer, but I didn't mind the question. I'd gamely try, with a borrowed lipstick, and drop the thing down the bottom of my shirt to the ground.

At the party there were newly graduated seniors from St. Paul's. There was beer. The former offered me the latter. I was astonished at the ease of it.

Also, oddly, I was infuriated. I felt apart from the other kids, as though they were in the coming-of-age movie and I was stuck in this real world where your father's best friend grabs you in your own home, and then the waters close over the event and nothing is there. I did not understand what I had come up against in Jed Lane—was that desire, or drunkenness, or some sort of insanity? I had started to feel ashamed of the way I must have looked. Of my light blue nightgown. Though I knew it was crazy, I worried that the kids at this party would see me that way too—compromised, caught out barefoot on the floor. As though he'd seen something in me before I could discover and contain it. I had new experience, but I felt newly skinless. Did these things happen to anyone else? Did they happen to everyone else? How could I ask these other kids without revealing something I'd been forbidden to share?

Worse, I was now worried about someday realizing that I wanted to have sex. I was frightened that if that desire appeared in me, it would confirm Jed Lane's ugly wager and make him right about me. Back in the springtime at school, when I had kissed Shep, my torso would begin a kind of humming that I liked to return to in memory. Was that what Jed Lane knew? Now I wanted to want nothing, ever, from a man.

I chatted away, drinking beer. Steph was a responsible soul, and I could trust her not to get too drunk to take me home.

Once I was tipsy I was seated on a card table, legs swinging, and at some point the recently graduated roommate of our host appeared in front of me. They had both started at St. Paul's as third formers, so by the time they were eighteen they had lived together for four years, and couldn't seem to quit each other even after graduation. The boy before me was visiting from the South and he would return there for college. We'd never had a conversation before, but observing him, I'd always found him charming and a bit goofy. The conceit was that he was unaware of his classic good looks and his pedigree. Given the list of his names, you'd never have guessed in which order they might appear, much less what to call him. (The truth was a nickname fit for a dog.) He was funny—I had known this—but I had not known that he thought I was funny, too.

I gave him a hard time about the girlfriend he'd dated at school. I still cannot picture one without the other: leggy young people in matched stride down a paneled hall, him smiling at her feathered wall of blond hair.

"That's over now," he said. "She's cool with it. Long distance is no good."

I nodded as though I had some knowledge of this.

"I always thought you were cute," he added, and I was dumb enough, or surprised enough, to consider it a non sequitur.

"You did?"

"Oh, totally. We all did."

I thought, *Then why everything (the fart with a face)? Then why nothing?* My mind was sodden with beer and hope.

"But then you were with Shep," he said.

Almost a year when nobody even talked to me. "I wasn't, really."

He shrugged, and drank his beer. "You excited to go back?"

"I think so."

"You think so?"

"Yeah."

"Come on. SPS is great. SPS is terrific. You have to be excited to be a fifth former. You're an upperformer now." He sounded wistful.

"Are you sad to be leaving?"

He finished his beer. "Aw, yeah. You'll see. You're going to go back and totally love it now."

"If you say so."

"I say so."

I'd have liked to hear more. I would gather details about precisely which good things awaited me back at school, as though his voice could deliver them to me. But I was aware that my longing for safety was the wrong note to sound beneath the banter of our exchange. This was a party, I told myself. Be cool. Stop caring. God, I was so tired of caring. I wanted the chatter and the froth. I wanted this tall boy to keep talking. I wanted to just drift a bit, and have it be fine.

He smiled, bent down, and kissed me. I was aware that the other kids had left the room. I didn't want the kiss, which surprised me, so I put my hands on his chest, feeling his shirt against my palms, and pushed him gently upright. He unfolded without protest.

"What's up?"

"Just, hang on," I said. I wasn't sure. No desire appeared, no simple appetite. I did not dare look at his face to work this out together, to share something of myself with him, or ask for something of him in return. I had the odd urge to tell him about Jed Lane. I was secure in my seat on the card table, my feet hanging down, hands firmly pressing his torso. I needed time. I hooked my fingers on his belt and rested them there.

"Oh," he said, like a child. "Oh."

I looked up. His eyes were wide. This sudden tilt of power from him to me rushed at me like the beer, like the awareness that we were alone in the basement now. I realized he was frozen. He moved my hands to his buckle. I undid his belt. It was black leather, with a silver buckle, and I liked the way the strap slid free—it felt purposeful, like I was untacking a horse. I still did not have a plan. He rubbed his hands on my shoulders and brushed one palm over my hair, awkwardly, as if he'd never touched a girl before, which I knew could not be further from the truth. He was pawing me to keep me going. It irritated me. I wanted to stay out ahead of his desire, rather than respond. For once, I wanted to be completely in the lead, as unpredictable to others as others seemed to me. I shook my head to toss his hand off my hair, and then opened his jeans, found the slit of his boxer shorts, and took out his already erect penis.

I looked for the first time.

This?

This.

I could not believe this man, this college freshman, would consent to stand in front of me, exposed as he was, letting me hold him, behold him, as I was. How convinced must he have been of my intentions? How certain of his own pleasure? I thought of him with near condescension, the entitlement of another man in his underwear in my dark house throwing a long shadow. What was this force that led men to break down like this?

I rubbed him for a bit, like I was warming up the arm of a child who had played too long in the snow. He adjusted my hands and modified my stroke. I did this for a while. He made encouraging noises. The train was stalling, though, and I was beginning to feel embarrassed by what was going on. I wondered if Steph might leave without me in her cool little car. I wondered what time it was.

There existed retreat, or advance. The former seemed to me to invite self-consciousness and shame. The latter showed clarity, even mastery. My old self was on one side and my new self—the fifth former, the girl on the stairs—was on the other. I lowered my head to his penis and took the end of it in my mouth. The noises he made were shocking. I did not feel my body respond, and he did not try to move me. His hands went limp on my shoulders. Periodically he squeezed the rails of my collarbone and leaned his weight toward me. My hair screened my face and my bizarre act. That's what it was to me: bizarre. I was taking the dimensions of some vector of power, poling to the bottom to see what was down there. It was surprisingly physical, salty, silly.

I didn't anticipate his coming, and it wasn't pleasant. I swallowed hard and hopped down off the card table. He was gazing at me with a lopsided smile, faintly confused, but quiet.

"Wow, Lacy," he said. "Thanks."

I was embarrassed for his sincerity. Angry that he thought that I had meant to do something for him, that this had been about him at all.

We climbed the stairs and found the others, and I gave nothing away. There was nothing to give. I folded up the experience like a receipt in my pocket—it might come in handy later, if I wanted to check the details, but the errand was done. I said nothing and switched to soda from beer. About an hour later, Steph and I left by the front door. My host, who had not been in the basement with us, hugged me goodbye. Just before I turned to head down the front walk, he patted my middle and said, "They're still swimming in there." It was some months before I realized what he'd meant.

Really, it would be so much easier to tell the story of what happened at St. Paul's and not tell this.

In the early pages of Alice Sebold's luminous and bold account of her rape while a student at Syracuse University, during which she was attacked by a stranger in a park at night and badly beaten, she writes wryly of the advantages she discovered when she arrived at the police station to have her testimony taken:

> The cosmetics of rape are central to proving any case. So far, in appearance, I was two for two: I wore loose, unenticing clothes; I had clearly been beaten. Add this to my virginity, and you will begin to understand much of what matters inside the courtroom.

The title of Sebold's memoir, *Lucky*, is taken from the line an officer spoke about how the last woman they'd found in the place where she was raped had been murdered and dismembered. It's a bitter term—evidence of how the same words have different meanings to a victimized woman and a world inclined to deny trauma. Where the word pivots is where Alice Sebold goes unheard. They called her *lucky*, which foreclosed the possibility of their understanding the impact of what had been done to her. I unheard her too, but in a different way: for a long time, I envied that she'd been attacked by a stranger. I thought that *was* lucky. And that she'd been an absolute virgin—not only a stranger to intercourse, as I was, but a stranger to any body other than her own. Unimpeachably pure. And, above all, she'd been injured. I actually envied her this. Nobody, seeing what happened to her, would say, *But you wanted this.*

Of course, her story was not that simple, because the criminal justice system is set up, at least in theory, to assume innocence until guilt is proven. A defense attorney made hay of the fact that Sebold, traumatized and intimidated by her attacker, chose the wrong man in a lineup. The defense came after her for her uncertainty but largely left the issue of consent alone. She had already won that one, welts glowing, hands down.

I could not earn my innocence with injury. Nor, I believed, could I earn it with—well, *innocence.* Because I was not wholly pure. Though to the best of my awareness that night at the party made nothing subsequent happen—nobody formed expectations of me as a result of it—still I held that I was guilty.

And in court I would have had lots of company arguing I wasn't pure. The reason I hate to write what happened on that card table—*what I did* on that card table—is because it's a defense attorney's dream. Aha! Desire! As though my choice on one night cost me the benefit of the doubt forever. The blanket projection of proto-consent, cast across all the days and nights of my life.

I don't owe anyone the telling of this. I never sued or took my abusers to court. Nor is it a matter of conscience. I did not want to write it because it should not matter, but of course it does, because a girl who is attacked will so often assume the fault lies with her. There is no escaping a primal culpability. I include the events of the summer I was fifteen in open defiance of this presumed vulnerability, and to force into view what is to me the chilling logic that a girl who has explored a boy's body, or permitted her body to be explored in any way, is thereafter suspect as a victim.

In other words: it's open season on her.

In other words: to believe in the perfect victim is to believe in no victim at all.

6

Fall 1990, Fifth Form

I returned to St. Paul's for my fifth-form year in the first sharp nights of September, a long week before classes began. I'd been invited early to practice with the varsity soccer team and quickly made the squad. I was released from far-flung Warren House and the claustrophobic double I'd shared as a fourth former, but swapped it for a lonely perch: I'd been assigned to a single in Brewster House, on the quad, while most of the Kittredge girls were all together with a few other girls across campus, in Center. Linley from Colorado had elected not to come back at all. She did not elaborate. She just didn't like it very much, she said, and her decision rattled me. I had considered people who came home from boarding school to have failed in some way, but Linley was fabulous. She had made a choice. It frightened me to think this choice was available to me too.

But the rogue housing lottery (which was not a lottery at all) had seen to put Elise—the sleepy artist from Kentucky—in my dorm too, in her own single three doors down the hall. She had been Linley's roommate, so she too was now on her own. I didn't know Elise well. None of us did. But her serious boyfriend from the year before had now graduated, and because we were the only two of our larger group of friends to be living in this part of campus, we took to each other immediately. Elise modeled a form of independence that thrilled me. She dismantled her bed, stacked the frame in our dorm's basement, and made up a futon on the floor. The carpet around it was strewn with sweaters and long socks, and the air smelled of linseed oil and turpentine from her advanced art studio. Her hair was often unbrushed. She carried books in her arms rather than in a woven tote like the rest of us, and when you read their spines you saw she was reading things not assigned for class. At the beginning of the year she took on Simone de Beauvoir in the original. I'd stick my head in after soccer practice, before classes had properly begun, and find her lying on her stomach on her mattress, with *Le Deuxième Sexe* and a French-English dictionary open in front of her and an uncapped blue Bic in her hand.

"Want to walk to eat?" I'd ask.

"Nope," she'd say kindly but without apology. "I'm dining with Simone."

Around Elise I felt saccharine and young, sporty and painfully earnest. She'd never have worn soccer shorts. Instead of cleats, she glided around in hemp sandals. Instead of holding crushes, she returned to Brewster House in the evenings trailing boys she occasionally deigned to date. Early in the fall term, a classmate of ours, Scotty Lynch, started turning up. He was distinguishable anywhere on campus for his pouf of curly brown hair and impish grin. When he smiled, his eyes narrowed dramatically and held a twinkle of sincerity that was unexpected, given the rat's nest and the slouchy cords. He was a true buddy, usually faintly redolent of marijuana and, like all his kind, masterly at affecting indifference to any form of authority or routine. I suppose Scotty went to class, but I never saw him in the Schoolhouse. I never heard him complete a sentence—he'd just scratch at the back of his hairy head and say, "Yeah, cool." Elise played modern blues on her stereo and kept her room dim by tacking scarves over the windows. She spent closed hours with Simone and open hours with Scotty. I, running stairs, running to the fields, running to the chapel for choir rehearsal, felt like a windup toy beside her feathery, breathy, French-philosophy wiles.

Within a few weeks of the new school year, I was fretting about whether to drop honors calculus for regular calculus. The decision felt monumental. Has a world ever been so small? The choreography of our curriculum and activities was, even in the early 1990s, tailored toward college acceptances—add Stanford and MIT, and one-third of my class would matriculate at Ivy League schools. As a junior I was already a year ahead of where the standard math sequence would have me, but would it demonstrate a failure of ambition to drop an honors class?

"Alternatively," said Mrs. Fenn, my fifth-form adviser, "would it be good to give yourself a little break somewhere?"

Easy for her to say, I thought. She taught regular calculus and was master of our dorm, living in the largest apartment, the one with a door that opened onto our common room, from which the smells of dinner cooking and the sounds of her children playing could sometimes make me weak. How could she understand how hard I had to paddle now? Academically, fifth form was a step up. Even if we hadn't felt the ground beginning to shudder with the approach of college, we all had a full year of Religion class, including the two dreaded exegesis papers; English electives that sent us deep into texts; conversational foreign language and literature classes; lab science; and so on. The only way to be high-achieving was to do everything, and because we never went home, there was nobody stopping us from working all night long, working through breakfast, studying flash cards in Chapel, rehearsing physics equations by the grassy defensive end of the soccer field, conjugating the *passé simple* while waiting for the alto line to enter Fauré's *Requiem Op. 48*.

"But Princeton," I said.

Mrs. Fenn pressed her lips together and puffed out her cheeks. My father had gone there. My grandfather had gone there. My uncle had gone there. My great-uncle had gone there. Dad liked to joke that I was welcome to attend any college I wanted, but if I went to Princeton, he'd pay for it. I did not experience these expectations as privilege; they terrified me. Besides immorality, the salient feature of entitlement, I think, is the total failure of imagination. The world of my adult life existed on the other side of a keyhole, and the shape of that lock was Nassau Hall. I could imagine no other.

"Princeton will be fine," said my adviser. "I'm more concerned about you."

I hung on to honors calc. There were ringers in that room, kids snapping their fingers before calling out answers, already chafing at their confinement to single-variable equations. I felt the chill of confusion, of being left behind, and it panicked me.

For English that term I'd chosen Modern Novel with Mr. Katzenbach, because as a debater I had watched Coach Katzenbach stand at a lectern and coolly prove to a student that he was not actually sitting in the chair he was sitting in, ontologically speaking. I'd had no exposure to rhetoric (only etiquette, brittle pretender). Mr. Katzenbach worked logic like a rope and used ordinary words to give the world the slip. The feeling of watching him do it was similar to the few times I'd been almost drunk, but better, because it was clear and cold. His coaching had been so good that the first time I'd traveled with the debate team to compete, back in fourth form, I'd returned with a trophy, a small personalized gavel with a metal plate bearing my name and FIRST PLACE, SECOND NEGATIVE. I'd gone on a lark. Mr. Katzenbach told me to consider law school. By fifth form I couldn't fit debate in my schedule alongside varsity sports, but I could take Katzenbach's English class.

For Modern Novel, he assigned Joseph Heller's *Catch-22*. On the first day, we settled around the lacquered round table—humanities classes at St. Paul's were taught at "Harkness Tables," in expectation of discussions, not lectures—and set our thick blue paperbacks like dead birds in front of us. Mr. Katzenbach hitched up his huge stained trousers and said, "All right, what's this? *They call me Ishmael.*"

We looked around the room. Blanks.

He shook his head. "Really? Okay. *All this happened, more or less.*"

More blanks.

He growled. "Okay. Come on. *All happy families are alike; every unhappy family is unhappy in its own way.*"

We were sinking into our shoulders.

"Argh! Are you there? Are you in there?" He shuffled around the room, panting, periodically tugging at his pants. "*It was love at first sight.*"

Nobody breathed.

"JESUS! Can you READ? Can you SEE? Open the BOOK!"

Fumbling pages. There it was, the first line of *Catch-22:* "It was love at first sight."

"So," said Mr. Katzenbach. "Who can tell me about love?"

Now, Mr. Katzenbach, by the time I had him in class, had been teaching at St. Paul's for decades, and in those decades he had touched several girls inappropriately, struck up unacceptable relationships with a few, and harassed many more. I knew nothing of this, and I include it because its presence in the generally aseptic report issued much later by a law firm hired by the school to investigate the history of teacher-student abuse on campus embitters my memories of him, as well it should. Among other incidents, the report details how, after he pawed one girl's breast beneath her sweater, she went directly to an administrator and coach she trusted, John Buxton, to complain, and Mr. Buxton replied by asking her what she had done to cause Mr. Katzenbach to behave in this way. This happened the year before I was born, sixteen years before I had him in class. Mr. Buxton had risen to vice rector by the time I was there, and Mr. Katzenbach seemed to me a very brilliant, very overweight and unhealthy man. Some combination of diabetes and dissipation gave him potent body odor, and his scalp was always running with sweat.

"A true *jolie laide*," said my mother, as I described him to her (I no longer cried into pay phones), which was not quite right, but I was happy to have a new phrase for this new character in my life. He made us talk about love. I didn't know what it meant to him, of course. I had no idea what it meant for anyone, but I was damned ready to learn. We spent that entire class on the first line. *The first line.* Nobody had ever directed me to read closely before. Nobody had ever been driven to yelling by words on a page. We opened all the windows and let him billow, like a sail.

I wanted to take Modern Novel all day long. Like Elise, I began checking out fiction and poetry collections nobody made me read: Alice Munro, Adrienne Rich, Ellen Gilchrist, Isak Dinesen. Here was a force to temper the lockstep urgency of the college-prep process. It was so simple: *pleasure,* the idea that I might find things I *wanted* to learn about, and follow in that direction. This momentum gathered fast. I dropped honors calc and, with an approving arm around my shoulder, Mrs. Fenn welcomed me into her regular calculus course, where I could plow through problem sets without much trouble. I was grateful for this bit of ease, and gratitude made me feel generous, particularly toward the few sixth formers in my new math class who were anguished and looking for help. I answered the pleas of hockey-playing Declan Brophy not least because my friend Maddy, still devoted to him, wanted to hear what his room looked like. For several weeks that fall I'd hike the wooded path to his dorm after Seated Meal, nights I didn't have choir rehearsal, and sit on the floor, back to a sofa, leading him through integral equations. I wished Maddy could have come with me—I don't think there exists a better way to untangle a girl's admiration for a boy than to try to coach him through calculus. Brophy squirmed and swore. His roommates laughed at him, which I took as an implicit expression of solidarity with me. His thighs were barrels on the floor. Neither of us could read the pencil scratches in his notebook. He tugged at his hair. "God, I fucking hate this stuff," he said.

I'd had no idea you could be at St. Paul's and have such a rough time with coursework.

"This is probably like cake for you, isn't it?" he moaned.

From the movies I had learned the popular archetype of the well-born dolt, whose pink sweater, tied over his shoulders, is the brightest thing north of his balls. You know, the one named Trip, whose loafers pass unchallenged through every door? The truth at St. Paul's was that plenty of high-born kids were terrifically smart. Students on scholarship were in my experience extraordinary too. Many athletes excelled as well, but by fifth form, it was becoming clear which of them would never again be part of an institution as esteemed, at least in certain circles, as St. Paul's School.

I thought of boys like Declan Brophy with equal parts derision and sympathy. I didn't know where the derision came from. I'd like to think it's because these boys christened my friend's breasts *the big guns,* or because they seemed unable to relate to any girl except to ogle her or screw her (or to have her as a tutor, I suppose). But I envied my friend her shape; I wanted to be ogled too. So I was grateful for the invitation to Brophy's room, even if it was only to run through problem sets.

Also, he was nice to me. We high-fived in the halls now. He nodded, passing me in lunch line or on the stairs, and after a little while his roommates started doing this too. It was perhaps a path to friendship, and I might have defended against my hope for it by deriding him, secretly, in my mind.

These were the last days before a teammate of his made the

late-night phone call to my dorm, asking me to come over. September and half of October, 1990. They were beautiful days on campus, as autumn days in New England always are. Wet salmon leaves on the redbrick walks. Marigold trees in the ponds. Sky so blue your eyes made orange. I loved how the slate steps of the Schoolhouse were scooped at the middle from years of feet. I loved the carillon in the chapel tower. Around Halloween every year, certain older masters told stories of a devil in a stained-glass window that was rumored to ring the bells at an off hour, in some homage—I can't remember the details—to Samuel Drury, the fourth rector of St. Paul's. The dorm where I tutored Brophy in calculus was named for Drury, and set off by itself in the woods, beside an open field. At night, when I left to head back to my room, the stars above this field were fantastic. I remember pausing to look up, and not being afraid.

I'm going to call him Rick.

He was tall, almost a foot taller than I was. Three varsity sports, including, of course, hockey. He skid-shuffled his feet down the hall like he was clearing a path. His girlfriend was one of the most beautiful human beings I had ever seen— fleet, fun, an excellent athlete in her own right. I didn't know her and I didn't know him, though he sat a few rows ahead of me in math class, crammed into the chaired desk like a caged pterodactyl. One day, after breakfast, he said, "Hey, maybe you could help me with calculus sometime."

I didn't know he was talking to me.

"Hey, Red."

He was so tall that his voice moved above me, on a different plane. This was in a high-ceilinged corridor. Gothic vaulting, shining glass.

"Hey."

He had caught up with me and matched my pace, so I understood he was actually talking to me.

"Yeah?"

"I said, maybe you can help *me* with math too."

"Oh. Sure. What's going on?"

"Just heard you're really good at it."

I didn't deny it.

"Sure, let me know."

"Maybe you could come over sometime," he said.

I didn't think of my problem sets in Brophy's room as "coming over sometime." There was a rounded feel to this expression of his, but it made no sense, because of the beautiful girlfriend.

"Sure."

"I just heard you're the best," he repeated.

"Um, not really."

"Do you mind being called Red?"

Nobody ever called me Red.

"It's fine, I guess."

"Or Lacy. Lacy."

"Yeah." I wished I had a more ordinary name, like Liz or Jen, so it wouldn't feel so personal, almost private, when he said it out loud.

"Cool." His smile was as big as the rest of him. My body felt uncertain, awake. In my mind was something like an electrical storm, fizzing across surfaces. I had no idea what he intended. He would not flirt with me, I thought, because of his girlfriend, and also because I was just *me*. But what he was doing didn't feel quite like flirting anyway. It felt like he'd issued me something that he might try to take back later.

Then, for several weeks, he left me alone.

The call came late on a Tuesday night. I have already described who was calling, and what followed—the ordinary cataclysm. Why don't victims bite or kick or scream? Because we aren't in a horror movie, we're in our lives. I was ready for bed when a third former named Stacey knocked on my door. "Phone's for you."

This was frightening. My parents would not call so late unless there was a problem. But, I reasoned, heading down the three flights of stairs to the basement, if there were truly an emergency they'd call Mrs. Fenn and have her collect me. So this was something else.

I passed younger girls coming dejectedly up. The line for the phone was long in the fall. To manage this, each girl would reserve her spot as next in line with the caller currently engaged. When the caller finished, she'd replace the receiver to sever the connection and then immediately lift the receiver again and leave it hanging by its silver cable so no new calls could come in while she pounded up the steps to alert the next in line that her turn had come. (The stairwell, far from affording privacy, magnified the speaker's voice, so we were careful to leave one another alone down there.) My call must have come in as a surprise the moment Stacey ended her conversation. This sometimes happened, and it drove us all nuts. She had answered, and because I was an upperformer, she'd had no choice but to come up and tell me the phone was for me.

I held the phone to my ear. It smelled of tears and morning breath. "Hey, Lacy," said a deep male voice that was not my dad.

"Yes?"

"I need your help tonight."

I searched the sound. Nothing came to me.

"Who is this?"

Did he laugh a bit? "It's Rick."

"Oh. Hi." It was strange, but maybe he wanted to go over a problem set on the phone. There was no compelling reason to do so before tomorrow. But that was okay—I was diligent too. I could run up to a new girl's room on the first floor to borrow notebook paper and a pencil to help work things out. "What is it?"

Then he made a sound in his throat, like a sob or a cough, I couldn't tell. So that hadn't been a laugh that I'd heard before. I pressed the phone tighter to my ear. "I really, really need your help," he said.

"What?"

"It's—I'll tell you. Not math. I need to talk to you. I need you to cruise. Please, will you come?"

"Now?"

"Please."

"It's late."

"I know that." He added, "It's a thing with..." and then his voice got very small and shivery. "My mom."

The way he said it, I just knew the diagnosis: either she was dead or would be soon. It was terminal. She'd just told him. And now he was this huge strong man about to lose his mom. I felt a surge of longing for my own mother, and then I settled back into an awareness that she was fine and I was her daughter, also fine, in a tiny way restored.

"What happened?" I asked.

"Please, just come. Please, will you?"

I had never cruised outside my dorm after hours before. I knew other kids did it, but I wasn't sure how they got away with it. Often enough they didn't. All year long we heard the results read aloud in Chapel. Nobody ever suggested *why* a student had left her dorm, but when the name of the suspended or expelled student was read, we all pretty much figured it out. Boys cruised to see girls. Girls cruised to see boys. Where else would they go? Nobody was stargazing. Security caught them and they appeared before the Disciplinary Committee to be, as we called it, D.C.'d. The committee was run by Mr. Gillespie, aka "The Rock." He'd been at St. Paul's for a hundred years and he would be there for a hundred more. He taught chemistry and coached varsity boys' lacrosse, and his trademark exercise was to make the boys start off preseason training running several miles of snow-covered trails in hiking boots. Rumor had it they vomited and bled. He had a military history nobody could identify, but his hair was buzzed and his shoulders wide. When he looked your way, you did your best to smile and scooted out of view fast.

"It's far," I told Rick.

"It's not." He named his dorm, a one-story building at the center of campus. "I'll open the window. You can come and I'll see you."

Whatever it was he needed, I could deliver it, but his girlfriend could not?

I found a way to make this make sense. She was a little cold.

Maybe not as quick. Maybe aloof. Maybe he sensed I was more thoughtful, more able to care?

I was working out the route: along the back path by the power plant, across a depression that flooded in spring. There would be one dangerous crossing of a lit road behind the rectory.

"It's late," I said. "I'll get caught."

"You won't. You're smart. Come on. Please just come."

Maybe that was why: I was smart. He needed someone really capable tonight.

"I don't know where, though." I had no idea where his room was.

"The last window by the path. I'll wait for you. Please."

I was a virgin alone in a basement stairwell, at the bottom of three flights of tile steps, and my grandiosity was colliding with my fantasies, all of them unnamed. I did not think of Rick as a potential lover, not then and not ever. So not that. And not math. But he wanted *something* from me, something that would save him and soothe him, and the fact that he was going to this trouble to convince me meant that I must have had that *something,* whatever it was.

The sense of a summons was hardly out of place at St. Paul's. *Now get up and go into the city and you will be told what you must do.* Our entire mythology was founded on our chosen-ness.

"Please," he said. I heard some shuffling in the background, and then he returned with a whimper in his voice. "I'm waiting for you."

My mom ministered to people. Why couldn't I?

"All right," I said, and I hung up the phone.

•　•　•

Elise had gone to bed. I didn't bother to knock and fill her in. I changed into jeans, a sweatshirt, and a pullover jacket, laced up my sneakers, and crept back down the stairs. Another girl was on the pay phone. I heard her sad voice as I pushed out the door silently, letting it close by millimeters but stopping it before it latched.

I remember my sneakers on the sandy path. That feeling, the whisper sound, was familiar, and a thrill. I had zoomed along trails in the North Woods, summers at sleepaway camp in Minnesota—I had been happy there, happy enough to shout and holler as I raced with my friends down the switchbacks to archery or the riding ring. I remembered the walk down to the beach after Jed Lane grabbed me. I was a feral thing, content in the dark. Here I am again, I thought. Here I am. I ran between shadows and waited, holding my breath, before taking the next angle and the next.

Coming up out of the marshy trail, I heard my whispered name.

"Lacy!"

I followed the sound to a dark window. The sill was shoulder height—too high for me to climb. He bent down and took me under the arms and lifted me in. I was on a bed. I felt bad that my sandy sneakers were on a bed, and tried to shift to the edge.

But someone else was there.

The only light in the room came from the rise and fall of equalizer bars on a stereo system. Its light was blue and traveled. The sound had been turned down very low.

They said, "Shhhhh," pointing to Mr. Belden's wall.

I worked out that the other person on the bed was Taz,

and yes, they were roommates—I guess I had known that. I'd never really thought about it before. I reasoned that if Rick was having a crisis, it made sense that his friend would be with him.

Taz was another sixth former. His girlfriend was on my tennis team. That's all I knew.

But I could see Taz's bare skin lit by the blue, a kind of chalky glow across his chest. And then Rick's bare chest, too—and I gathered this in the moment after I learned that Mr. Belden lived right there and I could not speak without the great danger of getting caught. A Disciplinary Committee action on my transcript in the fall of fifth-form year would take Princeton off the table, immediately and forever. The two boys were on their knees. I was folded on top of my bent legs, my sneakers stuck under me, and I was still worried about the sand on the bed.

I imagined a sort of benign confusion to this setup, not unlike what I used to feel playing Sardines as a child—that hide-and-seek game where each person, upon discovering the hiding spot of the player who is "it," piles into the same small hiding space to wait, silently. The last person out then finds everyone all together, and is next to be "it." I recognized the feeling of fumbling with other kids like this, being shushed and pulled into linen closets in neighborhood homes or under the porch stairs. It could take a while to work out where the bodies were and how to sit. That was part of the fun.

I tried to get my feet out from under me. This is when I asked what was wrong, and was shushed again. And then both boys put their hands on me and pushed me to the mattress. I did not understand. For a fleeting bright moment I thought it might be another wrestling move, like awkward Shep might have pulled—*Okay, okay! Let's play!* I'd go along. I strained to go along. But where Shep would have lifted his hands off me, they held me down. Then they (one? both? I don't know) grabbed my breasts and kneaded them, and it hurt. I still did not understand. Someone went for the button of my jeans, wrenched a hand under the zipper and stuck a long finger inside me. I shot my hand down there and cupped myself, to force him out. Another face was on top of mine now, kissing me hard. I say *kiss* but that's not right. It was a mouth pressed against mine, shoving and sucking, as if in preparation—with the same economy of force my mother used to cram halved lemons and heads of garlic into the cavity of a roasting fowl.

I had no idea this could happen to me—the pure prey I had become, without leverage, without recourse. This encounter with power was shocking and wordless and I did not understand.

What next? My jeans were unzipped. I kept my hand clamped over myself and thought *AIDS, pregnancy, STDs.* I'd had "health class" as a fourth former, and I remembered. If I could protect my virginity, I'd survive this.

"Just don't have sex with me," I said softly, as clearly as I could without Mr. Belden hearing me, and at that point Rick shifted his hips away from mine and up onto my face.

One of my favorite love scenes in print happens to feature this *just don't* construction, when the writer and cultural critic Maggie Nelson spends a first Christmas with her beloved Harry in a San Francisco hotel room: *"Just don't kill me,"* she writes, "I said as you took off your leather belt, smiling."

In which "just" means *please, everything up to.*

I don't for a moment believe they thought this is what I meant. But I do acknowledge that I did not choose my words more clearly, or name my terms more favorably. I see that now. I have always been terrible at negotiation.

Rick laid his pelvis across my face and fucked my throat. Taz grabbed and rolled my breasts. I had to concentrate on breathing, with the cock in my throat, and I did not move any part of my body.

After Rick ejaculated, Taz said, "It's my turn." Was he speaking to me? If so, these were the first words he'd ever said to me. Rick picked me up and angled me so that my face was in front of Taz's erect cock. It protruded blue in the light, and Rick put me onto it like I was a living socket wrench. Again I did not move my body. I worked on getting air into my nose and down into my lungs on the offbeat of his thrusting into my face, of Rick slamming me onto him.

Time got syrupy. I tried not to cry.

After Taz ejaculated into me, Rick let me sit back on the mattress and took his hands off me.

He said, "It's your turn now."

I got up onto my knees and pulled down my jacket, which they had not taken off. I zipped and buttoned my jeans. I remember thinking, *I am completely dressed.* As though something were still intact. But also this stood out for me, the illogic of it—that I was completely dressed. *This was proof, wasn't it,* I asked myself, *that none of this made sense? That we had not just fooled around, but rather that they'd treated me like I was not a girl, not even a person?* I dropped out the window, and they did not try to stop me.

•　　•　　•

Technically, as discussed, in the lexicon of criminal justice what had just happened was *felonious sexual assault* and *aggravated felonious sexual assault*. But these terms belonged to a system of discovery and response that I did not know how to access—it might have been a language spoken on the far side of the globe. Nor did I possess a vocabulary of psychological valence—words such as *consent* and *dissociation*—that might have helped me to understand. I walked back to my room slowly, as though something might come clear.

What they had done, I told myself, was *not that bad*. I had gotten away without worse, without the worst. I was fine. But I was shattered. Why? What part of me was broken? I rehearsed it over and over:

I broke school rules and went to the room of an older boy. He and his roommate, one at a time, put their penises down my throat until climax. I left the room.

It was not quite right.

The problem is a flaw in the chronology. "I left the room" does not belong at the end of the tale. It belongs right after "older boy." Because when they did what they did, I'd offered my body up to them in exchange for protection from greater theft. So:

I broke school rules and went to the room of an older boy. But there were two undressed boys there. I left the room. He and his roommate, one at a time, put their penises down my throat until climax.

Yep, that's it.

• • •

The simplest way I can tell the story of my assault is to describe how the boys made me feel I was no longer a person. Their first violation was erasure. I walked back to my dorm along the main roads, shuffling beneath every streetlight, as though to force the school to acknowledge me. I waited for Murph or Sarge in the white Security Jeep to accelerate from the shadows and stop me with a shout. But the world was different now, or I was, and nobody did.

Or maybe the remedy I'm looking for is not a telling, after all. Maybe it's a correction to that imbalance of power, a restoration of self to self. I went limp while I was in their control. Psychologists who study trauma and violence in all forms, across all criminal variation, identify responses like mine as normal, and have amended the old dictum to read "Fight or flight *or freeze.*" There is plenty of data. I was an ordinary possum.

In fact, I find it easier to try to imagine the boys than myself that night, even though I never spoke to them again. This is an exercise in fantasy, not empathy. If I can rehumanize them, I can offer myself something too. And I might not be wrong. I might find refuge in knowing, which is feeling's poorer relation, but perhaps a place to begin.

For example, what if I consider them from the perspective of social class?

Neither of the men who assaulted me comes from a family whose name is carved on school walls. Think of them that autumn. How exhausting it must have been to be strong and virile and powerful, and beginning to know that they were on campus (on the turf, on the ice) for perhaps exactly those reasons, and that this power was yoked to a system of legacy that would not admit them as men when they were through being boys. They were eighteen and seniors, and their time was already short. How exhausting it must have been to watch a girl, similarly (yet not in parallel ways) unstarred, striving and striving and striving, to hear her coaching your teammates on their calculus sets, to see her in cassock and alb singing a cappella, hair and cheeks shining.

She could be anyone, but this is someone you can hurt almost effortlessly.

You're captains now. It's your last year on campus. Why not take what you can, and kick the door down behind you when you go?

In bearing witness, we're trying to correct a theft of power via a story. But power and stories, while deeply interconnected, are not the same things. One is rock, the other is water.

Over time, long periods of time, water always wins.

What I want to know, even now, is: how?

7

October 1990, Fifth Form

I experienced the new morning not as a different girl, but in a different geography. I was the same. In fact I was even more myself, fretting about things, driving hard. The world was the same, too. But I had become aware of how it fit together in a new way. As though I'd come across a set of maps: here I'd spent all my life thinking the land contained the lakes, and just now discovered that in fact the earth is blue and we're lucky to be afloat.

As the nights grew colder from that third week in October, the news began to spread.

"Whoo-ee, Red," said one football player, slapping his lunch tray down on the conveyor belt next to mine.

As I walked into the reading room, late morning, during a free period: "Hey," said another, watching me enter, his voice sleek with suggestion. "You can leave your sneakers on. Anytime."

But when I tried to remember, my body reacted before my mind could think. My stomach hurt and there was a rushing sound in my ears, as though an elevator had begun to drop. I shut off these efforts immediately. The days were shorter, there was frost on the paths. It felt right to button up. *Batten down the hatches,* my father, the sailor, would say.

My plan was to keep quiet, be very good, work very hard, and slip through the net the night seemed to have cast for me. Above all, my parents must never, ever find out.

It's a curious thing how children are wired to ask for help when hurt or frightened—*Ouch! Help me!*—but shame turns this inside out: *I can survive this as long as nobody else ever knows.* As though secrecy itself performed some cauterizing function, which, of course, when it comes to the matter of self-delusion, it does. I couldn't talk about what had happened without having to let myself think about what had happened. The secret served me.

Plus I saw no logical reason to talk about it. Logic was the least of my modes of engagement with the event, but I was diligent. I was terrified their girlfriends would find out and hate me. I was terrified teachers would find out and have me expelled. I had no idea that what had happened in that room was against the law. I wasn't aware of the statutory legislation—that I was underage—and I knew that the boys had complied with my request not to have sex with me. Yes, they'd held me down. Yes, it had hurt. But I went to their room, right? And did I scream or kick or bite? Finally, the boys bragged about what they did. I was not old enough to wonder whether their grandiosity was intended to mask their own shame or to normalize what they had done. I just concluded that there had been nothing wrong with their part of it, which was why they spoke of it so openly. Hence the hisses along the chapel rail as I scooted to my assigned spot in the pew. And the sixth former Budge, who, as I've mentioned, promised to *pop my cherry.*

• • •

I began traveling with Elise. Her head full of de Beauvoir (and now Sartre, whom she thought a cad), she was unlikely to notice, or to care, what a bunch of thuggish athletes said in my direction. I copied her habit of wrapping a scarf all the way up my face and then pulling it down to offer a bon mot.

"I don't think women are actually meant to be with men," she'd say, her breath glinting in the cold.

"You don't?"

"I think maybe the best we can hope for is to be companionable without ever being truly reciprocal."

While I worked on this, I observed privately that Elise didn't seem to brush her hair much anymore, just let it tangle in her scarf, where it ratted enough to suggest the sophistication of a girl without vanity. She was skipping more and more meals, leaving me to venture out alone. Elise's skin was naturally the color of roasted almonds, but this morning it was ashy, and the early winter light made her hair brighter than her forehead and cheeks. She pulled at her scarf to give me her sleepy grin. "Don't you agree?"

I wanted to ask, *What about Scotty?* But our unspoken pact was to talk only about ideas, never people or events. I assumed this was what it meant to be mature and educated, and of course as a result we never had to so much as skirt the issue of Rick and Taz.

"When you say *companion,* I think of a big wolf," I told her. "Right by my side." I patted my leg where a heeling dog would be.

"Ooh, I like that. I think I'd like a leopard."

"What does Simone say about that?"

The entire school community was funneling toward the big

chapel: masters from their homes, students from their dorms and the dining hall, the tall, thin, long-haired rector crossing in an unbuttoned greatcoat, tails flapping, from the rectory.

Elise sighed. The bells began to ring. You had to not only be inside the doors by eight but be on your way to your seat, or you received detention. The several sets of doors—enormous wooden panels with Gothic studs—were policed by fifth-form chapel wardens. When the last of the eight o'clock bells sounded, things got interesting. Tina worked the left door straight ahead of me: one-half of a set of East Asian twins, she would let me slip through. But Morris, on the right, had two brothers, two uncles, and a father with St. Paul's diplomas, and he'd guillotine you.

"Simone would say go to Paris," Elise said.

"With my wolf."

"*Oui, avec le loup.* And books."

"And your leopard."

"Yeah. I think I'm going to break up with Scotty."

"You're what? Why?"

But she was cutting left, toward the entry closest to her pew.

"I don't know," she said, with her usual breathy detachment. "See you."

Morris, at the door, eyed me. "Well, good *morning,*" he said. The leer of a milk-toned, eyeglass-wearing Wasp such as this looks not unlike the result of a full ophthalmic exam. He held me in his dilated, unfocused stare, but he let me through.

When I could persuade Elise to come to meals, we'd swing through Center Upper, where Caroline, Sam, Brooke, and Maddy—along with two new friends, Meg and Tabby—would be sitting in the hall, notebooks out, waiting for us, and all together the eight of us would go to eat. This made the dining halls mostly safe. I walked to choir rehearsal with Sam, who sang too. Back in the dorm, I brought my books to Elise's room and joined her on the futon on the floor, blues playing, windows darkened, to work.

With the rest of our form, we were hacking through Paul Tillich's *The Courage to Be,* a mid-century existentialist's argument for affirmation in the face of such annihilating concerns as guilt and death. I was in my element. My Religion instructor was a new chaplain, Reverend S., a young father whose faintly protruding eyes always looked to me just on the verge of tears. Mom had met him as she did all Episcopalian clergy, introducing herself as "from the Diocese of Chicago," but his response was chillier than I thought that deserved. Reverend S. pressed out a smile and said, "Fred." *Come on,* I thought, *how many moms are on the inside? How cool is that?*

I resolved to be his best Religion student, for her sake if not for mine. *Because he was the school chaplain,* my thinking went, *if I was his best student, I'd be the best Religion student in the form.* I felt born to it. I loved thinking about language and being and faith, and the more I thought about such notions, the less I worried about my failure to harness them. Whatever small affinity I might have had for this form of inquiry was bolstered by my confidence in my years of exposure to liturgy and Scripture, and the grandeur of the concepts neatly eclipsed my true concerns, which were only growing.

When I called home that fall, as I did routinely so my parents would not worry, I was often surprised by an impulse to tell my mom that something bad had happened. My throat grew cottony with the threat, and approaching tears made it hurt more. I learned to defend against this by talking about Religion class. *How can we know God through the Gospels?* I'd offer. *In the beginning was the word,* Mom would reply, growing animated, and Dad would "ring off" to leave us to it. The world was made from language, Mom said, therefore the divine was immanent in language. God lived in books. She got out her notes from seminary to feed our discussion and mailed me xeroxed chapters of Mary Daly on feminist ecology and Paul Ricoeur on the nature of being. What I wanted, of course, not that I understood this then, was to make a connection with my mother so she could take from me the horrible pain I was in. But I could not do this, so I hoped instead to make a connection, however tenuous, to my mother via my teacher—also a priest, the chaplain, the young father. I knew a lot about a certain God, but nothing I could use. What to say to the boys harassing me? What to do with my throat or the fact that I found myself shivering when I was not cold?

I tried to formulate questions a chaplain would jump to answer:

What does it mean when you feel marked? What if you think hope is self-indulgent and foolish? What if God doesn't listen?

But Reverend S. did not respond to the questions I posed in my papers. I supposed he considered them rhetorical, or at least not meant to invite a pastoral response. The text sought an ontological conception of the notion of despair, and that's what Fred wanted. Fine. I had hoped Religion would offer me rescue in a form I recognized. Instead I worked Tillich's sentences the way I worked calculus sets: *Fear and anxiety are distinguished but not separated. The truth of the vitalistic interpretation of ethics is grace.* These constructions made sense, but they did not touch me at all.

Elise, sprawled beside me, wearing fetching reading glasses she didn't need, said, "Hey, listen to this: 'Be always drunken.... With wine, with poetry, or with virtue, as you will. But be drunken.'"

"Where's that?" I flipped the pages.

"Not Tillich. Baudelaire."

"Makes more sense," I said, and it did. I didn't need help defining despair. I needed help feeling like a living girl. "That one's not in *Fleurs du Mal,* I don't think. Is it?"

"Don't think so. But then it shows up in *Long Day's Journey into Night...* " Elise was, as usual, way out ahead of me. "Let's go to Paris and write plays," she said. I scribbled in my notebook: *Paris. Read plays.*

In Modern Novel, Mr. Katzenbach spent classroom hours forcing us to notice odd fragments of narration in *Catch-22,* places where someone complains of being cold. We were all cold. What was the big deal? The novel's unfolding was not linear, and this offended my new hunger for logic—a rigid, illiterate instinct that emerged the day after the assault, as if in open revolt against the girl with a head full of stories who had cruised to their room. Mr. Katzenbach hollered at us all: *there was a secret in this book, there was a haunting.* He made us identify every moment of this strangeness in the pages, what felt to me a tiresome scattering of ill-fitting detail, and list them all on the chalkboard. He wrote SAVE on the board so our list was preserved as it grew. The book was baffling—iterative and told from several points of view—and Mr. Katzenbach had us track each story line too. "And then what?" he fired at us. "And then what?" Character by character, we called out plot points, cracking the spines of our books so we could rifle faster. Sweat flew off his forehead onto the floor. After he had a student take over the chalk, he pounded on the board with his fist, sending up tiny yellow puffs.

What is to be said about the fact that the teacher who reached me—who made me not only think but feel, who ignited the material at hand—was one who was abusing his power of connection with other girls? Do we call that an unfortunate coincidence? Am I betraying the women he violated by writing about how he, almost alone and without knowing it, helped me that fall?

Mr. Katzenbach demonstrated how the narrative of *Catch-22* unfurled in a circular motion. He plotted every scene in space graphically, following chronology and character, using every last blank bit of board to reveal the spiral thus created. With his curled hand he traced the figure, drawing his finger in toward the center. Before us was a labyrinth, a closing in. What was at the center? What were we reading toward?

"What," he howled, "can you NOT ESCAPE?"

He directed us to open the book to a page near the very end and recited from memory the scene in which the hero, Yossarian, opens his friend Snowden's flak suit to find a hole has been blown in his guts. Snowden's intestines spill free. I thought his injury was tragic, of course. But I was haunted by the fact that the living man alone knew that his friend was dying.

Do something do something DO SOMETHING! I thought.

"I'm cold," said Mr. Katzenbach, softly, repeating Snowden's final words. "I'm cold." He waited, drawing out our attention, which was entirely his. Hushed, he continued: "'There, there,' says his friend. 'There, there.'"

Our eyes were shining.

"That, my friends, is war."

Then, mopping his brow, he released us to the bell.

Walking into breakfast one morning, Caroline sidled up to me and said, "Lace, did something happen with Rick Banner?"

"No." I said it before I even thought it. It emerged reflexively. And then there was ringing in my ears.

She was silent.

We stepped up into the common room outside the upper dining hall and then fell into the line along the hallway that led into the kitchen. There were notices pinned here on a bulletin board, and I pretended to read them. Schedules for laundry collection, community service opportunities. An athletic calendar showing home and away games.

"Okay," she said quietly.

In my mind I begged Caroline to say something else. I had no intention of deceiving her. It was a rejection of our friendship to refuse her question the way I had. It would make her angry, as well it should. But what else could I do? How could I help this?

At the beginning of fifth form, the sixth-form heartthrob Knox Courtland had declared, first through back channels and finally open proclamation, his love for Caroline. But she'd had eyes for someone else: a fellow rower, enormously strong, with what she called "floppy hair." She loved the way his hair bounced around when he walked, the contrast between this and his oversize smile and muscled body. In a few years he'd be an Olympian, but at St. Paul's he was just a sixth former named Dave. And not fit to date Caroline, thought the friends of Knox Courtland.

One evening in lower dining hall, not too many weeks before Caroline asked me about Rick Banner, one of Knox's friends had stood suddenly at his seat, as though to give a toast, and shouted, "Hey!"

All the tables looked up. We were in our usual circle— the Kittredge girls and now Meg and Tabby, too—and we all turned. Knox's friend was staring hard at Caroline.

"You could have had *him,*" said this minion, pointing to Knox. "Do you understand that?"

Caroline was pale, her eyes pained. She'd been hanging out with Dave the rower for a few weeks, but she hadn't said anything unkind, hadn't rejected Knox to his face—she had just taken up with someone else. We girls were uncertain how to react to this boy's eruption of righteous anger. Brooke was gape-mouthed, already starting to laugh. The rest of us were horror-struck. Now this sixth former pointed at our friend Caroline and yelled, "Do you have *any idea what you're doing?*" He picked up his tray and kicked back his chair, and his friends, Knox among them, followed, heads hung. As he passed us, he leaned low and added, "Dave is a *tool.*"

Caroline would have been able to understand domination. She'd have accompanied me to tell a teacher. She'd have listened.

Why could I not tell?

The memory existed behind what I can best describe as a narrow and tensile membrane that felt more than anything like a part of my very body, and I had a pure, instinctive

171

unwillingness to break it, as though to push through it would be to tear open some part of myself. I'd tried so hard not to crack, and now my friend, my dear friend, was asking me a question that felt like yet another invasion. I could not answer her.

We made it to the kitchen, picked up our trays, and skipped the hot meal line for the coffee and tea tanks. I popped a frozen waffle into the toaster. Caroline made her tea. She had a green apple on her tray, and she stood with me by the bread and toasters and gobbed some peanut butter onto her plate with a spoon.

Ordinarily she'd wait for me there, chatting, while my waffle wound its way beneath the heating coils. But today she picked up her tray and walked off toward our friends.

By the time my waffle dropped down I was no longer hungry. I buttered and loaded it with cinnamon sugar anyway. I always ate like a toddler. I wore my parka and gloves, like a girl visiting Grandma. I was ridiculous. I set my tray down at my friends' table, ashamed of my own food, and dropped into the seat behind it.

I got a few strained smiles. My heart might have stopped. The news had reached my friends; here it was.

My throat had been hurting for a few days, which was a good enough reason not to eat. Brooke was complaining about a class, and Maddy was giggling. Caroline hacked slices off her apple with a dull cafeteria knife. I scoured my brain for a clue about how to handle this, the slipping away of my confidants, but I couldn't find any solution save saying the thing I absolutely could not say. There was nothing else that could cause them to see.

At five minutes to eight we tossed our trays on the belt, slung our bags off the floor and onto our shoulders, and pressed out the door onto the path. Students were everywhere, surging into the day, and if you'd been watching, you'd have seen me walking with a bunch of girls, as though I belonged. But the stain had touched them, and now I had failed Caroline, too. I sensed that from here the descent would be rapid indeed. I had no idea where it would lead.

As I've said, first, I got sick.

My initial visit to the infirmary was useless. I have only slivers of memory of being feverish in an infirmary bed, shades drawn against the fall blaze, hearing the voices of my schoolmates on the walks. I thought I was crazy, and that my throat was either swelling up to suffocate me or peeling away to rawness, as though what had passed there had to be sloughed off indefinitely.

Finally they prescribed the medication I needed, but without telling me why I needed it. The Zovirax, an antiviral, did its job. I never saw a sore (I still never have; there is no way I can examine a place so deep). The outbreaks would recur every six weeks or so, because I was not taking Zovirax prophylactically, which would have been medical protocol for my diagnosis. But the doctor at St. Paul's did not, would not, tell me what was wrong.

When I arrived home for Thanksgiving, Mom was there in the pickup lane at O'Hare, hazards flashing, with a basket of strawberries waiting for me in the car. She hugged me quickly in the pools of exhaust. "Get in, get in! It's cold! You're home!" She handed me the fruit. "Figure we'll start getting you vitamin C right away!" I had been so sick, after all.

Her face betrayed nothing but pleasure, so neither did mine.

That year we spent the day of Thanksgiving itself at the house in St. Louis where my father's parents had lived for more than thirty years. Our family traveled to accommodate the varying urges of an extended group much longer on obligation than affection. What was inviolable was that my father should snap his Christmas card picture of his children before Thanksgiving weekend got away from him. He'd have forgone the feast if necessary, but never the three-by-five matte of his two redheaded, freckled children in their holiday finest. He'd then spend every evening of the first week of Advent humming carols and pasting copies of the photograph into hundreds of cards. His list, groomed from year to year, included fellow parishioners from the Episcopal church in town, club friends, parents of our childhood classmates, tennis partners, colleagues on charitable boards, and certain business associates and old classmates (including Mr. and Mrs. William Jefferson Clinton). I wasn't wild about the thought of Jed Lane having a picture of me, but how could my parents leave family friends off the list? Many of us were subjected to this, growing up in my town and in towns like mine. I might have been okay. But then I put on the dress.

Mom tightened up her face and said, "Oh."

Dad said, "Gosh."

"What?" I asked. That summer Mom had accommodated my adolescence by buying me a black velvet Christmas dress with a square neckline that belted tightly at the waist. I was quite thin—I couldn't think what was wrong.

"Just...bodacious ta-tas," Mom said. She covered her mouth with her hand.

I worked out what that meant. My skin flushed sharply, and I shivered into the velvet. I looked down so my hair hung across my chest.

"You can say that again," said Dad.

Now, I have never been buxom. In spite of my fervent youthful hope, that is not my fate. I was raised on the old line about needing no more bosom than could fill a champagne flute (a very narrow vessel in my home) and had resigned myself to a braless existence. I'd started the physical process of puberty relatively late, and consequently my body had continued to change while I was away at school. Some combination of being almost sixteen and losing some weight around the rest of me had given the impression of larger breasts than my parents remembered. The dress was gorgeous. It set off my hair in a way that made me proud. I had planned to take it back to school to wear to the Christmas formal dinner, and then, beneath my choir robes, for the service of Lessons and Carols.

"We can't send that out," Mom said, still looking at me.

"No, I guess not," said Dad.

My brother was staring. "What?" He had just turned eleven.

"Your sister's figure, is all," said Dad briskly.

My brother was unmoved. "Oh."

"What do you want me to do?" I asked.

Mom had recovered. "It's no problem, sweetie. It's just that it's inappropriate for a girl your age to have breasts that large. Maybe we could try another dress? Let's go up and look."

Upstairs she held out hangers for me. I dropped the velvet and slipped into red wool. She pulled my hair in front of my shoulders and smoothed it flat. "I have all these zits," I said. "And my teeth are too small."

"Oh, no," said Mom, still moving my hair. Her touch made my stomach hurt. I wanted so badly to cry. "Oh, you're exactly the girl I used to hate in high school. The blond one with the big boobs."

Hate. I grabbed onto that word like the fin of a shark. I wasn't blond and I didn't have big boobs, but I was fascinated by the thought of my mom as the girl doing the hating because, I realized, it was exactly what I feared: that my mom would learn what I had done, and hate me.

I tolerated the veneer for the duration of a photo shoot. Mom swept blush on my cheeks and gloss on my lips, and finger-combed the hair at my temples. My brother grinned his new grown-up-tooth grin. I put my arm around him. Such a good girl, hanging on by a thread.

Given the chance, I would finish her off.

Then we drove the six hours to St. Louis. I was back in jeans, and I brought into the back seat a pillow from my bed, a yellow Walkman with several mixtapes, and the remaining rag of my baby blanket, Nigh-Nigh, which had come home in my suitcase. I had no books in the car because I got carsick, so I smashed the pillow against the cold window, spread my blanket over my shoulders as best I could, and listened to Linley's Colorado mix (Clarence Carter, the Eagles, the Steve Miller Band) while we drove south the length of Illinois.

In the passenger seat Mom was tense. I didn't know whether it was fact or myth that my father's family disliked my mom, but the resulting conflict was part of my earliest memories and that made it true. I had cousins I had not met. My father had a brother who lived twenty minutes away, but we did not see him. Dad, aiming for balance, landed on evasion—"I think it's just such a shame all around"—and his equanimity felt to me disloyal. I had long before taken my mother's side. As I got older, I looked forward to discovering what it was that they did not like about Mom because, I assumed, it must be true about me too. I was her girl; I meant to do more of whatever it was. I saw my grandparents once a year, and they did not appear to enjoy it.

"They hate me, and they hate my children," Mom said, in the car on the way down.

Dad just said, "It means a lot to me to see my parents."

My father had grown up on a small street in suburban St. Louis called Black Creek Lane. Behind it was an actual creek where as a boy he'd pulled newts from the mud. When I went down there to look, there were only rocks ringed by wet earth. There was always something evading me at this house, some animal truth I could not put my finger on. I figured it lived like the dried-up creek, in the past.

My grandmother Ginny had birthed three sons in the immediate postwar years while my grandfather, whom we called Big Jim, was in Asia with the merchant marine. My father, their eldest, was expected to be born during one of my grandfather's leaves, but Big Jim's stay at home came and went, and the baby did not arrive. "The doctor told me October," said Ginny. Dad was born in the last days of December. "He was in there for eleven months."

Not until I was older did I realize that my grandmother, who had a bachelor's degree in child psychology from Sarah

Lawrence, had spent her entire life thinking my father gestated for eleven months. There was no question about paternity—no reason for the doctor to lie or be cavalier except that he simply didn't know or care. And my grandmother apparently had had withheld from her enough information about the female body to not understand that the doctor was wrong. I could not believe, when my grandmother told me this, that she had been subjected to such crap; either the doctor was crazy or the 1940s were hell.

But then, after my brother was born at the end of the 1970s, my mother's obstetrician joked that he had put in an extra stitch or two for my dad. So.

Once my father finally arrived, in late 1945, Big Jim requested leave to visit his firstborn son. My favorite story of my grandfather's is the only one he ever told me: "I put on my dress whites to go meet your dad in the hospital, so he would be proud of me."

I see it so clearly, it's as though a photograph survives. Big Jim, six feet and change, with his narrow, handsome face and bright blue eyes, standing at attention before a hospital bassinet, waiting to be admired.

We arrived at Black Creek Lane and piled out. My grandparents came to the door. Ginny was a square woman with blunt-cut hair and a set jaw, no bullshit, the sort who ran all the ladies' boards and golfed in culottes wide enough to upholster a loveseat. She leaned toward me and said, "Mwah." My grandfather, tall, thin, and twinkly-eyed, like an emaciated Santa Claus, leaned back and stuck out his hand. "Well, hello there!"

My brother and I were toting our stuff. "Whatcha got there?"

asked Big Jim, and my brother began showing off whatever handheld game console he'd traveled with that year.

"Oh, this is just my blanket," I explained, holding it up. "I've had it forever."

My grandmother's face soured. "You're what? Fifteen?"

I nodded.

She frowned at me. "Much too old for that stuff."

She turned for the kitchen. The turkey had been cooking for a while, but there was no lovely aroma. Mom sensed trouble. "When did the bird go in?"

"Oh, I don't know." Ginny was a disaster on the domestic front, but she did not pretend otherwise. My dad told a story about the harried night she took cans from the wrong shelf, opened them into a pan, and served warmed Alpo on noodles to her sons. Ginny laughed. "And you liked it."

My grandfather had a few tricks with children, most of which involved snookering us about our bodies. He'd tweak your nose and then exclaim that he'd taken it, displaying his fist with the thumb protruding from the fingers—such a reasonable facsimile that anyone under six reached a hand to her face to check for damage. Or he'd threaten, if you angered him, to lift you up by your ears. No child could resist this, so we'd anger him right away. The way to make my grandfather mad was to call him "Grandpa." The title made him feel old. We walked right up to him and said, "Hi, Grandpa!" so he'd do his trick—stand behind us, grab our earlobes one in each hand, and lift us up, bearing the weight of our bodies by pressing his chest against our backs, even though it looked like being hung by your ears. But the business of not being made to feel old was deadly serious. "Don't you all rush to my hospital bed," he liked to instruct us. "If I wake up and see you there, I'll know I'm dying. Don't you ever do that."

When my grandfather really was dying, in his eighties, my father and his siblings visited his hospital room one at a time. Big Jim also specified that to avoid competition none of his children should be permitted to speak at his funeral service, so no one did.

My grandfather's greatest trick, though, and the one that made us squeal, was the one he called the Indian Death Lock. We'd sit with our legs crossed, in the position called Indian style by white families like mine. He'd reach an arm down between our legs and grab the bottom ankle. Thus clamped, it was impossible to uncross your legs. You ended up just grinding your joints into each other—there was no way to free that bottom leg with his hand there. The claustrophobia was quick and terrifying, and his release a moment later made a kid giddy.

My brother was going through just this exercise, my grandfather pinning him on a chair, while I tucked away my bag with my mixtapes, Walkman, and Nigh-Nigh. Mom confirmed with my grandmother that my uncle Michael and his family would be joining us too.

"And the turkey is how big?"

Ginny rounded her arms. "Oh, like this."

"Only one of them?"

"Anyway," said my grandmother. "Who'd like a drink?"

My parents didn't care for martinis, but my brother and I got soda pop. That's what it was called in St. Louis. Our favorite was Mr. Pibb. It made Mom wince.

My grandfather released my brother and turned to me. "So, how's that school in, ah, New England?"

"It's fine, thanks."

"You learning a lot up there, are you?"

"Yep."

The fuse sputtered. "Well, good," he said. "Virgie, I'll make drinks."

I wandered back into the kitchen. I always paused before coming into this room, where my father had been a child, as though if I were quick and quiet enough, I could catch a glimpse of him hopping up into his chair—big-eared, athletic, a legendary student. I'd have settled for a scribble on a wall or a ding in a baseboard.

We were greeted in the kitchen by Rose, the African American housekeeper who had worked in my grandparents' home for more than thirty years. Rose moved silently and had no front teeth. Her hair was a tiny knot at the back of her head. By then she would have been well into her fifties, and her skin was unlined, creamy to the touch. Beside her we were a snappy, swaggering, mottled crew. Rose had been night nurse to all of my cousins, most recently Alison, who that year was just four, and she had sat long afternoons with two of my great-grandmothers before their deaths—one the January prior, and one just that spring. I can't complicate the Mammy cliché with any information about Rose's life or character because, of course, I don't have any. She was an angel to us. And I knew nothing about her except that she was the only person in my grandparents' house who came down to the floor to talk to a child.

I showed her Nigh-Nigh. She rubbed a corner between her fingers and said, "I remember." I believed her. She hugged me and my blanket close, my bodacious ta-tas smashed against her thin chest.

• • •

In her elegant and sophisticated memoir *Black Ice,* Lorene Cary, St. Paul's School Form of 1974, writes of her bravado upon arrival as one of the first African American students and one of the first girls to enter the school:

> I had no idea that wealth and privilege could confer real advantages beyond the obvious ones sprawled before us. Instead, I believed that rich white people were like poodles: overbred, inbred, degenerate. All the coddling and permissiveness would have a bad effect, I figured, now that they were up against those of us who'd lived a real life in the real world.

I'd have been the first to agree with Cary: if I was not a poodle, I was certainly a fool. But sensing how little I understood about the world outside my small life made me timid rather than wise. I knew that Rose lived in the real world. She was missing teeth, for heaven's sake. But I also saw proof of a rougher existence in her unearthly skin: her beauty seemed to me related to loss, as though her agelessness had been earned by years, her wrinkle-free eyes proof not of ease but of the extreme hardship she had transcended. This was a Christian fantasy. That it was founded in paternalism made possible by my race-based privilege did not change the fact that she nursed every cousin from the cradle and then, when it was time for my grandparents to die, showed us how to handle that, too. It was Rose who took the phone on the Sunday afternoon in February when I, holding a six-week-old, was unsure whether to book an emergency flight to St. Louis because my grandmother was failing. "She's awaiting on you, Miss Lacy. She's gonna meet that baby."

His entire life, my grandfather made a quiet project of supporting Rose. Her children and their children had their educations funded, no questions asked. Physician appointments. Rent, cars, winter coats. Nobody ever talked about this.

Lorene Cary also writes, in *Black Ice,* about falling apart when she learned that her mother, back home, was ill. The rector, concerned, summons her and asks why she doesn't just go home to visit. "I'm sure your teachers would be more than happy to excuse you to go home to see your mother." He doesn't imagine that Cary doesn't have the money for a weekend jaunt. I would not have imagined it either. The thought would never have occurred to me that kids didn't go home for Thanksgiving for any reason besides not wanting to. Cary describes how the school came up with the money for her to go see her mom. She accepts it uneasily; in the context of a sense of tokenism she shared with the few other African American students on campus, it was hardly a simple gift.

But she also writes, of boys at St. Paul's:

Some talked over us as a matter of course; others were pointedly deferential. I remember being glad that I wasn't one of the white girls. Boys stared at them. I watched them looking from one to the other and then back again to one particular girl or some part of her: her hair, her arm, the nape of her neck.

When I think of what it might have been like (what it might *be* like) to be black at St. Paul's, I consider that my experience of the assault might be useful: by taking the measure of the loss of what, at school at least, I had imagined I was entitled to, I can see what I had assumed would be mine. From here I might begin to consider what was not meant (was never meant) for others.

Only one of the boys who assaulted me was white. I don't think there's anything more to be said about that.

After a few more uneventful hours in the kitchen, my grandmother, poking at the dull bird, asked my mom whether it was finally time to take it out of the oven.

"Are the juices running clear?" asked Mom. She was sitting on her hands to avoid taking over.

My grandmother said, "What juices?"

The bird, never thawed, was a carbonized shell. We made a late-night Denny's run. I had never seen my mom in a Denny's—she did not believe in franchised establishments—but she slid into that banquette like she'd been born to it. My brother and I couldn't believe our luck. We got bottomless drinks with lots of ice. The plates ran with gravy. There were chocolate sundaes.

On the way home the next day, Dad announced that he wanted to push through, so we would be stopping only for gas. We never spent more than a single night with my grandparents, and this was one of the few times we stayed even that long. A pall beyond the ordinary covered us: my grandparents, having buried the last of the previous generation, were putting the family home on the market and moving to Florida. This concession to time had unsettled my parents, and they were snappish. I put my headphones on to avoid the fallout in the front seat.

"They are terrible," Mom said, because she wanted my father to apologize.

It was the last thing he'd do. Dad said, "They're my parents."

"Well, they're still terrible."

"Alicia, please."

"Did you hear them ask about Lacy's classes? Or James's soccer?"

Dad softened. "Oh, no, I didn't—"

"Right. Because they didn't."

"Ah. Maybe they forgot?"

"They hate us."

Dad did not respond.

My brother fell asleep.

Outside the windows, the cornfields were overwintering like farms of pins, a whole horizon full of matchsticks. If I had somehow managed to open the door and jump out of the car without dying, without anyone noticing, could I have run off into those fields? How far would I have had to travel before I came to a place where I could start a new life? I remember visualizing the perpendicular angles of momentum: how our car was barreling forward, Dad at the wheel, hands at ten and two, mirrors minutely adjusted, and how my door—against which I was curled—would open out, at ninety degrees. What if I just shot off in that direction? I pictured moving away east while they continued north. Our lines would never, ever converge.

In Grundy County, Illinois, about a hundred miles south of home, Dad pulled into a gas station. We all got out to stretch our legs. With Mom watching keenly, I sprinted across the freezing tarmac to use the foul restroom at the back of the service building. Enormous trucks rocked on the pavement. Still more were pouring north, heading toward the first major interchanges south of Chicago. I was grateful to tuck back into the warm car and let Dad nose us onto the entrance ramp and speed toward home.

When we arrived, I carried into the house my pillow and my Walkman, my little bag with its set of mixtapes, and the trash from our snacks. Nigh-Nigh was not there. We looked under the seats. We looked in the trunk. We emptied our duffels to the canvas. The blanket was gone.

"Do you remember having it this morning?" asked Dad. "It must still be at my parents' house!"

We called Ginny and Big Jim. Nope, they said. Absolutely not here. Lacy must have taken it with her. We set everything by the door. She takes that thing everywhere, doesn't she?

I didn't remember. I couldn't picture it with me on the way back home, but then again I'd been so absorbed in my fantasies of running off into some other life that I hadn't noticed much of anything at all. I must have brought it with me, though, right?

"Well," said my grandmother, "it's not the end of the world. It was time to be done with that."

I'd kept my blanket with my things, I knew I had—I'd been so embarrassed by my grandmother's reaction that I hadn't left it out anywhere. I hadn't even slept with it that night. I did not myself remove it from my bag.

"But how could it just vanish?" asked Dad. "It's the strang-est thing."

Mom's eyes got huge. "It must have fallen out at the gas station!"

Dad held his face. "My gosh, Alicia, you're right! That's the only explanation!"

I could have cried. The rocking, roaring trucks.

The next morning at dawn, Dad popped his police-radar detector on the dashboard and sped to Grundy County. He taped MISSING BLANKET signs all over the gas station, plus those at other exchanges and in a few nearby towns. He even listed a reward for the return of Nigh-Nigh.

It never did turn up. For a long time, before I figured it out, I hoped the terrible prairie wind had blown my blanket off the pavement and into the cornfields, just as I had imagined running into them myself. That would be an okay fate, I thought, beneath the skies and the stars. Better than beneath a tire.

Around sunset, Dad came home from Grundy County dejected. "I'm so sorry, Say-see," he said, rubbing my shoulders, as if he knew what was gone.

Christmastime at St. Paul's was glorious. In choir rehearsal, the sopranos were working on the full King's College descants, so that my friends sounded like the live BBC broadcasts of the Cambridge Festival of Nine Lessons and Carols that my mother played, as loud as the radios would go, throughout the house every Christmas Eve morning. We wore our holiday best to Seated Meal and poured hot chocolate into plastic mugs to carry across the starlit paths. Masters spangled their doorways with blinking fairy lights. During the day, Murph and Sarge, the surly Security guards, wore red Santa hats on patrol.

One morning Budge, the rooster-headed hockey player, strode up behind me and said, "I think it should be tonight."

I thought, *Bodacious ta-tas*. I thought, *Round yon virgin mother and child*. I thought, *Fuck you*.

If I'd had Elizabeth Bishop in my arsenal by then, I would at least have had a road map for this descent. *Practice losing farther, losing faster*. When I finally read her "One Art," I recognized the defiance of the devastated overachiever. Of course! Chuck it all. But I wouldn't read Bishop until sixth form.

Instead I looked, permitted myself to really look, at Budge.

His mouth protruded in a way I found vaguely aggressive, almost like a primate's. He swung his hips like a lion. Except for the spray of hair, I could not see the boy in him. This was exciting—the cruelty of it, his cruelty, was exciting. This was the truth. About the world, I mean. When he hissed about needing to finish what his friends had started, I didn't have to deny anything to him, or pretend to be someone I wasn't.

"Tonight," he whispered, coming in close.

"I don't think Candace would appreciate that," I finally replied. His girlfriend had grown close to many of my friends. She was on our hockey team. I liked her, too. She had thick blond hair and a practiced brusqueness that stood out in contrast to the glamorous frigidity of so many of the prettier girls. A New Yorker, private-schooled, no one's fool, already planning for an MBA and an island summer home. Her roommate was Nina, the angelic chorister who sang with me in Madrigals. I couldn't guess why Candace had chosen to date Budge, but I didn't give it much thought. One hoped for the pleasures of an idiosyncratic harmony.

"Candace will never know," he said.

God knows she didn't need protection from me. I couldn't protect anyone. My friends were already acting strange. I wasn't going to police a girl's boyfriend. Those sorts of scruples belonged to a world that was too precious for me.

At the same time, I believed Budge when he said that no one would ever know. After all, Rick's and Taz's girlfriends still, two months later, did not seem to know what had happened in that room. They passed me in the hallways same as always, long-legged and indifferent. I understood from this one of the rules of war: what happened to girls like me did not matter, did not even register.

All sorts of things were possible at school. Behavior that was dignified and visible rode atop a wild landscape of unspoken thieving and mischief. I wasn't wrong about this. Years later I learned which girl's terrible mononucleosis, so severe it had sent her home for a term, was actually the third trimester of a pregnancy. I learned who was avoiding faculty come-ons after check-in, and who was courting them. In the moment, unable to shake Budge, I thought I grasped this about sex at St. Paul's: some girls got to be girlfriends, and they were escorted and protected, even if they had not been chaste for years. Other girls got abused. On this path from held to hurt, you could move in only one direction.

I kept walking. We pushed through the doors and into the Schoolhouse. The steps were loud with bodies rushing up and down.

He leaned into me. "You and I are kinda friends," he said. I considered whether this was true. "I don't think Rick and Taz should get the last word. You know what I'm saying?"

I didn't.

"I think I can show you how it should be. Done right."

I ignored this and turned the corner for class. When I looked back, just before heading into French, he was still standing there, in the hallway, watching me.

By that point, halfway through my junior year in high school, more of my friends were sexually active than weren't. There was nothing particularly momentous about having sex at St. Paul's. Third formers did it in the shower, fourth formers did it in the back of Memorial Hall, everyone did it at some-one's house over a long weekend away from school. I hadn't made a fetish of my own virginity, and had no fantasies about how and when I would give it away. Nothing much beyond protecting it from Rick and Taz, at least—but that was not for the metaphor of innocence. That was because I didn't want to get pregnant or die of AIDS.

Budge's dark genius was to speak only of my virginity. He didn't even say "have sex." His repetition—*I am going to pop your cherry*—made the idea of virginity itself seem absurd. You're going to deflower me *now?* I was already a step ahead of him. I knew virginity to be the teacup construction of a world that holds female sexuality to be a possession. And it hurt me. The thought hurt. It reminded me only of what I had lost. To speak of my virginity was to mock me, and Budge knew it. It was the glass slipper without the ball.

Furiously, almost feverishly, I ran in my head a mathematics of dominance. I would hold on to and cherish and groom this splintered lack of experience only to hand it over to a man, who would—listen to the words—*take it* from me? (No man *receives* a woman's virginity, no matter how freely given.)

No, thanks.

If it was something they wanted, then by God it was nothing

to me: *Render unto Caesar that which is Caesar's.* Nothing to see here. Nothing to steal.

He followed me. He showed up in every doorway. "Fine," I told the boy called Budge. "Fine."

After that our encounters became something almost darkly sweet. We were conspiring to take away this thing that we both knew was a lie. It was like planning a surgery, a bit grueling but necessary, with the inherent power differential that one of us would be wounded and one of us not. I moved from class to class in a bell of silence, resting my throat (which had broken out in sores again) so I could sing at evening rehearsal and avoiding the eyes of people who might have been my friends. I needn't have bothered—they weren't trying to make contact with me. My friends didn't exactly speed up when I joined them on a pathway, but they no longer waited for me, either.

When I saw Budge, I could relax into the candor of his brutishness. He knew everything there was to know.

"Your room or mine?"

"Not mine," I said.

"You on top or me?"

"Me." Definitely me.

"Tonight?"

"I have Madrigals."

"After?"

"That's check-in."

"Tomorrow?"

"Budge, I have to go. I have a math quiz."

It was almost protective, the way he watched me walk away.

•   •   •

When I was twelve and in the eighth grade, my best friend, Wendy, was five foot six and I was four foot nine. She had started her period. I did not have even the beginnings of breasts. My hips were as narrow as my brother's. There was not a womanly hair anywhere on my body. I was miserable.

"Mutt and Jeff," said the teachers, as we girls walked down the hall.

"Mutt and Jeff," said Wendy's parents, picking us up from skating or soccer.

"Mutt and Jeff," said my mom. I figured, incorrectly, that I was the mutt.

Still, my parents started to worry. My dad wasn't tall but he wasn't short, and my relatives on my mom's side were quite big. "I just don't understand it," Mom said. "My grandfather was positively *statuesque.*"

I had been an average-size child, so we'd never had reason to worry about this. "Just hang on," Mom said hopefully. "I promise you things will start to change."

When they did not, she took me to see my pediatrician. He was close to retirement by then. I did not like him, but I don't remember him being unkind. Mom thought he was brilliant (he'd had a fellowship at Harvard; he was on the faculty at Children's in the city). The fact that he was old was what she loved. "Intuition is worth more than anything," she said. "Once, when you were little, he heard you talk and said, 'This child has strep.' And he was right. I'll never forget that."

I was measured and weighed, and Dr. K. plotted these points on a standard growth curve. It was true—I was falling quite demonstrably behind. He leaned into my mother and said something quickly and quietly to her, and she left the room.

The doctor put his head out the door and then returned with a nurse. While she stood by, he had me undress to the waist, lie back, pull my knees up, and let my legs fall open. I remember exploding with misery at what I was being forced to reveal. I squeezed my eyes shut. Gloved, he used his fingers inside me and a palm on my abdomen to confirm that my reproductive organs were in place and intact. There was blood on the paper when he was done.

"You can get the mother now," he said to the nurse.

Later, Mom said, her eyes sideways, "It's all fine. Your parts are all there, they just haven't started to develop yet. So that's good! We just have to be patient."

I'm told they use ultrasound now, along with basic blood-work and X-rays of growth plates in the hands, to resolve questions regarding the onset of puberty. I'm old enough to appreciate such progress. There is nothing to hold against the pediatrician; my grandmother, after all, was pregnant for eleven months. And my mother was stitched extra tight for my dad.

I was still growing fast on the late-December morning I went to Budge's room to lose my virginity. I knew my hymen was already broken, so I wasn't frightened, and I had no wishes for connection or affection, so I couldn't be disappointed. I had never felt stronger at St. Paul's School than I felt that morning. There was a dark lashing force inside me, and I thought this was something I could use. The sense was that Budge and I were teaming up to kill someone.

He lay back on a rotting sofa. His dorm was one of the single-story, 1970s-era, squat buildings on campus, and it glowered like a bunker at the downhill edge of the Schoolhouse lawn.

On the sofa we were at ground level, looking up at the row of masters' houses on the hill. Frost sparkled on the grass. A thin sun was rising over campus. He was not expecting me to appear in his single room then, long before Chapel, and I appreciated having the element of surprise. This was my doing, all of it.

He used a condom. It stung a bit. He looked at me as though I were something he needed to retrieve, a puzzle, a football caught in a tree: far away, mouth pursed, frowning. I looked back and hated him. We would never so much as have a conversation again, and I wanted him to hurry up.

When he was done I pulled my jeans back on and walked back to my dorm to get dressed for the day.

Then for a while nothing happened. I have no recollection of Christmas that year, except that I was very sick again. My pediatrician's office tested me for mono. It was negative.

In January I returned to school, and one morning in that dead second week of January—flat light, rutted ice—I again left Elise in her dark and overheated room and walked alone to breakfast.

I crossed the low edge of the quad and continued onto the frozen path along the Library Pond, from which the dark trail snaked up toward Drury House and my former calculus tutees. (I was no longer asked for extra help with problem sets.) I came to the road and crossed back up the hill toward the Wing entrance of Upper House, pulling open the great wooden door and hearing it squeal and slam behind me. Cold air followed, and still more of it pressed in from the wall of windows on my right. The name panels on the left were dull. It was icebox light, blued with shadow, and even in this pretentious Gothic corridor you could feel the forest all around you.

I found that going to breakfast was a better way to start the day than not. The kitchens were warm, and the bustle of people feeding themselves helped me feel less lonely.

I turned off the hall and climbed the stairs to Center Upper to pick up my friends. The fire doors were always closed (the terror of fire was the sole constant of the buildings crew, who'd have quit and left the state if they knew how many candles and bongs were lit around campus each afternoon and night), and when I pulled open the door onto my friends' hall, the wheeze of the self-closing hinge caused them to look up. Caroline, Sam, Brooke, Maddy, Meg, and Tabby were sitting on the floor as always, backs to the wall between their respective doors, books in their laps, preparing for the day.

"Morning," I called out.

Whatever withdrawals on their friendship my deviance had made, these girls had sustained some affection for me until just now. I had finally reached the limit. All of my friends, every one of them, looked down as suddenly as if the floor had vanished beneath them. It was Budge, I understood. Candace was their friend, and I could not be excused. I had no idea how they'd found out. Again, I'd said nothing. I had thought what I'd done was only about destroying myself, and that no one else would discover it, or care.

I waited a moment longer. It was excruciating, standing there, but also fascinating: an entire hallway of wonderful young women, friends I had laughed with and skated with, friends whose heads had balanced on my shoulder when the winding shivers of the soccer bus put us to sleep, friends whose adventures with boyfriends and lovers I knew in minute detail—these friends were refusing to acknowledge me in any way. They were performing something for me, I knew. Indifference is easy. It takes a surprising amount of energy to shun a person.

"Fine," I told them. I turned, and went down to breakfast alone.

The day warmed and water dripped from rooftops and tree branches. Crossing back to my dorm after classes, I passed my urban friends from fourth form walking together arm in arm, shiny and brittle with their usual conspiratorial glaze. Twin miniskirts. Fresh lip gloss.

"Hey, ladies!" I said, passing them.

They stopped on the walk and grabbed each other's forearms, aghast, and then began to howl with laughter.

I thought, *For walking? For saying hello?* Their cruelty was clear, but I was agitated by what seemed an absurd irrationality: I could find no reason for their reaction. It breaks my heart to write that—I was looking for the rules, as though my situation were a chess position I needed only to study long enough. I am not sure anything speaks more clearly to my naivete than this. Because I knew—I felt, as surely as we all felt the rumbling of the steam wending its way beneath the lawns—that beneath the strictures of gentility at St. Paul's School was a hunger for excess. Nowhere on its campus, or indeed in the world it purported to prepare us for, could you lose your head. Rage was inappropriate. Desire was inappropriate. Grief was inappropriate. Even joy was inappropriate. All you should want, or need, was your *goodly heritage*—this was from the school prayer, the psalm appointed for April 3, 1856, the first day that boys received instruction at St. Paul's School: "The lot has fallen unto me in a fair ground; yea, I have a goodly heritage." We heard this regularly from the chapel pulpit. How convenient that it should reinforce privilege, this notion of *heritage,* which slipped so effortlessly from the fruits of biblical lands to the fruits of American race- and class-based striation. Students tossed around the word *goodly.* Got a *goodly* bagel there, huh? A *goodly* cigarette, by any chance? A bland adjective made even more arcane by its unusual form; nobody really wanted a *goodly* anything, but ingratitude was not an option.

The contours of my downfall were so spectacular that they permitted the luxurious pleasures of scapegoating. There was something in my story for everyone: the kids who felt marginalized because they were not white, or wealthy, or academically excelling; the kids who felt the heat of their own indiscretions, whether discovered or not; the kids who felt ignored by boys or by girls; the kids who needed reinforcement that they alone belonged at St. Paul's School, and all the rest of us were impostors. You could laugh at me, rage at me, gape in disbelief at what I had done or allowed to be done. I could do nothing about it except hoist up my book bag and walk away, sporting my freckles and a hankering for the Ivy League.

I worked through the variables like they were homework. Hate-sex on a single occasion with Budge was not acceptable, but sex from the age of thirteen with numerous boyfriends was fine. You could put a bra in a boy's mailbox, okay, but you could not get taken advantage of by two sixth formers you'd never speak to again. Was it the combination of Rick and Taz, followed by Budge? Was it as simple as *not having a boyfriend*—in which case my problem was not what I had allowed to be done to my body, but that it had been done by the wrong men?

Or was it something else about me—something everyone but me could see?

If you go to their room, you get attacked. If you permit yourself to get attacked, you get sick. If you do something that would break your parents' hearts, your grandparents will toss your baby blanket. *Lose farther, lose faster.* It was like chalking the names of the dead on the blackboard wall. I'd fucked Budge the way firefighters torch the remaining grasses so the inferno has nowhere to go. But this thing kept getting bigger.

I listened to those girls' mad-hatter laughter ringing off the pavement. They were giddy with hate. I had thought, *I will be less and less and less.* I had thought I was basically nothing now. But I inspired such fierce emotion, and these reactions were in inverse proportion to my own sensate awareness of myself. I couldn't eat much, or sing much. I walked everywhere alone. I changed for hockey in a corner of the locker room, not wanting my teammates—who included Budge's girlfriend, Candace—to see my body. On the ice I was largely benched, too sick and too uncoordinated to win a spot on the lines, though I traveled everywhere with the varsity team. I appeared in my assigned seats for Seated Meal and for Chapel, and always in class, but nowhere else. I made myself as silent and as slender as I could. But I was a wick, held fast and burning. I could not seem to put it out.

A week or so later, I was walking from my room to class when something detonated at my feet. I stopped. There was nothing there. But yes, there was: water, or something dark, spreading across the sunlit walk. Then another *crash* hit behind me. I turned. Now I saw the shreds of latex scattered around. They curled ugly and gray as toenails in the grass. A third *crash*— close enough to sting—and I looked up.

I was walking behind Simpson House, the girls' dorm opposite mine in the quad. Budge's Candace lived there, and I spotted her and a friend in a second-story window. They ducked down and then reappeared, and Candace hurled another condom water balloon my way.

"Cunt!" they screamed.

"Disgusting slut!"

"Whore!"

I waited until they had to reload, then kept walking.

There is a contemporary inquiry into shame that suggests that shame is not as deeply rooted in guilt as in power. Considering the work of evolutionary biologists, psychologists studying the physical manifestations of shame noted that they closely resemble the behaviors of mammals trying to demonstrate subordination to a more powerful individual. Unshackling the notion of shame from ideas of right and wrong strikes me as helpful, at least where sex is involved. In my experience, shame is not the wholehearted burn that follows a realization of guilt, which we consider to be shame's obvious antecedent, but rather a surplus of displeasure that adheres to one party—and always the less powerful one. Shame is messy and pervasive. It does not attend to the course of misbehavior. Often enough, in fact, I think we have the order on this reversed: shame goes around seeking its object. I found Budge. There was nothing of pleasure in that for me.

I thought about the condom balloons in my fourth- and fifth-period classes, French Lit and History of the Second World War, and while I walked back to my dorm (via an alternate route) to eat some crackers out of a drawer for lunch. I was lucky it wasn't colder, and that I hadn't taken a direct hit and had to go back to change out of wet clothes. I looked out my window across the meadow. We'd had early hockey practice that morning, so a long free afternoon stretched ahead, and the sun was still cold but high. It would have been nice to nap. But I'd made a decision.

I crossed the quad again and went into Simpson House, where Candace lived. I turned left and climbed the stairs to the hallway where I figured her window must be. With the same undirected impulse to clarity with which I'd unbuckled the pants of that Southern graduate at a party in Chicago a lifetime before, I needed to identify what was so ferocious here. I thought if I could just know, I could stop the falling apart. It all seemed a big misunderstanding. Nothing I had done was motivated by carnal desire, and wasn't *that* supposed to be the sin? Couldn't we work this out?

Candace's door was propped open with a shoe, and I could see that she was in her room. I stood outside for a moment. She was folding laundry, opening and closing drawers. There were no voices, so I thought she might be alone, which meant I'd chosen a felicitous moment.

I knocked.

"Hello?"

She leaned her head to peek at the door.

"Oh, my God," she said, face darkening. "No."

I kept my distance in the hall. "I'll go if you want me

to. I just thought there might be some things you wanted to say to me."

"I have nothing to say to you."

"Okay, well, you're throwing things at me."

"You deserve it."

I didn't necessarily disagree.

I said, "Can I come in?"

"I don't even know. I guess. Whatever."

"Thank you." I pushed through her door, let it close gently again on the sneaker, and stood there just at the threshold. She was in front of her dresser, so that it blocked her body from mine, and I sensed that she would stay there. Across the room were three windows—she'd lucked into a bright room—including the one she'd have been sitting behind to hurl condom balloons at me. I wondered if the condoms were otherwise kept in the top drawer of the dresser she was now reorganizing. I'd never bought condoms. Where did she go to buy them? Were they for Budge? Of course they were.

"Candace," I said, "I'm sorry. I had no intention of hurting you."

She folded furiously: turtlenecks, long-sleeve tees, short-sleeve tees. She did not look at me once. "You are a slut. Do you understand that? And you have no friends. None. All of our friends hate you now. You are disgusting. Do you understand?"

I did not reply.

"And then you go and fuck my boyfriend. Are you kidding me? Did you think you could get away with it? Did you think he was going to break up with me for you?"

I said, quietly, "I have no desire to be with Budge."

"Hunh." She snorted. "Then why did you screw him?"

Well, the truth, even if I'd had it, was not going to come out here. Not to someone who would bag it up and hurl it back in my face. I thought for a moment, watching her ball socks, and said, "I can't explain that. But it wasn't just me, Candace. I wasn't alone in that room. And I'll never talk to him again, if that helps any."

"Yeah, well, it doesn't. But don't worry. He hates you too. He'd never talk to you anyway."

It hurt to consider whether this was true.

"I don't want anything from him."

"Oh, yeah? Who's next? Seriously, who are you going to fuck next?"

"Okay," I said. "I'm going to go now. I just wanted to say I'm sorry. And I understand that you're furious, and I don't blame you."

She exploded. "Don't blame me for *what?*"

I got even quieter. "Nothing. It was a figure of speech."

"You're a fucking joke."

"Okay. Thanks for letting me come up." I turned and wriggled through the space between the door and the jamb. I didn't want to touch anything, as if the whole room were electrified with her hate.

She called out, "Don't ever talk to me again."

"No problem."

There was a moment.

"Lacy."

I paused in the hall.

She was looking my way, and there were tears all around the rims of her dark eyes. "I love him. Okay? I love him."

Now I was crying too. "Okay," I said, through the wobble in my throat. And then I turned and left.

I do not remember any hour that winter so cold as ice-hockey practice. The dehydrated air of the rink scored my throat, and when I sprinted I tasted blood. I was sick, too, with the endless colds we passed around, often feverish. I could not cough for the pain. It felt as though I inhaled alcohol instead of air.

I had made the varsity team, but I rarely saw playing time; our team was led by Sarah Devens, the closest thing to aristocratic athlete Hobey Baker that St. Paul's School had seen in eighty years. She was from Massachusetts, not Main Line Philadelphia, but you could picnic beneath a statue of her Devens forefather in a Boston park, and she demonstrated joyful, graceful mastery of every sport she attempted. I saw her spiral a football fifty yards into the arms of a football player who wasn't expecting it. On an all-school trail run, she covered root-tangled forest miles in five minutes and forty seconds each. When we played other teams, their coaches arrived with strategies to contain her, and they looked up at Sarah and down at their clipboards as though there were no one else in uniform. The few other female pre-Olympians in New England knew who she was, and they met Sarah, and she them, with the dignity and mutual respect of generals on a battlefield.

This prowess would have made her enormously popular even if she hadn't also been kind. It seemed impossible, seeing her in action, but inside those torrents of competitive energy spun a bright, steady self, held almost gyroscopically still and centered. I did not know Sarah Devens well enough to call her "Devil," as her friends did, but I knew, as everyone did, that the sporting nickname worked precisely because she was anything but evil.

I sat on the freezing bench during hockey games all over New England and watched her play. She had a slapshot that hooked the back of the net from across the rink. I was a little bit frightened to share the ice with her. I had not developed a sense of where I was out there, so although I was fast, it seemed skaters came at me from nowhere. My helmet made me feel not protected but constantly in danger of ambush.

Candace had made the varsity team too. She was a strong player, much better than I was, and her jocular wit suited the physicality of hockey. My friends had rallied to her side. I sat alone, dressed alone, and did not attempt to talk or cheer. I never pretended to belong. Our coach, Ms. Royce, was Candace's adviser. Royce, as we called her, was just out of college, and with us she sometimes made the mistake of trading on collegiality rather than maturity, aiming for affection rather than respect. Royce liked to know who was dating whom. She commented on new dresses and haircuts. She lamented not having a beau herself. She was dismissive of me, which might have been because I was useless to her as a player. But I suspected it was just as likely that Candace had told her about my transgression with Budge.

One of Royce's favorite exercises for us was a sprint game called Categories, in which groups of skaters, identified by some code, would sprint to the end of the rink and back. We'd line up, she'd shout, "Anyone with blond hair, skate!," and off would go the blondes.

"Anyone with brown hair, skate!"

"Ponytails!"

"Bangs!"

And so on.

(If you're wondering if she ever called out *locs* or *dreads* or *braids,* the answer is of course no.)

It was important that we all get the workout, so if you were the only redhead, you'd wait patiently until your category was called, then skate like hell while your team watched.

Deep January or early February, we had been losing games despite having Sarah Devens on the first line. We did not have a deep enough bench to compete against the bigger schools closer to Boston. Sarah was frustrated. Royce was frustrated. We were all exhausted and unwell, tired of the term, tired of the cold. To liven things up, Royce created new sprint categories.

"Anyone who has ever been kissed, skate!"

Laughter broke out across the line, then every girl skated. We returned to the line and waited.

"Anyone who has ever kissed...Reid!"

This was surprising, but then again Royce was young and we could see she was aiming to be fun. Reid was a sixth former. His girlfriend, Jess, skated.

"Anyone who has ever kissed...Miller!"

A fifth former skated.

"Bart!"

These were the easy ones, the long-term, highly visible romances. Royce knew enough of our histories to get most everyone out on the ice. One by one, delighted, girls skated. I saw it coming but could not escape. Did I imagine the moment's pause, the intake of ice air, before she came to it?

"Anyone who has ever kissed Budge, skate!"

With sharp cuts of her blades Candace started off down the ice, but they were looking at me. Royce too. From my spot at the end of the line of girls, I could not read the expression on her face—whether this was payback or accident.

I considered skating. I considered digging my edges in and sending myself off, just to say, *Yes, I did it, I thought it would save me.* But then I'd have had to turn and skate back.

But also: I had never kissed Budge. We never kissed. I leaned on my hockey stick and looked up the line at my helmeted teammates, their long ponytails dull in the blue-white shadows. A sob was cupped in the base of my throat. I could not breathe myself free of it. I heard the canister lights buzzing over us. Candace carved a quick and triumphant lap out and back, and our friends cheered her return.

Royce looked down the line. I was the only one left. I hoped she didn't care whether I sprinted or not, that she realized it hardly mattered for our team whether I took that extra lap.

She called out, "Anyone who has ever kissed Rick Banner, skate!"

No one on the team had kissed Rick Banner. Everyone on the team knew this. He had always dated the girl he was dating now. Her roommate was on the ice with me. My belly lurched; I felt bile creeping up my throat, and the burn was remarkable.

My father once told me something about the legendary hockey player Hobey Baker. It was commonly known that he was the last casualty of the war, dead in a plane crash that followed the armistice, tragically, by hours. Dad looked up at the plaque that bore Baker's name there in Gordon Rink and said, "Hey, Lace, you know what? People only *think* Hobey Baker died in a tragic crash." I followed his eyes, listening. "People think it was a terrible accident. But actually that might not be so."

He explained that there was no good reason for the crash that killed Hobey Baker. The war had ended, and Baker had his papers to go home. He'd asked to fly one more time. His squadron objected—why take the risk?—but he insisted. The weather was fine. He was an expert pilot, the very best.

"People who know the story," said Dad, "think it was not an accident. That he had come to the end of his time as a flying ace, which was the highest accolade a young man could achieve. He was on top of the world. After St. Paul's, after Princeton, after being a hockey star that famous—well, there was nowhere left for him to go. And people think he realized that, and crashed his plane because he could not face going home to a normal life. He just said *It will never be better than this* and flew right into the ground."

I knew why my father told me this story. Dad had been a member of the Ivy Club at Princeton, the eating club Hobey Baker had joined back in 1912. Dad would have learned his insider's mythology there. Writing from Cottage Club, the eating club next door, F. Scott Fitzgerald had borrowed Hobey's middle name, Amory, for the hero of *This Side of Paradise*. The story my father told was not to him tragic. It was about a kind of mastery.

I too found self-destruction more interesting than bad luck. I admired it. Nothing was taken from Hobey Baker, I calculated, nothing visited upon him that he didn't ordain. The only thing he'd ever had to give up was his own future.

I could die. That was a choice. My father might even understand.

I didn't skate to Rick Banner's name. After Royce finished the kissing sprints and let us go, I changed in silence and left the locker room alone. When I was halfway to the rink doors I heard someone behind me, quietly, sneakers on the rubber mats. I stiffened, waiting. Would I be hit? Spit upon? How soon until they laughed?

My follower caught up and threw an arm around me. It was Sarah Devens, superstar. She had never touched me before. We'd never exchanged more than a friendly hello.

"Hey, Lace," she said, resting her arm heavily across my shoulders. She was shorter than I was and seemed endlessly powerful.

I did not reply, just waited.

Sarah sighed, a long and sad sound. We walked together. After a few more paces, she pulled me in to her in a kind of sideways hug and stayed with me like that for a moment. I ached to hear what she would say next. I could not so much as offer her a word of my own.

But she withdrew, and when I looked back she was with our team captains and others, including Candace, and they were stony. I was no glutton. I would not ask for more. I took Sarah's moment of solidarity and turned it over in my mind. I remembered the weight of her arm on my shoulders.

I still don't know what she might have meant to say, if there was anything else she had meant to confer. I never asked. Sarah Devens killed herself four years later, but we haven't gotten there yet.

Crack-ups at St. Paul's were almost always observed in retrospect, beginning with the rector's announcement in Chapel that a student had withdrawn from the school, for the rest of the semester or for good. A brilliant ballet dancer would get thinner and thinner until one day we learned she'd gone home on a health leave, and then, on the walk to the Schoolhouse from Chapel, her hallmates would reveal the details. A suicide attempt with pills, usually—she'd swallow everything she could get her hands on, prescribed and unprescribed, and wait to be found. One student arranged herself holding her mother's picture on her chest, as though she were in her coffin already. Nobody succeeded while we were students there.

Or a boy would get caught "partying"—alcohol or drugs—in such a conspicuous way that it was clear he wasn't even pretending to adhere to school rules. It was difficult to know when behavior was truly manic, because we all worked all the time anyway in our fever to perform, and sometimes this pace extended to rule-breaking, too.

Withdrawal from the world was the final course of action, and this was the progression I'd been witnessing in my hallmate Elise, close up, without realizing it. When I felt her starting to disengage from our friendship, panic moved in my stomach. It couldn't have been disapproval of me—she was anything but judgmental, and sex was a field she considered expansive and ill-suited to shame. I hadn't wronged her, had I? I wondered whether she might, hearing great gossip about me, have felt left out, not learning from me what everyone else seemed to know. In a similar position, I might have suffered such a petty injury. But that wasn't it either.

Elise refused breakfast, lunch, and most dinners, managing to buy snacks from the student Tuck Shop during its open hours mid-morning. She stopped carrying Simone and Jean-Paul around with her. Because I was so impressed by her, I found a happy explanation for everything: She wanted to be left alone with her sophisticated thoughts. She had moved past French existentialism and was weighing which intellectual movement to embrace next. She realized that the quality of our existence is only a matter of perception. And so on.

Then, in February, Elise withdrew completely—left the school and went home.

I got a note. She added our favorite quotations at the bottom: "Be always drunken." And, from Religion's latest assignment, T. S. Eliot's *Four Quartets:* "We shall not cease from exploration, and the end of all our exploring will be to arrive where we started and know the place for the first time." Her handwriting was elegant, long and sloping, almost masculine in the way she compressed open spaces and crowded her lines to take up room on the page. In my large, careful hand I copied her quotations onto separate pieces of paper and taped them over my bed. Down the hall, Maintenance retrieved her school-issue cot from the basement and removed the tacks that had held her scarves over the windows. They dialed down the radiator and left the room bare and cold.

I was again nominated for the Ferguson Scholarship. I cringed when my name was read. I worried that the sound of it, released in the chapel, would remind people how they hated me.

My sixteenth birthday was approaching. What did I want? *Sweet sixteen,* my parents said. *Sweet sixteen,* said Mrs. Lane. *Sweet sixteen,* said my adviser, Mrs. Fenn. Did I have any requests?

I am not sure if it was before or after the actual day, but

one night around that time I again received a late phone call. I went down warily, disbelieving.

It was another male voice.

"Johnny Devereux." A student who had already graduated. I hadn't known him at all, but I knew about his family. His parents were nationally recognized humanitarians who had addressed the school in Chapel. Their son's name was listed on award plaques for character and athletics. I was pretty sure he was in the Ivy League now.

"Yeah?"

He'd heard I was amazing in bed. He'd heard I was the sexiest thing at St. Paul's School. He'd always wanted to try me out. He was going to drive all the way to campus and pay me a visit.

"Oh, right. Okay. Whatever."

I ended the call. Where did this stop? I climbed back up the stairs, finished my homework, brushed my teeth and washed my face, and went to bed.

I don't know what time it was when he came through the door. We had no locks; I don't know who let him into the dorm. I don't know why I didn't realize he'd meant what he said. He came in smelling of the cold and did not switch on a light. I sat up, my heart crazy, not sure who this was or what he meant to do to me. I'd been sleeping on my stomach, as I did. He sat on my bed and took off his shoes, his hand on my back.

"Baby, it's Johnny." He pulled back my sheets and ran his hand along my body.

There wasn't time to think. I had to stay quiet. *You started this. Sort it out.* He'd driven all the way to St. Paul's. He was an adult. An Ivy League star. I remembered his father's face addressing us from the lectern in Chapel. And I remembered that his father had been—might still be—a St. Paul's School trustee.

What would this man do to me if I said no to him now?

Shame drowned me; more of it meant nothing.

I lay back down on my stomach and cried into my pillow while he fucked me from behind, and then in no time at all he was gone.

In math class, I began doodling on the edges of my worksheets. First I worked Elise's quotations in elaborate Gothic lettering that made them look taken from tombstones. Then I sketched out landscapes behind them: a castle on a hill, a bare-branched tree. I silhouetted a big black bird in the tree. I wrote lists of words that moved me: *dovecote, awakening, remedy.*

Moving between the rows of desks one day, Leighton Huhne—the happy augur of a good term from the year before—caught sight of my page and said, "Dude. You are a *freak.*"

As expressed in the school vernacular, this was a near-total compliment. To be a freak of this sort was to be creative, independent, *interesting.* Leighton was a buddy, and he'd have appreciated the morbid scenery and script I was embroidering all class long because it was consistent with the buddies' fascination with the Grateful Dead and the aesthetic that surrounded the band.

I looked up. "Yeah?"

"Totally. Dude. Check this stuff out! What's your deal?"

This was a complicated question. I knew better than to pretend to answer it.

"No deal," I said casually. "Just passing time here."

He tapped two huge fingers on my page. "That's way cool."

"Thanks."

"Vidster." (Affectionate derivation of *vid,* which itself comes from *video,* as in *good vid* or *bad vid.*)

I let this wash over me. There was an opening here, and I couldn't believe I'd lucked into it.

He continued on up the rows, shaking his shaggy head in slow appreciation.

Some of the buddies managed to exist at St. Paul's without appearing to invest in anything. They shuffled to classes by day and got high at night. A few played squash—shockingly well, given their lack of focus—and a few were in school bands. But for the most part they existed in their own good-natured fog of odd wit and poor hygiene. The masters granted them clemency on these and other counts. One day that fall, a buddy who was Muslim (one of the very few Muslims I ever knew at St. Paul's) had stood up in class and shouted, over the teacher's voice, "LOOK AT THAT TREE!"

Everyone turned to find one of the thousand sugar maples right outside the window, perfectly crowned, aflame with fall.

"THIS ONE MOMENT BELONGS TO THAT TREE! THAT TREE IS INCREDIBLE! THAT TREE DESERVES TO BE LOOKED AT! STOP EVERYTHING AND LOOK AT THAT GODDAMNED TREE!"

The teacher waited until this outburst was complete, then quietly asked everyone to get back to work. Nobody said much beyond that. It was just what this guy did, just what some students did: they'd see a tree and be so moved they had to shout about it. *Total freaks.*

I savored the moment with Leighton Huhne for a day or two. I was so hungry for kindness that his compliment felt like a proposal. Why had he been friendly? Why was he not appalled by me?

My problem, I figured, must have been one of allegiances. I was a tri-varsity athlete, a top student, a chorister—I wanted to be admired. *Of course* I would become a pariah for any break from this routine. But what if I didn't want any of those things? What if I just drew crazy moonscapes and spouted poetic epithets and pretended not to care about anything?

If I simply went crazy, would they leave me alone?

"You should come hang out sometime," said Leighton.

The first time I visited his room, I sat on the floor in front of the big easy chair where he was slumped. Dead bootlegs played on the stereo. His wall of tapes made the room look like a bank vault. He was from Colorado and knew Linley. (The coordination of social class around St. Paul's meant that most everyone from a certain city or even state would know everyone else from that place, and the farther you went from New Hampshire, the truer this was. Choose a student from Hong Kong, he or she would know every other St. Paul's student from Hong Kong long before setting foot on campus.) Leighton told me Linley was doing well, was happy back home, that she and her brother were good people. I said I missed her.

He never mentioned Rick or Taz or Budge or Candace. I was keen to make sure *that* version of me was never invoked—not in the slightest. I asked about the music, and he talked for a while about some concert venue called Red Rocks and a crazy bridge between "Dark Star" and "Brokedown Palace."

While we chatted, I reached over to his giant socked feet and began to rub them.

"That feels amazing," he said.

"Doesn't it?"

The point was to be nuts. I was aiming for a kind of beatific vacancy, as though I could return to innocence by way of insanity. I rubbed his feet for a while, then got up, utterly aloof, and went back to my room in time for check-in. I felt certifiable. But my act worked: Leighton, disarmed or otherwise unconcerned, invited me to meet him and some other buddies in another sixth former's room to get high. I'd never even seen pot before. On the appointed evening I ducked under the tapestry that was hung, in open defiance of fire-safety rules, across the threshold, calling out, "Hello?," and was immediately and loudly shushed. Two dressers faced me—another obstacle to any faculty member who dared to venture in. I cut right around them and found a cavelike space beneath loft beds, where a group of guys huddled toward what I gathered was a bong.

It was red plastic, the size of a child's telescope, and translucent. It bubbled in a pleasing way. The closest referent I had was a lava lamp, or the tiny red oil lights that my childhood friend Wendy had on her Christmas tree and which made my dad hysterical with fear. "Boiling oil is basically a bomb! That tree would go up in a heartbeat!" I recognized the smell of pot, and for the first time knew what it was.

"'Sup?" someone said.

"Hey."

Leighton patted the floor beside him. "You're up next."

I scooched into place and waited. The bong was held

to my face. Across the circle, a student I'd never spoken to flicked open a lighter and held the flame to a little metal cup at its base.

I stared.

Leighton whispered, "Inhale."

I pointed to the mouth of the bong. "There?"

Everyone laughed. "Yeah."

I lowered my face to the red plastic opening and inhaled as best I could. The snap-snap sound of the student's lighter flint pleased me, like a train clicking over its track, like we were together helping me arrive somewhere else.

My cheeks puffed fat as a chipmunk's, I raised my head.

Everyone laughed again. "No, *inhale,*" said Leighton. He patted his chest and filled it, to show me.

I had never so much as smoked a cigarette, but I gulped some of the fiery air in my mouth down into my lungs. The moment I did, I realized my mistake.

My throat tore open. I was ignited, I was sure of it. The pain was astonishing. I hadn't remembered. I hadn't thought.

I burst out coughing and crying, and the first smiles that had appeared around the circle closed quickly into faces of concern.

"Dude. Is she okay? Are you okay?"

I had to cough, but coughing was awful. Tears were running down my face, and I was waving a hand in front of my mouth as though to cool myself.

"Jesus."

"Okay, no tokes for you, kiddo."

"Christ."

"Is she, like, allergic?"

"Maybe she's just super-wired to weed."

Someone laughed. "Totally. Like, built for it. Like, a Polaroid with weed. Just show it to her and she lights up."

Leighton clapped me on the back. "Awesome. Welcome."

I didn't even have to talk. I sat there, watching the red bong glow from hand to hand, listening to the laughter and the crackle of the flame in the bowl, the endless, low, insipid tones of some long-ago Dead concert on the stereo. I waited to get high, but nothing happened. My throat hurt so much that I let spit pool in my mouth before I worked up the courage to swallow. One guy across the way smiled a particularly large smile at me. He had long red hair that fell in a lush drape over his face, and he kept pushing it aside so he could see me. I thought how funny it would be if we became girlfriend and boyfriend, how much shit people would give us for both having red hair. He had the same idea. This was Timothy Macalester. He was interested in social justice, Northern California, and smoking weed. In no time at all he was walking me to class and home at night, and I never again had to pretend to try to get high.

I don't remember what we talked about, Tim and I. He was thoughtful and independent and funny and mild, and I remember best his enormous smile. It took up half his face, and he coupled it with the longish red hair in a silly way, but because he was not self-conscious, all you saw was a really nice guy whose face could make you smile. Everywhere we went, we were told we'd have redheaded children. I was just happy not to be alone.

He never asked about Rick or Taz or Budge, and I never volunteered anything about them. He liked to kiss. This was fine with me, though my body remained cold—whatever high glitter had swept through me the spring before, kissing Shep beneath the lamplight, was gone now. We did not engage in much beyond this. I recall only vaguely our intimacy. It was my duty as his girlfriend, I understood, and it was a small price to pay for the fact that other boys had stopped promising to, say, fuck my freckles on the way to Environmental Science class. No more calls from college men seeking a quickie.

But when I think of Tim, my stomach twists with a sense of guilt, and a memory of betrayal I can't quite place. It wasn't about a person. It was about the absence of a person. I liked Tim well enough, but I was using him, plain and simple, for protection, and he was far too emotionally aware to pretend that I was an active participant in this couple we were forming. I remember him saying my name, as though to wake me up from a trance, and then, after watching my face for a moment, shaking his head as though I'd disappointed him. I remember him gradually spending less time with me and more time with his roommates and friends.

I was pretending to be nuts, but I was actually cracking up, too—utterly disconnected and careless. In choir I had almost completely lost my voice, so the only time I could hear myself was in the empty stairwells of my dorm, where the acoustics were so sharp that the tiniest tone was amplified. I didn't talk much, but I did practice alto lines in the stairwells. My grades remained almost perfect. I slept around five hours a night. I arrived at the rink for hockey practice and watched the last of the varsity boys' practice—Rick Banner was terrifically tall on skates, taller than Budge and his sidekick, than any of them. I watched them to prove I could, to prove to them, and to myself, that I was not afraid. Their blades cut and cracked the ice. They sent sprays of shavings in every direction. The rink's coldness was so dry I could barely breathe. I saw those men as sharply as if they'd been etched onto the air. I heard every sound of their skates. I could not seem to lose them in a scrimmage or a crowd. But Tim I saw as though he were on the wrong end of a telescope, small and wobbly, smiling his huge smile.

By spring break, we had fizzled out. I was aware that he was angry but didn't try to determine why. I just couldn't bring myself to act.

"Lacy *must* be happy," Mrs. Fenn wrote to my parents in her adviser note that semester. "She sings in the hallways."

8

Spring 1991, Fifth Form

When I told a therapist in my mid-twenties about how I fell skiing in New Mexico on spring break of that year, fifth form at St. Paul's, and broke my hand, she suggested that I'd done so intentionally. "Not that you planned for that particular bone," she said, to clarify. "But that you needed a visible injury to allow you to admit to harm."

I'm as open as anyone to the notion of the unconscious working the borders of intention, and I appreciate the line of authority she was trying to offer me—to suggest that some part of me was aware of my situation and powerfully able to alter events to draw attention to it. How tempting it is to fold accidents into our own narration. To think that it wasn't as simple as sitting back on my skis at the end of the day, on a mild slope, and stumbling onto my outstretched right hand, my ski pole acting as a lever to hyperextend my thumb so that the tendon pulled away a bit of bone. But in fact, it was. It took less than a second and very little speed. It's called *skier's thumb,* and I went home from the mountains and back to school in a bright pink cast.

"Crawford Curse," said my mom.

I am not sure a dumb fall on a rich ski hill qualifies as bad luck. On balance, I think that if you're a sixteen-year-old on skis on spring break, you are still officially in the good-luck category.

Mom added, "But at least it was the last day, right?"

I didn't tell her that if I'd known how easy it was to break a bone, how much power you could generate from sliding just a little bit fast, I might have found a way to die. Could it be done gently? Could I have it happen before I knew it was happening, just disappear without having to do the dying?

The morning I fell, I had been walking across our rented condo in full-body long underwear, heading to find my ski socks, when my father, already dressed and eager to get on the lift line, looked up from his newspaper and said, "Lacy. Where did you *get* that figure?"

I froze. Mom shouted from the bedroom. "Jim!"

Dad's face was guileless. He meant it only as a compliment, an impulsive expression of surprise. My shape was mature, attractive, and this shocked him. It was such a simple slip. But my skin felt iced. He'd seen me as a woman, not his child. Not even a woman: a body. So I was right: even here, even to him, the girl I had been—the *person* I had been—was gone.

I did not answer my dad. The question seemed particularly cruel because my figure would have come genetically from him and my mother, so that he was, in a way, complimenting (implicating?) himself. I'd had nothing to do with it.

"What?" Dad asked, in response to my mother—half puzzled, half defiant. He wore a fallen smile.

I was in ski school all day, buried in fleece. Our instructor, Blake, was something of a local legend for his freestyle skiing. He was raffish and attractive, in his mid-twenties, and when he wasn't teaching teenagers in ski school he hurled himself off cliffs and did full-layout flips on the way down. At lunch in the busy cafeteria he was high-fived so often he just stopped making his hand available. The rest of my ski-school classmates competed to come up with a story or a joke to catch his attention, but I thought he was dull.

"So, ah, Lacy...what grade are you in back in—what did you say—Chicago?"

"I live in Chicago," I said. "But I'm a junior at a high school in New Hampshire."

This was on the ski lift. He took turns riding in the quad chair with us, striving to be inclusive. Our feet dangled over evergreens. The sodden quiet of snow cover. Distant peaks.

"New Hampshire, huh? Is that like for juvie?"

"Ah, no. It's for academics."

"Oh, like tutoring?"

"Yeah. Sorta like that."

"Got it. So what subjects, then? Like, math? Reading?"

I was pissy, hungry, arrogant. "Actually, I'm putting together an independent study project looking at the relationship between biochemical depression and the creative genius."

"Oh. Sweet."

"Yeah." I felt lousy, listening to myself. The girl on the other side of him on our chair was applying ChapStick. "I'm just interested in why poets are always killing themselves."

"Oh, right. Rock on. That *is* cool."

"Isn't it?"

I was following with his other students in a line down the last slope of the day when I sat back, overwhelmed with something I could not name, and fell on my hand. Blake took me to the first-aid clinic himself. He'd skied enough to know what it meant that I could not move my thumb.

Not a big deal. I might need surgery, I might not. An orthopedist could determine this later.

"Rock on, poet girl," said Blake, once they'd read the X-ray. "I always give a prize to the kid who manages to ski hard enough to land a fracture." He patted me on the head, then high-fived the emergency-room physician on his way out.

It wasn't until after they casted me that I worked out there was no way to hold a pen, much less a tennis racket. No playing my best sport, no shot at the No. 1 singles spot, no joining my team. How would I write my essays, do my homework? I could type, but it would have to be one-handed, and back then the only computers were in the computer lab. I took my discharge instructions and a bottle of strong pain relievers back to the condo, where Mom helped me get out of my ski clothes and taped a Ziploc bag over my hand so I could shower.

It hurt. As my hand swelled I felt my heart in my palm, and at Mom's suggestion I took a few painkillers. I remember how they softened the edges of my peripheral vision. I sat on a stool in the little eat-in kitchen turning my head swiftly and waiting for things to line up. When Blake rang the condo to ask how I was doing, my parents were grateful—and more than comfortable with his offer to take me out for a hot chocolate to cheer me up.

Nobody carded me, walking into a bar with Blake. My cocoa was spiked and delicious. There were shots, too. One of Blake's friends, also an extreme skier, joined us, along with a girl from ski school named Tori. She was blond and enthusiastic, with glittery pink lips, and I both judged her for being cheap and drew courage from her cheer. I can still taste the liquor in the hot chocolate. I welcomed the nausea and the spinning. I wanted to launch off a cliff. *God's country.* I remember being led through the snow and wondering if I could lie down in it and never wake up. How hard could it be to die? Truly, how hard? And what loss would that be? One less prep-school girl on spring break. One less suburban doll. One less Princeton applicant, one less aspiring fool. They'd turn down the radiator in my room and leave it dark, just like Elise's.

At one point Blake was having sex with me while his buddy had sex with Tori just a few feet away. I saw them and I saw my cast, which was bright enough to shine in the dark of their filthy living room. That's all I remember. I no longer cared.

Mom was wrong about the curse. My hand was a terrific blessing. I couldn't have chosen a better tiny bone to break to release me from the usual school routine. My hand was casted at rest, fingers and thumb in loose parallel, and there was nowhere to lodge a pen. This meant I couldn't take notes in class. Teachers threw too much material at us for me to simply try to remember it all. "You could bring a tape recorder," said Dad, but then what? Sit in my room and replay entire classes? It would take all night. Instead I used what I could—my left hand—and, working with intense concentration, taught myself to write with my opposite paw.

It meant being slow. It meant being deliberate. I had to choose what to record or I would lose the thread. The effect was an engagement with classroom discussion I'd never forced on myself before. I stopped worrying about other people and started listening to them.

I pressed out French papers with new focus and math sets with greater clarity. In Religion, I cut out the fat of pseudo-philosophical musings and said only what I meant to say. Reverend S. remained unmoved, but to hell with him. I was finally understanding what it meant to pay attention, and he'd been gassing on about that all year.

I needed more time to do my work, and I received it. Because I could not play tennis, I was given the afternoons free to exercise as I wished. (As a fifth former with two other varsity sports, I'd have been given this opportunity anyway, but I never would have taken it otherwise.) "You could come warm up with the team," suggested Coach Schiff, and for the first few days I did, shivering through laps around the blustery courts and stretching for no reason. "You could ride the exercise bike in the training room," she offered, and I tried that, but Rick came in to ice down after lacrosse practice and his half-naked body in a tub made me quake. The training room was nauseating, a cesspit of overcompensation: four orthopedically designed tables on one side for administering pulse therapies and wrapping joints, and on the other side a whirlpool and the ice basin, as though we were all Olympians. Everyone, it seemed, got taped up at the trainer's. Everyone needed to be stretched or examined. Pedaling the exercise bike smack in the middle of the room with my hot-pink cast, I felt like a sitting duck—actually sitting, my legs actually paddling, all these athletes coming and going.

On the day Coach Schiff took the team for the long run we called Blinking Light, I joined them. It seemed like the right thing to do, though I had always hated these training runs. There were shorter routes through the woods, but they were narrow and full of sticks and chipmunk holes, best left to solitary walkers or kids looking for a quiet place to bone or get stoned. Varsity captains preferred to send their teams up the road toward the boat docks—a mile from the gym— and then ordered a left turn to a major county junction, where a single stoplight was strung across the intersection. The small pleasure of being able to leave campus was far offset by the uphill climb, two miles out, to that stoplight, which blinked red—there was not enough traffic to require anything more. We passed through woods and came out into farmland, with a house in the distance. I dreamed of seeing another human being in the world beyond school. A nice farm wife with a graying golden bun and a tray of biscuits or a pitcher of lemonade. I had always been a slow runner— that is how I am made—and I was miserable, trying to keep up. The damn stoplight never seemed to get any closer. On the soccer team in the fall our pace had been set by Coach Green, a six-foot-four ectomorph trotting alongside Meg, whose first New York City Marathon, which she would run on a whim, would earn her a racing sponsorship. Days I threw up, I was patted on the back and told to keep working on my aerobic capacity.

Now, the early-spring sky was slate. Our tennis team was small and the girls had on their tennis skirts, which would have been a silly sight to a local resident on that country road— fourteen or so preppy girls in pleated skirts, like an image from *Madeline's* Parisian orphanage. I pounded along behind them. Running made my hand ache and turned my throat raw, but when this run was over, I knew, they had to return to the courts and follow orders, while I could do whatever I wanted for the few hours before supper. This bit of time felt un-imaginably indulgent. After we reached the light and turned around, I fell well behind. The woods to my left were dark, the bark of the leafless trees wet with the thaw. The pavement had no curb. Again I imagined slipping away, into the woods. How cold would it be at night? Would the farmer's wife take me in? It was quiet enough to hear squirrels climbing. My own breath sounded explosive. I considered being frightened—I conjured the usual misshapen country recluse who might hack me to bits with the ax he happened to be carrying. But the thought didn't take. My cast was hard. I swung it a few times as though I was hitting a forehand. It was pendulous and made me feel curiously powerful.

When it came time to turn back toward campus, I went left instead and found the top of the trail into the woods. Ice still glazed the muddy hollows. I'd been running longer than I had ever run before, but on these curves I wasn't tired. Instead I felt propelled by them. The earth was springy beneath me. I got faster, or it seemed I did, clipping the bigger, closer trees with my cast. I knew this path as Long Ponds, but I'd never run it in this direction, and never alone, and certainly not when the trees were bare, so I hadn't had the chance to work out what I was working out now: where the dining hall was in relation to the chapel, with the ice rink behind; how the edge of the forest was actually just a strip before a parking lot here, and a utility road here; where the bridges ran, and why water rushed over the waterfall by Simpson House; how the entire campus was basically just wedged between the boat docks on Turkey Pond and Pleasant Street. Not much of anything at all, really. The trail emerged like a secret by the chapel, onto a path so narrow between the pond and the trees you'd worry there wasn't room on the shore to keep from falling in.

Maybe a student with a better sense of direction would have been in possession of this vision of her home much earlier than I was, but that was the first day I realized the shape of the school. With it came the secondary realization that the school was a place, like any other place—stationary, platted, with boundaries. It was possible to leave it. One day I would.

I was late coming in to dinner. Caroline happened to be in the hall. She said, "Lacy-o."

It was a surprising kindness. I had given up on Caroline, on all of them, because of their loyalty to Candace. "Hi, Caroline."

"How is your arm?"

"I just ran six miles." I'd worked it out. "Blinking Light, then Boat Docks, then Long Ponds."

"Wow. That must have felt terrific. Didn't it get dark?"

"Not quite."

She reached for my bright pink cast and held it up. "Though this thing is like a torch."

"Or a club."

She smiled, weighing the plaster. "Yeah, you could deck the shit out of someone with this."

We walked into the dining hall together. Our schoolmates clocked this small progression in diplomacy. I saw Sam's eyebrows go up.

That night before bed, I dragged my old camp footlocker out from the floor of my closet, where it held shoes and sweaters and spare shampoo, and pulled it in front of my door. All student doors opened in. I leaned across the trunk to test the knob and was able to slam the trunk with the door hard enough to let in a few inches of hallway light, so for good measure I tossed a few heavy textbooks inside. We were forbidden to block the doors, of course, in case of fire, but I reasoned that if I had to I could just open my ancient mullioned window and drop two stories to the grass. Whereas nobody could climb in.

My reckoning with the land continued. I ran every road. Out the white gates and left; up Pleasant Street, facing traffic; across the way to a far hill, at the top of which I found a house with mountain views and a Labrador retriever who let me sit with him in the grass and look around. I went past the blinking light beneath a major interstate and into the next town before I lost my nerve. I found a quarry, a cemetery, and a park. I didn't risk running toward Concord, where my presence might be misunderstood as leaving campus without written permission. But I pounded everywhere else. I got barked at and honked at. I remember trampling mud and new nettles. I spotted lady's slippers, which I recognized because my mother had pointed them out carpeting damp woods in Illinois. Sometimes I imagined I was circling the place as a wolf might—as *my* wolf might, to mark her territory—but I never did feel I possessed St. Paul's; more often I imagined a kind of stitching, as if I was ensuring the perimeter could never pick up and expand. As if I was nailing the place down for good.

I didn't think about the boys. Not any of them. I thought about the school, and whether my small catastrophes in so vaunted a place meant the world itself might wish me ill. (I was wrong to imagine a malevolent rather than indifferent world, but I had no idea how right I was about the school.) Perhaps growing up with the Crawford Curse had given me my propensity to understand what had happened to me as something broader and crueler than two boys in a dark room. Seen one way, my interpretation was paranoid—a child's conflation of incident with environment. Seen another way, it was an easy instinct—which I believe all children have—to identify the power structures that animate any institution or society, and particularly one as preening and self-possessed as St. Paul's.

I'd never had much interaction with the people who in fact wielded power at the school. The rector, Kelly Clark, was to me an oddly tanned, constantly intoning priest, one of many Episcopal clergymen I'd heard from pulpits all my life. To many of my classmates he was a benevolent paterfamilias, standing beside his smiling wife with her blue, sugar-spun hair. At our every encounter he called me "Lucy," so I felt no particular affection, but I didn't hold it against him— why should he know me? There were five hundred of us. Leadership of St. Paul's was the last position of his career (as it had been for almost every rector, being a pinnacle appointment), and he seemed tired, almost addled. I didn't expect anything more.

Around him was a ring of men: Bill Matthews and John Buxton and Cliff Gillespie. The vice rectors, who served as our deans, were not academic but sporting, their energy not pedantic but avuncular. Mr. Matthews was a legendary hockey star from St. Paul's himself and now a championship coach. Two of his sons had played for St. Paul's. The younger of them, who had graduated before I arrived, had a popular reputation that was burnished even in his absence, and this interested me enough to watch from beyond the boards while Matthews yelled at his hockey players. He was pug-faced and seemed angry, yapping up at them, his breath visible, the skaters towering over him on their blades. I saw his absence of gravitas as a normal, if alternative, presentation of masculine leadership—not for him the churchly bromides. He wanted pucks in nets and points on the board. I don't remember him having much of a rapport with girls. He signed off on our requests to leave campus, and his signature often appeared on formal school communications. If you got into a tangle with the administration for complications of any reason—leaves of absence, failed courses—you'd likely be dealing with Mr. Matthews. I'd had nothing to do with him at all.

Mr. Buxton, another vice rector, coached wrestling; had I not gone to watch Shep's meet that long-ago winter, I wouldn't even have known his face. Mr. Gillespie was, as I've said, The Rock. It was his verdict I imagined immediately and with terror when I thought I might get caught in Rick and Taz's room and sent to explain myself to the Disciplinary Committee. He coached lacrosse and taught chemistry, neither of which I pursued.

I don't know by what process the deans decided that Mr. Gillespie would be the one to try to solve the problem of the Ferguson Scholarship exams. Mom and Dad thought something should be done to help me sit written exams with a broken hand, but the faculty considered it unfair to give me extra time. After all, every nominee was going to be challenged to the height of his or her personal ability; how could they know that my extra time would benefit only my motor skills without boosting my performance otherwise?

"This is a little bit ridiculous," said my mom on the phone when I told her no accommodation would be made for me.

"It will be fine."

"It's not fine. You can't *write.*"

At that time, I didn't know the history of Henry Ferguson, eponymous patron of these scholarships: how he'd been shipwrecked at nineteen and forced to drift in a lifeboat across three thousand miles of the Pacific. Desperate, pounded by the sun, Ferguson had, of course, kept a journal of his trials (as any good St. Paul's student would), which was promptly published in *Harper's* upon his return (as any self-respecting St. Paul's alumnus's work would be). This man was no ordinary example of Puritan austerity and forbearance. By the time he was a trustee of St. Paul's, Ferguson was regarded as an almost holy survivor. They even made him rector for a while.

"I'm not going to win, anyway, Mom," I said into the phone. "It's really not worth the fight."

But at home in Chicago, Mom howled for Dad to come to the phone. "She can't write!"

"I know," I heard Dad say. "But they make a decent point."

"How is that decent? She has to use one hand!"

"But how much longer would be fair, given that? How could they calculate that? I understand it's sort of impossible for them to be fair to all the other kids. And she's the one with the injury."

"Exactly! *She's* the one with the injury!"

"Yes, but—"

"This is outrageous. I'm flying out there."

"Please don't," I said into the phone.

"Please don't," said Dad.

Mom came back. "I just want you to have a shot at winning," she told me.

"I know."

"And you can't do it orally? Like defending a thesis?"

"Not if writing is part of the evaluation, and it is."

"But what if you can't write? How fair is that?"

How sweet it was, I thought cruelly, that Mom somehow had in mind that St. Paul's was fair.

"I will write left-handed and I will do the best I can."

Mom was beginning to cry. "All right, love. I know you will."

But the next day a typed note appeared in my post-office box: Mr. Gillespie was requesting to see me in the chemistry lab that afternoon.

I had never spoken with The Rock. He was, to me, unapproachable and uninterested at the same time, someone who sat and waited for us to fuck up, at which point he decided what portion of our futures we had forfeited. I was the broken-handed, novel-loving humanities girl summoned to meet him in a science building where the doors slammed shut on their own and the walls hummed with unseen machinery.

I found the chemistry lab for the first and last time. The Rock was at one of the high tables, the ones topped with a black waxy substance you could carve with a fingernail. His feet were tucked into the bottom rail of his stool, and he patted the stool beside him.

I hopped up and felt like an impostor, as though my ability to do that belied my injury.

"It's just a tiny piece of bone at the base of my thumb," I offered, tapping my cast at the spot where the break would be. Hardly a shipwreck in the South Pacific. I thought he'd appreciate an impression of toughness.

"I understand."

He had in front of him on the table several plastic tubs filled with Styrofoam balls organized by size and color. "Okay, now," he said. "Let's see it."

I held up my arm, feeling embarrassed by the fact that all of my running had made my cast begin to smell.

"It's a little bit, um, old," I told him.

"What's that?"

"Just, I can't shower with it."

He shook his head to dismiss my concern, gripped my cast at the wrist with one hand, and tried half-heartedly to wedge his other fist inside the casted space between my fingers and thumb. This hurt. Then he held his fist up and eyeballed it— first in front of a tub of blue balls, then green. He took a green ball.

"Let's try this," he said, and fit the ball inside my casted hand.

It fell to the floor.

I said, "Sorry."

"Nope. Not carbon. Hang on." He reached back across his bins and pulled a blue ball, marginally bigger. He set this in my cast. It rested against my thumb, but when I waved my arm, it too fell out.

"Oh, sorry," I said again.

He ignored this apology too. "Okay, so not oxygen. Hmm."

He stood up and perused the table. It was odd to be alone in a room with any teacher, but particularly this one. I studied his back. His shoulders were broad and round, with his square head poised between them like a great gate hung on two

pillars. His shirt strained against his torso. He was coaching
Rick that spring. Also Budge, and so many of the others who
had catcalled and propositioned me, who had made every hallway a gauntlet. In an hour or so, this man would be out on the
field shouting things that Rick had to obey. It was intoxicating
to be near someone who had such power over them. I felt
urgently that I should be doing or saying something.

He was murmuring. "I'm just trying to think which will be
exactly..."

"Sorry, but what are these?"

He did not turn. "Elements."

He returned with a larger Styrofoam ball, fire-engine red.
"We use them to make models of molecules," he said, tucking
it into my casted hand. It made a small crunching sound as it
went in, and held fast. "Bingo."

With a firm tug on my arm he pulled it out, then took up
a sharpened pencil and began to drill it through the center of
the Styrofoam.

"You could do all sorts of things with this," he went on. "A
fork. Maybe even a tennis racket." Once the ball was speared
with the pencil, he wedged it back into my cast, pencil lead
down, and slid a piece of paper in front of me. "Okay, try."

I moved my arm, and the pencil moved.

"How about your name?"

I wrote *Crawford*. I had very little control, but the word
was legible.

"Good! That should do it."

It wasn't good. Nothing was solved. I could not outprint
a preschooler this way. And in fact it hurt, because my hand
inside its cast pressed against the ball at the precise spot at the

base of my thumb that was broken. But how could I complain to The Rock about Styrofoam? He was on his feet, restacking his bins.

"Okay, thanks," I said. "Thanks so much."

"You're welcome."

I was desperate for something more. "Um," I stammered. "So, which is it? Helium?" The only element I could pull up.

He frowned. "Helium is tiny."

"Oh, right."

"No, that's sodium. Which you generally know in part as salt. Everyone in my lab will know you're working with a salt there. Good luck."

I sat the Ferguson exams. Religion was first. I began printing each essay with my salt ball, but it was slow and my thumb ached. I switched to my left hand and used a normal pen to write several more paragraphs on that side. Finally, running out of time, full of frustrated ideas, I turned my pages upside down and left the room. It was worse in the afternoon, for English, when my hand was already sore. Back in my dorm, I tossed the silly salt pencil into my footlocker before dragging it back across the door.

On Sunday evenings at seven o'clock, a small, optional Vespers service was held in the Old Chapel. The cornerstone of this building had been laid in 1858, in the field alongside the Lower School Pond. Ten years later they'd sawed the place in half and expanded it north and south, adding a transept. The cross shape it formed was still contained by the roundness of the space, wholly unlike the enormous thrust of the new chapel just up the grassy way, which had itself been deconsecrated, sawed apart, expanded, and made holy again, as the school grew in size and stature. We did not use the Old Chapel often. Until the spring of my fifth-form year, I'd been inside only twice: for the First Night Service, when the rector gathered us newbs to bind us up and attempt to distract us with prayer from the car doors slamming in the lowering light; and on the cold night in January 1991 when the United States invaded Iraq, and the tolling chapel bell invited students to gather there. Where the new chapel was magnificent, it was also domineering, and the site of too much daily turmoil to offer solace. I didn't even need to enter the Old Chapel to draw a sense of quiet—just its shape in the middle of campus, curled and impervious as a sleeping cat, was enough.

Sometimes I'd thought about going into the Old Chapel by myself to sit. Maybe I'd try to pray. But I was worried I'd be discovered there and forced to reveal something I'd rather not. I never so much as tried the door. Was it unlocked? Could we go there whenever we wished? I wouldn't have known whom to ask.

I took a long run almost daily that spring, and each time I would finish jogging just as the path turned past the Old Chapel. I used my runs to begin to dream of a world not colored by St. Paul's—surely there were cities not dominated by alumni, offices where I could work, little coffee shops I could waitress in where nobody would care. I pictured one by the beach, maybe in California, which I had never seen. Another in a European city, likewise unseen, its narrow street ribbed with light. If one of the great sources of misery for all high schoolers is the illusion that high school will never end, the reach of power implied (and wielded) by the alumni and trustees of St. Paul's School threatened that in our particular case, that nightmare was real. It's odd, because the Old Chapel was an original building—core to the campus and its history—and might have been the root of the place. But with the completion of the new chapel, it seemed to me that the school's soul had jumped across the green to inhabit the soaring new expanse. Ritual always did love majesty. What was left in the Old Chapel was humble and patient. I aspired to both virtues. And I sympathized with a space that seemed unmoved by spectacle.

I was finishing a late run on a Sunday in April when I emerged from the woods to find Marion, our choir's star soprano, walking alone down the path to Vespers. I called out to her.

Marion offered me her trademark smile: gap-toothed, wholly sincere. When she sang she tilted her head and softened her eyes, as a mother does singing a lullaby, so that her sound was made more beautiful by the pleasure you saw on her face. I was always embarrassed to be singing alongside her, but she encouraged me.

"How far'd you go?" she asked. It was exactly the right question.

"I don't know. I ran for ninety minutes."

"Blinking Light?"

"Fisk Hill, then around and back to Long Ponds."

"Wow," she said. "Want to come to Vespers?"

"Now?"

"Yeah. At seven."

"But—" I gestured to my sweaty clothes, my dumb pink plaster cast.

"Oh, who cares about that? Come on." She took my good arm. "Nobody goes anyway."

I pictured the priest. "Is it Reverend S.?"

She screwed up her face. "God, no. Do you think I'd be going? Radley."

It was rumored that Marion's parents were geniuses who were also unwell, and that she might have had her own apartment in New York, or Boston, or Maine. Her aunt was a powerful trustee of the school, and Marion seemed to have special knowledge of everyone on campus, from the third-form Japanese exchange student whom she knew because they were both virtuosos on the violin to the women who sorted our mail in the post office. "Marion!" I'd heard one of them rasp, seeing her enter. The postmistress was usually glimpsed only through your open metal box, if she happened to shuffle past at just the moment you were peering in.

"I'll sit far away, then," I said. Between my shirt and my cast, I was pretty sure I smelled horrible.

"You'll sit right next to me," said Marion.

Inside, the chapel smelled softly of dust. It was still warm—the day had been sunny, the wood had taken it in—but I knew it would be cold by the time we left. Ms. Radley stood quietly with her prayer book in her hands. I recognized that the slim, red-bound volume must be her private copy—my mom used hers in services too—but Ms. Radley rarely wore her clerical garb. She taught Religion and violin, and was mother to two students at the school, a girl older than I was and a boy younger. There was no Mr. Radley, as far as I could tell. She wore her dark hair short, with sprays of gray creeping out from her temples. Her lean body and utilitarian clothes were mannish in a way I found appealing but did not yet recognize as queer. All I sensed was a quiet objection—an objection to everything collared and exalted. I had watched her carefully from my chapel seat but had never been lucky enough to have a reason to talk with her. I couldn't think what to say—*Hey, my mom's a priest too?*

Ms. Radley embraced Marion and nodded her head in greeting to me. I sat quickly.

We were the only two students there. No matter. Ms. Radley led us as if there were a hundred people in the space, speaking the service clearly and carefully.

What a nice thing, I thought, to come to Chapel on Sunday evenings. What a quiet hideaway this is. Again I had the feeling I so often had at St. Paul's, that I had stumbled upon a dedicated practice that my peers had discovered for themselves—in the art studio, on a playing field—and thought it remarkable not least because I had failed to find such a practice of my own.

When Ms. Radley spoke certain prayers, her voice, already a bit hoarse, took on extra air. I leaned in to listen:

> *Keep watch, dear Lord, with those who work, or watch, or weep this night, and give your angels charge over those who sleep. Tend the sick, Lord Christ; give rest to the weary, bless the dying, soothe the suffering, pity the afflicted, shield the joyous; and all for your love's sake.*

Marion and I said, "Amen."

It was not a prayer I'd heard before. I decided that anyone who spoke the words *work* and *watch* and *weep* the way Ms.

Radley did was someone I needed to be close to. She said them with her whole mouth, intently. I had never thought about the word *weep* much before. I'd considered it for wounds, perhaps—something unsightly. Nobody I knew *wept*. When we were upset, we *cried*. We *sobbed*. We *blubbered* or *bawled*, we *got hysterical,* we *freaked out.* Her voice made me consider whether there might be honor in sorrow.

But the words that stirred me most were *shield the joyous.* I said goodbye to Marion and walked back to my dorm with my arms wrapped tightly around my core. The sun was down and I was chilled, walking across campus, and far from joyous. I couldn't remember the last time I'd felt even halfway happy. Maybe this is why the phrase struck me as so generous and so wise. Of course the weeping needed protection—but the joyous too? I considered the notion that good fortune was tender. It soothed me to think that compassion might be aimed at the lucky. Maybe it gave me a way to feel I mattered. Even if I was not reveling in the riches of school, even if I was not among the dancing heirs, I might serve as a shield for those who were. Caroline. Samantha. Brooke. Maddy. Marion. Everyone who belonged there, everyone who was kind. I thought I could settle for that.

Every Sunday I went back to hear the reedy tones of Ms. Radley's *work or watch or weep this night.*

I asked Marion how I should approach Ms. Radley about advising my Independent Study Project, or ISP, on biochemical depression and the creative genius. It was a pretentious topic, I knew—just the memory of myself on the ski lift, hand intact, pride inflamed, rattling on about aesthetic sensibilities made me wish a blizzard had come up just then. But in the proposal I was working up, I didn't intend to claim either depression or genius. I meant to construct the inquiry to have enough novelty and grain to pass muster with the faculty who approved such projects. The main point of it all was to be left alone. (Hence *independent project*.) And it was informed by my own experience, however flimsily. I had, after all, taken Prozac for about ten months, which allowed me to borrow a small portion of authenticity, though I mentioned nothing about this to anyone. The drug hadn't made me feel any different. But the experience had caused me to begin to pay attention to the fact that a new, partially scientific notion of "biochemical depression" had taken root in the popular imagination, or at least in as much of it as I could monitor through periodicals in the school library.

This was all before the internet, with only a newly computerized card catalogue and a librarian to help me access databases better suited to doctoral candidates. I followed book to article to book like a set of torches on a tunneled hall. My investigations began, of course, with *The Bell Jar.* Sylvia Plath was every sad Waspy girl's patron saint. We all but knew her: look at her face! She'd have been on the field hockey team! After Sylvia's dreadful end I moved on to Ted Hughes, imagining it was sophisticated of me to leave the girl and join the men. Everybody knew "Daddy," but who knew "The Hawk in the Rain"? From there I encountered a range of English poets: Stephen Spender's crew, including Auden as a young man, before he'd been bloodlessly anthologized. I glanced past Virginia Woolf, whose intelligence and self-possession frightened me—I placed a marker there, to return to when I was older—and came back the long way to the T. S. Eliot of our Religion class.

Still, women's verse appealed to me more: Anne Sexton, Adrienne Rich, Maxine Kumin. Mom told me that as a child in Rome she had played with a girl named Jorie Pepper who was now the poet Jorie Graham, and I figured this would help me somehow. I imagined them: one girl growing up to make these poems, the other growing up to make me. Carolyn Forché taught me the beginnings of the language of witness, though all I understood at the time was the jolt a reader felt when a writer described crisis without mediation.

I read Van Gogh's letters to Theo. Biographies of Michelangelo, Mozart, and Beethoven. I had no clue what disciplines I was paddling in, nor even on what shores a discipline might form. What I was watching, with all the fever of a voyeur, was the practice of passion. These examples were startling alternatives to the life of my own mind, to the steady, frozen-rain fear that made everything glassy and fragile. I was terrified to break through. All I wanted was to break through. I thought I recognized the feeling contemporary artists recalled when asked how they felt in treatment with new psychotropic medications and they described being dulled and divorced from themselves. They wanted off the drugs and back into the storm. I envied them their sense of direction, even if it led to unspeakable misery.

I returned to Plath and her men with a love of the rack and the screw. Sitting in the soaring alcoves of the new library, I read to myself, softly but out loud. If I studied keenly enough, could I borrow these writers' fire? It was not so different from my little girl's logic that kneeling on hard wood made God more likely to hear my prayer. I did not understand how a person fashioned a self. But the books I found seemed to lead from one to the next as though someone had gone up ahead and laid them out for me. *I rise with my red hair.*

I finished my proposal and prepared to present it to Ms. Radley. I hoped from the way she led Vespers that she would agree to supervise me. I just couldn't begin to think how to explain why I was doing this project, or why I was asking her.

"Just come to my Religion class," suggested Marion. "Eighth period Monday. You can ask her right afterward."

"And say what?"

"How about just tell her what you want to write about?"

"But won't she want to know why?"

Marion's smile was almost pitying.

I asked, "Will you stay while I talk to her?" I needed so much from Ms. Radley that I was frightened to approach her.

"Um, if you want me to."

"She has no idea what this is about."

Marion said, "Do *you* know what this is about?"

Of course not. "I've got a very thorough proposal," I said.

"Then I think she'll be happy to say yes, Lace. But I'll stay if you want."

When I appeared at the door to their class, Ms. Radley was shrugging into a sweater—it was still chilly in the evenings—and on her way out she suggested we meet at her home when we might have more time.

"Just any time?" I asked, feeling panicky.

"Well, unless I'm on duty. If I'm on duty, you can come talk to me in the dorm, but we'll have more privacy at my home."

Marion gave me her lullaby smile.

This planning of Ms. Radley's attention was a revelation. My encounters with faculty had almost always taken place in a check-in scrum or while walking in a crowd. Halfway through each semester, Mrs. Fenn handed me my interim grades on a small piece of computer paper and said, "Congratulations." It hadn't occurred to me that a teacher could invite me to her home for a conversation. I was grateful for this.

I waited until a Tuesday night I thought she'd have free and walked across campus to the little white house where she lived.

She was among the faculty who did not live in a dorm, though she was assigned to one for check-in and advising, as almost all masters were. Somehow, the truly mild girls ended up in the dorm she oversaw—the musicians and poets, girls like Marion. I wondered again who decided housing assignments. For the sixth form I was planning to request to live with the Kittredge girls, though it wasn't likely they'd put my name down too. We had arrived at a passable détente, as thin-lipped as the new spring over the lawns. I could sit with them at breakfast if I wanted to. I could join them on the path between classes. My company was welcome so long as Budge's Candace (they were still going strong) was not with them. If I saw her there, I kept my distance.

Ms. Radley heard me on the step before I knocked.

"Come in."

The room was cozy and low. She sat beneath a floor lamp with a brown satchel at her feet, yarn twining up into her lap. Her knitting needles were ice-blue and flashed beneath the lamp. Books and papers were stacked everywhere, and musical instruments leaned on stands in a corner. There was a golden retriever on the floor. The dog's tail thumped.

"Good girl, Raz," she said. And to me: "Now, what's the plan?"

She gave me so much space, it did not occur to me to wonder what she knew.

"Well, I want to do an ISP. About the connection between biochemical depression and the—"

"Yes, yes," she said. She let loose a knitting needle and held out a hand. "Give me the form. I'll have a look."

"—the creative genius. I was thinking to include three subjects, namely Sylvia Plath, Mozart, and Van Gogh—"

"Sure." She set the page down, unexamined.

"—and I've got several texts lined up that address the pharmaceutical research, which is really new, and I can contact this psychiatrist at Northwestern if I need to for an interview..."

She nodded, eyes on her work. I spun faster, but I was running out of impressive things to say. Finally the dog groaned, and I stopped talking.

"Oh, Raz," said Ms. Radley. "I bet you'd like a scratch." She looked up at me.

I went and sat next to the dog and pushed my fingers into her fur. There was a dangerous unraveling in my chest. I sensed it beginning and I tightened my entire body against it.

"Where are you living next year?" asked Ms. Radley.

"I don't know. I know where I'd like to be, but so far I haven't had much luck with the housing lottery."

"That can happen."

The dog scooted closer and heaved herself upside down. I rubbed the pink skin of her belly.

"Raspberry is very happy," said Ms. Radley.

I was beginning to cry. I fought it, swallowing and blinking. I thought about Cliff Gillespie and his elements. I thought about the bike in the water. Nothing was enough to stop the tears.

"Are you looking forward to sixth form?" she asked me.

"I'm looking forward to my ISP. I mean, if it's approved, if you're comfortable with it, of course. And I'd like to start Italian, if they can find a teacher. And it'll be good, I guess, to be at the top of things." By which I meant that Rick and Taz and Budge and all of them would be gone. I was almost there. So close. "And college, of course..."

"Yes, yes."

The dog was snoring. Ms. Radley said, "You've got free afternoons with that hand, do you?"

"I do. I run."

"Where?"

"Around campus. Blinking Light. Boat Docks. The woods."

"Hm. I wonder if you might take this one with you sometime." Ms. Radley aimed a tethered needle toward the dog. "She loves the woods."

"Really? I could do that?"

"Her leash is right over there."

"That's great. That would be amazing. The woods can be kind of creepy. I'd feel so much safer with a dog with me. I'd feel so much better."

"Good." Ms. Radley raised up her knitting and examined something close under her lamp. "Sweater for my daughter."

"I wish I had a dog in my room," I said suddenly. "At night."

I heard the needles clicking again.

"I wish you did too."

She hadn't asked me any of the questions I'd been sure of. *Tell me about your plans for the project. Tell me how you will balance this with your course load as a senior. How many pages? With what supporting evidence? What outside sources? Initial bibliography? Tell me about yourself. About your mother, who's a priest, like me. Prove yourself.*

"Lacy," she said. "You know that I have to be a chaplain to everyone."

I didn't understand. "Of course . . ."

"So you will see me being friendly with people who have been horrible to you. That is my job and I cannot change that."

"I would never ask you to—"

"But," she continued, still without looking over at me, "if you ever feel unsafe, at any hour, you just come right in through that door." She gestured with her needles. "It's unlocked. The guest room is just there. There is a bed made up. No need to wake me, and you know Raspberry. Just come up and you may sleep there. I will vouch for you."

I couldn't talk. My tears fell onto the dog's fur. Ms. Radley knew this, and did not look my way. It was generosity on top of generosity, delivered without fanfare and without any expectation of reply. I hardly knew what to do with myself. I was silent, terrified of the flood.

She went on knitting for a while, until I found the courage to thump the dog twice in valediction, stand up, say thank you, and get out of there. Any longer and I'd have dissolved. She had me bring her a pen from a table so she could sign my ISP form, and I held that page in my good hand all the way back down to my dorm.

• • •

I was at the Tuck Shop, buying myself a blueberry muffin. The shop sold highly processed baked goods wrapped in cellophane. They were wet to the touch when you unwrapped them, and I liked to microwave them for half a minute to make them even softer, so they wouldn't hurt too much when I swallowed.

Because I still didn't know what was wrong with my throat, I considered each new outbreak of sores to be a punishment. This time I wasn't so sure what I'd done—I hadn't had much to do with any boys lately—so I figured it must be that I'd thrown in the towel on the Ferguson exams, especially after The Rock went to so much trouble to help me. But the weather was finally warming. The air was humid, raising steam over the meadow when the sun broke through. Afternoons were properly hot. So close, the end of the year. So close.

"Hey, Lacy," said a voice behind me. The tone was sly, on the tilt, and I braced for an insult.

But when I turned it was just Scotty, Elise's Scotty, the boy she'd left behind when she'd withdrawn from school. He gave me his impish smile and made a little wave.

"What's up?" I said. I marveled that his hair was still shaggy, a giant pouf all around. It hadn't gotten any bigger all year, which meant either that it grew that long on its own but no longer, or that he carefully trimmed it to exactly this mess. Either way it was interesting, nonthreatening.

"Have you talked to Elise?" he asked.

I hadn't. It hadn't occurred to me. Do soldiers still in fox-holes write to the ones who got to go home?

"No. Have you?"

He shook his head.

He wore low-slung cords that were covered in what looked

like plaster. Hand-swipes were visible across his thighs. But his shirt was an Oxford button-down that still bore the sheer planes of an iron, and seeing him in it I imagined his mother, how her loving him kept all of this together.

"What's that you're eating?" he said.

I held up my paper plate.

"Oh," he said, and scratched at the back of his head. He did this absentmindedly, when he was anxious or without a thought, not because something itched.

"Want some?"

"Oh, naw. I'm good."

His accent was almost Southern. "Scotty, where are you from again?" I asked.

"Philadelphia."

I knew nothing about Philadelphia. I wasn't even sure where it was.

"Cool."

"You're from Chicago."

"Yep."

"Cool."

"Yep."

I balanced my plate and waited.

"All right, well, see you around," he said, and smiled at me again.

"See you around."

I missed Elise, too. I was moved by how much Scotty must have loved her, to approach me like that, out of the blue. I wished I could conjure up something of her, but now that the school year was almost over and she'd been gone for a few

months, it seemed almost like I'd imagined her—dreamed up a
kind intellectual girl just down the hall who would walk places
with me and read beside me at night. Maybe I *had* dreamed
her up. She was the perfect projection of my better self, but
she had disappeared right around the worst night of my life
so far, the night Johnny Devereux came to my room. Even a
fantasy can put up with only so much.

Then at lunch Scotty's roommate, Gus, bumped into me,
on purpose, nudging me in the side with his plastic tray.

When I turned, he was smiling.

"Um, hi?"

I'd never spoken with Gus before. He was a buddy, like
Scotty, well-ensconced in the community of them. As rising
sixth formers, my classmates were beginning to gather force,
and Gus and Scotty, who had been well-liked by upper-
formers, would now be much admired as seniors. They wore
a new confidence on their shoulders, and swung their hips
the tiniest bit more as they moved down the halls, taking
their time, ensuring they'd be seen.

"Scotty's got a crush on you," said Gus.

This was the last thing.

"On me? What?"

"Don't tell him I told you."

I was sure they were messing with me. Someone wanted to
lure me somewhere, see me naked, goad me into some new
and vile compromise.

"Okay, I won't."

Gus was grinning. "What do you think?"

"About what?"

"About Scotty."

"Oh. Um, I think he's nice. He's from Philadelphia. Elise loved him a lot."

The grin wavered. "Yeah. That sucked."

"I'm sure she's much happier at home."

"No kidding."

Students were moving all around us, gathering food or dropping off their trays. Cutlery clacked and chairs scraped across the floor. Odors of tater tots and ammonia mingled and soured. The halls were a zoo. Our conversation would not go unnoticed, though—Gus talking to me, like this, in the open, would not go unnoticed. His attention would benefit me. I wondered what mine would cost him.

"Well, anyway, about Scotty," he said.

I waited for him to say the *anyway* thing, but that was all he'd meant to convey.

He put a hand on my shoulder and squeezed it before moving away.

I found a note in my post-office box that my ISP had been approved. *Advisor, the Reverend Molly Radley.* A shiver ran over me. I walked out of the post office and into the sunshine. The flag snapped high on its pole. Students crossed everywhere. I was stitching hours into days like the boards of a rope bridge: I'd go to lunch, then go pick up Raz for a run through the new-leafed woods, then shower before dinner, and then when I left the dining hall to head to the chapel for choir rehearsal (we were working on the pieces for the commencement services now) there would still be lavender light in the sky and in the ponds. Then tomorrow, and the next day, and another few weeks, and this was done.

The prospect of sixth form I would tackle after I'd had some rest.

Scotty's roommate, Gus, had gotten into the habit of knocking into me or elbowing me or in some other way offering a slightly aggressive note of affection whenever he saw me around campus. I had no idea how to react. I'd met a few of Gus's and Scotty's friends during the brief spell I'd dated Tim, but their attentions panicked me. I had gone from too shy and intimidated to talk to boys I didn't directly know to paranoid about who hated me or wanted me to suck his cock. I could not tell, just looking at an approaching face, what he intended to send my way, and it seemed any given student could switch back and forth, depending on his mood and the moment when I happened to cross his path. The consequences for guessing wrong were extreme. The sixth former who lived next door to Rick and Taz, whom I had never met in any capacity, set on me daily a steady glare. And once, as I passed alone, he said simply, "You're awful. I hate you."

Gus persisted in his good-natured, little-brother way, and Scotty, appearing in the hallways or on the paths, would follow up with genuine questions: How was my hand? Where did I take the dog? Whose dog was it, anyway? When could I play tennis again?

Though he was not big, Scotty had a spot on the varsity lacrosse team, which made him dangerous. I was spikier than I might have been because of this. I never watched him play, but sometimes as I headed out for my runs I saw him with the rest of the boys, pouring out of the locker room on their way to the fields. Lacrosse players wore full pads above the waist but only athletic shorts below, leaving them top-heavy as bulls,

the broadest and tallest among them—like Rick Banner—
appearing to be superior creatures still gathering from the
head down, like you'd caught the djinn just at the moment
it bloomed from the lamp. Scotty's shoulders were already
surprisingly broad, given how slight his body was, and of
course his hair made his head seem huge anyway. The lacrosse
gear just emphasized the shape he already had. I saw him and
laughed, and then, as I left through the white gates and onto
state roads, I wondered about this laughing.

I was beginning to see why Elise had kept him around. His
absentminded goodwill was cheering. He was an antidote to
so much intention.

Scotty asked me to meet him one night at the Tuck Shop. I
arrived after choir. The streams were alive in the meadow; the
grass rustled. He bought a pint of ice cream and set it between
us, then plonked down two plastic spoons. I didn't know he
had the munchies, and he didn't know ice cream was about
the only thing I could eat without pain.

We polished it off. When our spoons clicked in the ice
cream, he dug in further and smiled up at me. There wasn't
much more to say about Elise—we'd been over that—but I
understood our abandonment of her as a topic to mean something about a development between us.

Just before check-in we wandered down the path, back
toward Brewster House. My belly was jumpy with ice cream
and gratitude, though I didn't understand the full mechanics of
the latter. Spending time with Scotty—and more to the point,
being seen spending time with Scotty—had had a rehabili-
tative effect on my reputation around campus. He was popular
enough with other boys to command respect, and when I was

with him, this extended to me. Caroline asked me what was up with Scotty, how it was going. Sam mentioned something about my new beau. I didn't comment, not least because I didn't actually know what was happening. Scotty and I had nothing in common, he was kind to me, and he hadn't tried to fuck me. It might have been some sort of celestial accompaniment, as though Elise were looking out for me from afar. Whatever it was, I did not ask questions and I did not boast.

Walking through the low point of the meadow, Scotty and I came to a pocket of cooler air that had gathered there like a winter ghost.

"You know," I heard myself say, "something really bad happened with Rick Banner."

Scotty said, "Yeah?"

"Yeah. And Taz too."

"Well, like what?" He put his arm around my shoulders.

"Like, they called me," I blundered. "I mean, Rick called me. To cruise. And, like, Taz was there, which I didn't know. And they told me to be quiet. And did stuff to me."

"What kind of stuff?"

"You know," I said, because I was sure he did. "Stuff."

He was quiet. Our feet shuffled on the sandy path. It was re-gritted by the grounds crew every winter, for the ice, and melted off into tiny dunes in the spring.

"Not sex," I said, to clarify, and because I was afraid I'd frightened him off.

"Hm."

"Just oral stuff."

After a while he said, "Yeah. I'm sorry about that. That sucks."

Scotty wasn't cruel or quick enough to intend the pun. I sensed a foggy bit of regret, some concern. Most important, he did not remove his arm from my shoulders.

"So anyway," I said.

We climbed back up out of the meadow, into the warm evening air, and stopped by the back door to Brewster House—the door I'd snuck out, the one where, shattered, I had walked back in. The door that opened to the power plant and the meadow and the back of campus and that shared a view with my window, one flight up.

"Hey, Lacy." He sounded eager, and I understood we were starting a new conversation now. "Wanna hang out?"

I looked at Scotty in the sulfured light of the utility bulb mounted over the stoop. He was cute. His hair was haloed. A little cloud of bugs swirled above us, like an echo of his hair.

"Sure," I said.

He smiled at me for a long moment. "Cool." He kissed me.

I consider now that he might have been stoned out of his mind, that he might not have known how to respond to what I'd revealed. (What I'd revealed! And the ground did not open up, and the trees did not splinter and collapse, and the moon did not slip, and I did not explode.) But somehow he knew enough to open the door for me, and then let me go in, up to my room, alone. I figured that was perfect. It irritates me now that I needed to be desired in order to be able to tell, but I understand: if my shame emerged from the sense that I was dirty, ruined for love, then a person I could talk to would be one who looked at me and thought he might love me anyway.

But is this really true? Or was it that the words were welling up in me, as the season was, and it was only a matter of the right company on the path?

In any case, nothing more happened that night. I couldn't have worked it out myself, but if you'd done the math—how to care for the girl I was just then—you'd have come out exactly there.

Years later, after I graduated from college and moved to California, I acquired a trained security dog, a sleek and leonine Belgian shepherd whose leash I would slipknot around my waist before going out for very long runs. I swore up and down that her fearsome presence had nothing to do with my personal safety. I just liked dogs, and I particularly liked this breed. We'd run for three or four hours without stopping. At that time in my life I liked to choose a difficult route and then double it—add a mountain, say, or every set of stadium stairs in the arena. I'd put some mad money in my sock, and off dog and I would go.

I learned that there wasn't a contest I set for myself that I could not finish unless I made one critical mistake: to look up before the end. The moment I scanned the top of the hill, my legs lost their courage. The instant I saw the chutes at the finish of the marathon, my chest tightened like an asthma attack. The trick was to never know how close you were, because relief was the killer of drive.

With about two weeks remaining in the school year, my fifth-form spring at St. Paul's, I finished a run in the woods, dropped a panting, leaf-dragging Raspberry back at Ms. Radley's house, showered, grabbed a bite of supper, and headed for the library to continue studying for finals. I had exhausted myself on my exegesis for Reverend S., a grand thesis on the feminine aspects of the Holy Spirit for which I had drawn heavily on outside sources and even corresponded with an old professor of my mom's from seminary, a classicist who preferred the Coptic Bible but would work from the ancient Greek if he had to. The resulting thirty-eight-page masterpiece, heavily foot-noted, stacked and stapled and multiply blessed, felt as weighty to me as a slab of my own flesh. I was sure Reverend S. would be knocked out. I had calculus nailed; French would be fine; English was always fine. Eutrophication of lakes and streams for Environmental Science? No problem. I could formulate acid rain in my sleep. The year was mine. The cast was off my hand, but I'd gotten good at writing left-handed anyway; my right thumb was so weak it was easier to do so. I was happy to shower properly. Scotty knew, when he took my hand, to approach from the left.

In the evenings, after Seated Meal, we were allowed to wear denim. I had cutoff shorts like all the girls did, with long white strings fraying from the hems. By late May it was warm enough for these. Scotty and I took heartbreaking chestfuls of the spring night before surrendering to the library. We set up on a red couch and pretended to study. I'd review a bit, and he'd ask me questions and run his fingers along my arm. He'd just asked me to come visit him that summer—maybe in Philly, maybe at his family's house in upstate New York—when he drew his finger along the C scar on my thigh and said, "Whoa. What's this?"

I told him about the bike. He hadn't been there that day, but he'd heard about it. His shaggy head went up and down, and he laughed, his mouth hanging open. I told it lightly, feeling embarrassed by all the misfortune I'd encountered, as though it spoke to some secret desire or need of my own.

"Lots of bad shit happens to you, huh?" said Scotty.

"Not really." How could I say it did, lofted high in the Robert A. M. Stern–designed library, studying my little notebooks, overlooking the grounds of my elite boarding school?

Scotty twined the threads of my cutoffs. His fingers were blunt and always a little grimy, but I admired this as a mark of his ease in the world. I was grateful to him for not abandoning me when I had told him what little I did about Rick and Taz. I ascribed his steadiness to a sense of safety he would have acquired between the gabled estate on the Philly Main Line and the lake house in the Thousand Islands. He didn't talk about money, and he certainly didn't look much like a boy with money, but in his ease was a confidence I was learning belonged to a certain kind of heir.

"I don't think more bad things happen to me than to anyone else."

"Oh, well," he said. "Seems like they do."

He never really disagreed with anything, just set his idea up there next to yours, as if there was plenty of room on the shelf.

He traced my scar. I considered being shy about the shape of my thigh spilling out beneath my cutoffs on the red sofa, but I liked the feeling of Scotty's fingers.

I remember the sunset over the pond out the glass wall, and the clouds reflected in the water. I permitted myself a softening. Something like a valediction. *You made it.* Scotty's stillness beside me, his hand on my skin, let it open up in me like a flame.

"Gus said it was kind of nasty," said Scotty, nodding at my scar. He was talking about the injury that caused it, but I was thinking of something else.

"It was kind of a big deal," I admitted. "It hurt. And it was scary."

"That sucks."

"Someone had to carry me to the infirmary."

"All cut up? Wow. Who?"

And in that moment, all at once, I remembered. I hadn't known him then, when he'd carried me, and I'd been so distracted and dizzy. But now the knowledge just appeared, like a person who had arrived to speak to me.

Scotty felt it. "What's up?"

It was Rick Banner. He was the one who had wrapped a towel around me and lifted me up in his arms and brought me to the infirmary door. I remembered his voice, how I'd been aware of his arms and height while he carried me, how strong he was buoying me up. I saw how we'd looked. Like the fucking Pietà he'd carried me.

"Nothing," I said.

"Cold?"

"No, no."

"Does that tickle?" Scotty made everything easy.

"A little bit, yeah."

"Sorry." He rested his hand, then took it back. "Let's go."

We pressed out into the air, and the air pressed back—humid, turgid with spring. I wanted to grab it in my hands and hurl it away, it was so soft, and I was so mad. I would not be buried in new life. I would not be swamped by hope. Winter was as rigid in me as my spine.

"Maybe let's take a walk," said Scotty, steering us toward the woods.

I had not remembered. Not in math class, not when he called me, not when he lay on my face did I realize Rick was the one who had carried me up from the water. Not when I left their room, not when I ducked as he came down the hall, his head high and menacing above the carefully mussed hockey hair of the boys who surrounded him. Not when my throat was searing. Not when Johnny Devereux was fucking me. Not once had I remembered that I had been in his arms. He had *helped* me.

Is that why he called me? Is that why? Because I'd gotten hurt, or because he'd been there to rescue me?

He had been gentle. This above all broke me.

If a person with a heart had been kind and then cruel, had chosen me...

We were people on this earth. This life was all we had. It was all we fucking had, and life, my life, could not be determined by cruelty like this. It could not be allowed to stand.

"Scotty," I said, "I'm not feeling well."

"Oh. What's going on?"

"Don't know. I think maybe my tummy. I think I ought to go lie down."

We veered right, around the Old Chapel settling into the dusk, and back down the road toward the quad. The grass was already damp with dew, and tiny gnats buzzed at our ankles.

"Dinner?" he asked.

"Probably."

"Next time skip it and order pizza."

"Yep."

"You need anything?"

"I think I might be sick. I think I need to be alone."

"Okay." We crossed over the waterfall. "Now?"

"Yes, now. Sorry." I pulled away from him and started to jog across the lawns, shaking to my fingers. The long metal door pull was cold. The air in the stairwell was cold. I went down to the basement, generously empty on an evening so close to the end of the year (even the most miserable girls could make it another few weeks), punched out my home telephone number, and waited, hoping nothing happened to disrupt this plummet because I could not start it again. *Please ring. Please be home.*

Once I heard my mother's voice, my mind got very clear.

"I have to tell you something."

She offered to go get my father on the line, but I said no. I told her some boys had done something to me. Two sixth formers. They'd called me and asked me to come over, and it had been a trick. A trap.

"Lacy," said my mother. "Were you raped?"

I breathed when she said this, because it meant she could handle the sharpest part—she said it, not me—and because I thought I could honestly answer no.

"Only my mouth."

Then her voice dropped low—ground-floor low, everyone-off-here low. I had never heard this tone before and I wanted to weep with gratitude for it. She said, "What are their names?"

I told her.

"Was this last night?"

"Um, no. October."

There was a pause. Then she said, quietly, "Your throat."

I was nodding. That was all I could do.

"Okay. You did the right thing, telling me. We are going to bring you home. Can you pack a bag? I am going to make a few calls."

"No. Please don't tell anyone." I had no idea how ridiculous this request was.

"I need to talk to the chaplain." Here her voice wobbled, and the sound panicked me. If she talked to people, *told people,* all the work I'd done would be undone. All the precarious stacking of hours and days, all the silence and shrugging, even the lying still while they'd done what they needed to do—all of it would come apart. And everyone would talk again, and everyone would know.

"Reverend S.? No, you don't. Please."

"Fine. The rector. Or Dean Matthews. We need to tell them."

I saw that I had made a terrible mistake. "But there's a few weeks left, we have—"

"*Lacy.*"

"You can't tell anyone."

I heard her sigh. I thought of her with almost patronizing sympathy, the poor thing, just learning what I had known all year. Whereas I was a pro. She'd get used to it. She'd see that I hardly needed to come *home,* for heaven's sake.

She said, "I'm going to do what has to be done. Right now, that means calling the airlines. Go on upstairs and pack. Just what you need. You don't need anything else."

I needed to finish out the term, with its flourish of ceremonies and award presentations, the sixth-form graduation on the lawn, the last dwindling hours of this unholy year. I needed to say goodbye to my friends so they didn't think anything was awry, and I wanted everything smooth with Scotty so I would still be on track to visit this summer, and as a down payment on his company for next year.

"I have five exams," I told her. As I had suspected, this gave her pause. "I've worked really hard and I'm prepared and I want to get them done."

"Oh shit," she said. "Exams."

She was not in thrall to the St. Paul's School registrar, but to the same sense of discipline that lived in me, the one she'd raised me with. She knew I'd *want* to take my exams. I wasn't a kid who would ever be grateful to get out of them. And the prospect of making them up somehow, or taking incompletes? Not in our lifetimes.

She said, "You're ready for them?"

"Absolutely."

"God, Lacy."

"It will be fine. I'll just finish them and come right home."

She was wavering. Exams at St. Paul's were administered in the gym, which was set up in endless rows of desks with small stacks of blue books and nothing else. The acoustics were terrible—God help you if your stomach growled—and the canister lights, way up in the cobwebby rafters, burned holes in the top of your skull. These small miseries brought me to new heights of focus and recall. Between my left hand and my right, I could get through my exams. I knew everything. I was going to set them on fire. This year would not beat me.

"Listen, Mom. It'll just be another few days and then I can be finished and come home."

"Okay. Okay. But the very next day."

"That's fine."

"Are you safe?"

My eyelids prickled.

"I'm fine, Mom."

"There's a five p.m. out of Logan. How about that?"

"That will be fine," I said.

"*You* will be fine. We are together now. Okay?"

"Okay."

The morning after I finished my exams, I returned to my room from breakfast and dragged my blue duffel bag up onto my bed. I'd made the bed, unsure what to do with my sheets. Usually at the end of the year we took a few days to box everything up. Those of us farther than a car ride from home borrowed handcarts to haul boxes and duffels to the post office to be shipped, and underformers dragged other boxes, as many as possible, out into the hallways for Maintenance to load onto landscapers' trucks and store over the summer. There was a lengthy process of probate executed by graduating sixth formers, who left campus a few days before the rest of the students, during which prized (and often multigenerational) items were awarded to friends: floor lamps of particular distinction, or an especially soft and not fetid armchair. The unwinding of the stuff paralleled the unwinding of the year.

I was frantic at the thought of just leaving. Would I be coming back?

I was staring at my stuff, paralyzed, when Reverend S. knocked on my door. He opened it before I'd said *come in*.

"Lacy?"

He slipped around the door in work boots and khakis,

landing in the awkward, slender space where my footlocker sat. He picked up his boot and set it on the top, meaning to slide the trunk sideways, for room, but it hardly budged.

"God," he said. "What've you got in there?"

"Could you just walk around it?"

He did. As I watched, he pressed his hands to his face and peered through his fingers. He looked at my walls, lingering on the quotations: "Be always drunken." He looked at my dresser, covered, as all of ours were, in a cheap Indian tapestry and littered with hairbrush and lotions and little pots and pencils. He scanned my closet, which had no door: dresses, pants, skirts, parka. Boots akimbo on the floor. My bedside table with its little lamp. My books everywhere.

I figured this wasn't a good time to ask him what he'd thought of my magnificent final paper for Religion class. He said, "Your mom's asked me to help you get packed up."

I didn't hear in that what I might have—what was true— which was that my mom had called him after all, the night I'd called her, and spent two sobbing hours on the phone asking for solace and support. He said nothing of this to me either. I wouldn't have begrudged her the need for an advocate of her own, but I'd have suggested she call lots of people before she called Reverend S. I honestly thought he had no idea what was going on. How could he, and stand there looking at my things and not at me?

"Okay," I said.

"Have you started?" He was still staring at my walls. T. S. Eliot: "Here, now, always." De Beauvoir: "One is not born, but rather becomes, a woman."

"Just now."

"Okay. Well, what do you need?"

What I needed was underwear, bras, blue jeans, shorts, T-shirts, and a jacket, but I was not about to open my drawers to pull these things out with Reverend S. standing in his boots in the middle of my room. He bent to a stack of books along the wall and began half-heartedly moving them to the middle of my shoddy carpet. He stepped back out into the hall and returned with some cardboard boxes, which he wrestled into shape on top of my footlocker.

"Let's just start loading things up," he said absently.

"I don't think I should be going home today," I told him, half to get him to go away.

"Oh, I think you should."

I had got it in my head that there was a strong chance I'd be awarded one of the subject prizes for my year, and particularly in Religion, at the awards ceremony. I felt I needed to be there to collect my prize. And I thought Reverend S. would understand this, that this is what he and I were talking about without saying it.

"Just a few more days," I said.

"No. Today is good."

"But I think I need to stay for the awards ceremony."

He gaped at me. His eyes bugged, as they always did, but because he let his mouth hang in a small *o* he looked frankly disgusted with what he was seeing.

Then he looked away, at my bed. "You don't need to be at the awards ceremony," he said sharply.

I was stunned. So there would be no prize. I took in this disappointment like all the rest. Particularly bitter because it was Religion class, which I had thought I was born to. But why this cruelty? Did he not like my paper, did he not see how hard I had worked all year?

I turned to my dresser, eyes burning, and got to work pulling out clothes. I bundled my underwear tightly inside my shirts so I could pack it all without him seeing. He began moving my things into boxes, indiscriminately, without asking, without sorting, going as quickly as he could. I cringed to see his hands on my things. "Wait," I said frequently, and pulled something from his grip to pack myself somewhere else. "Hang on." An antagonism, tentative at first, grew between us into something hard. Ever the student, I thought I could see what he had found to hate. Mine was a dusty, small, overcrowded room, full of the sorts of decorative excesses that teenage girls preferred: a plant with a ribbon tied around it, a case of diet soda, stacks of hand-decorated mixtapes, a mirror covered with pictures of friends. It was an almost baroque combination of sentiment and appetite, longing and grooming. Yes, I should have been packing for days. I'd known I was going home. But this was my nest. He had no idea what I'd gotten through here. I wanted him out.

He checked his watch. "We need to keep moving."

I zipped up my duffel and hauled my backpack up onto my bed. "All set," I told him. He quit packing immediately, which gave me the impression he'd been sent for another reason—to supervise me, perhaps, rather than to get anything done. He never asked me what had happened, or how I was doing, or said a word about how he'd come to be in my little room. I didn't know who would finish bundling my things. I didn't know when or even whether I would see them again.

"Right, then. Let's get you to the post office to meet your car."

I didn't even have a chance to look a last time out that window over the meadow. I glanced, but couldn't engage the colors till they formed the trees and gaps and brush I knew. How could I feel sadness? I had forged a self in this room. And it had been hell, but it was mine. Those trees, that expanse, formed the horizon of my courage, small as it might have been. I loved them.

9

Summer 1991

In early March 1878, when St. Paul's was not quite twenty-five years old, a measles epidemic swept through the school. Dozens of boys fell ill, confined to their rooms, and one came so close to the brink that "the whole dormitory was awake and watching as brandy was administered and he was barely saved from death by strangulation and spasms." We learn this from August Heckscher's *St. Paul's: The Life of a New England School,* a comprehensive history from its founding to the year 1980, when Scribner's published the book. (The Scribners all went to St. Paul's.) Several of us had this red-jacketed hardback on our shelves at school, often a gift from godparents seeking to impress upon us the honor of our matriculation. I never knew anyone to actually read it. It served to prop open doors on warm days, cushion coffee mugs on late nights, and elevate the little bowls of Siamese fighting fish that languished on our desks. Opening the book finally, as an adult, I recognize that not even the adolescent grandiosity we displayed as Paulies could touch Heckscher's fire: "In writing about St. Paul's, I have felt at times that I was dealing with a minor nation..."

If I had bothered to read *The Life of a New England School* as a student, I'd have been knocked out by the story of the first-form boy who went to the infirmary later that spring of 1878, not with measles but with a sore throat. He was, Heckscher reports, "otherwise apparently in good health." He was likely ten years old. Shortly after ten the next morning, he was dead.

A letter to school parents advised them of the tragedy but encouraged them not to bring their living children home. "The risk of infection seemed remote," according to the rector, Dr. Coit, whose name I knew because it belonged to our oak-paneled, high-table, Oxford-style dining hall. Coit appended to his letter the opinion of the school's doctor and its founder, also a physician, arguing for no change in routine. In spite of the shocking loss, they wrote, "it was in the boys' best interests to remain at school."

And so scarlet fever spread. Two more children died. With three bodies, "no choice now existed but to close the school." Nevertheless, in announcing this closure, the rector reported that "the best authorities pronounced the sanitary conditions at the school satisfactory...and could find no cause for the recent afflictions."

Even accounting for the peril of childhood before anti-biotics, this self-exoneration seems to me remarkable. It's got both the knee-jerk, sputtering detail of the guilty, and a kind of fantastical entitlement too. Winter was cause enough for illness, surely. Not even an institution as blessed as St. Paul's School would be delivered from ordinary dangers. Children had died there—one particularly haunting scene involved a third former who failed to show up to breakfast on the day he was to go home for Christmas, and was found dead in his bed. But the obligation of the school, which is first and foremost in charge of the care of children, is to react—immediately and generously—to prevent further harm. August Heckscher suffers no sadness or frustration on behalf of his minor nation of a school for failing to do so.

I hadn't reported to the infirmary with a sore throat and died. I suspect that what I did was worse. I kept living, and then a few months later I went and told people about a sexual assault. My parents called the school. I wasn't on that call, nor on any others between my family and school leaders, but I can imagine their tone. Mom and Dad called, worried and deeply upset, and assumed that the people they spoke to would share their concern: two boys on campus had assaulted their girl. What could be done to address this?

After my mother called the school to explain what had happened, the administration, as the school itself would later tell the Concord Police Department, conducted its own "internal investigation." I was still on campus, since the year had not ended, but their investigation did not include talking to me. I have had to put together these few weeks from documents that remain—medical reports and what has been shared with me of the criminal case file from 1991. I was studying for my finals, knowing that the events of the night in Rick and Taz's room were formally known to everyone now. The priests knew, the teachers knew, the deans knew. There was nothing left to hide. I felt exposed and exhausted. I thought I was almost finished with everything.

School leadership talked to people about me. They had conversations with students, but not with my friends. They talked to the school psychologist, the school's lawyer, and the physician in the infirmary. I do not know the substance of these conversations, but in the third week of May, the school psychologist, Reverend S., Vice Rector Bill Matthews, and the rector, Kelly Clark, sat down with the school's legal counsel and arrived at the formal conclusion that, despite what I had claimed, and despite the statutory laws on the books in their state, the encounter between me and the boys had been consensual. They also concluded that they would not abide by state law and report the incident to the police. The authorities were not notified. They remained in the dark.

When I heard about this meeting for the first time, decades after I'd left school, I remembered Reverend S. standing in my room, half-heartedly packing my books. What had he heard that helped him conclude I was promiscuous and had desired my statutory assault? No wonder he never asked me how I was doing. No wonder he wanted me gone.

If the first violation of the boys who assaulted me was the way they made me feel erased, it was exactly this injury that the school repeated, and magnified, when it created its own story of the assault. This time the erasure was committed by men whose power over me was socially conferred rather than physically wielded, by men who—some of them—had never even been in a room with me. They still never have.

But I knew none of this then. The school never said anything to me. They did, however, apparently find reason to enlighten my schoolmates about one thing. Before we all left campus that spring, the vice rector sat down with members of the boys' varsity lacrosse team and told them that he didn't want to ask any questions, but if any of them had ever been intimate with Lacy Crawford, he should go to the infirmary right away to get checked out.

I have been told, variously, that this happened on the

lacrosse field and in a teacher's apartment. Where was I, at that moment? Certainly not at the infirmary. I still thought my throat hurt because I was a bad person who had done a terrible thing.

Even once I found out a few months later about the vice rector's bit of patriarchal counsel to his boys, I did not do the math to arrive at the realization made by a detective investigating the school more than twenty-five years after the fact:

"So the students knew about the herpes before you did."

Yes, they did.

Back in Lake Forest in early June, Mom took me to see my pediatrician. This doctor was new to the practice, and a woman. I was desperately grateful on both counts. Mom had called to set up the appointment, causing a note to be added to my file before I visited the office: "Child sexually assaulted by two boys last October. Child confessed this to mother last week." The verb "confessed" is useful, nestled in the pages of this caring clinician—not that she thought I was guilty, but that she anticipated the guilt I was feeling.

There was, by this time, a river of shame inside me. It curved and snaked and fed all manner of dark snapping certainties about who I was and what would happen to me. I considered what had occurred in that room to be my fault, and afterward I had gone and done what I'd done. It was clear what sort of girl I was. And if this conversation proceeded, I would be forced to say so.

Dr. Kerrow asked me to tell her exactly what had happened. She wrote it all down, and my pediatrician's office saved this report beyond the usual threshold of a patient's reaching the age of twenty-seven. Every time I read it I remember: Yes, they did tell me, after they had both ejaculated into my mouth, that it was "your turn now." Yes, they did warn me not to leave before they assaulted me, and said I would get caught if I tried. Yes, Rick did hold me down on top of Taz's cock. All of that.

Then these details disappear again. For decades I forget them, if *forget* is the right word for the white blast of nothing the mind deploys like an air bag at the memory's approach. I have wondered if I'm able to lose these particulars again and again because I know they're written down, so I don't have to take care of them—but this is a curious piece of anthropomorphism. In fact, I murdered details by the thousand that spring and summer. I don't remember, for example, how it felt to greet my mother when I came home. I don't remember the look on my father's face. What I do remember is sometimes difficult to categorize—why this bit and not that one?—such as the decorations in our kitchen when I heard my mother speak the boys' names. I don't remember who she was talking to. I do remember we had a nature calendar and an old *New Yorker* cartoon about "Mommy needing to go to seminary now."

I remember the kindness of Dr. Kerrow, who held my chin delicately in her fingers and said, "Hang on tight, this is going to hurt." She did what was called a "blind swab"—she couldn't see far enough down my throat to find anything worth scrubbing with a cotton bud, so she just dug around. "Just bear with me."

I didn't tell her about being fingered so she wouldn't insist on examining me there.

I still had not realized that I had contracted any diseases.

Over and over, I'd cataloged what I knew. I still had the text-book from fourth-form health class because I saved all of my books. Herpes was blisters on the penis or vagina, and I did not have that. Gonorrhea and chlamydia gave you discharge. Syphilis was for drug users and nineteenth-century composers. I knew the word *chancre*. I thought AIDS would have killed me by now. None of it made sense. I just submitted, as I had before, and was grateful to the doctor for saying it would hurt. Because it did.

I gagged and retched. She had the nurse fetch me a cup of water. Results would take about a week, and she would call as soon as she had them. She'd send me for blood work, which was for HIV and syphilis, but I didn't know this.

Then she turned to me, and there was a new force in her voice. "I am going to have to report this to the State of New Hampshire."

I pictured the state itself, narrow, stacked like a book on a shelf alongside *Vermont*. "What?"

"To the police. I am mandated by law to report this assault to the police."

As I remember it, this was the first time I'd heard the word *assault*. It did not contain the events I remembered. It seemed to clothe them in armor and send them out into the world to do more damage.

I begged her. Throat raw, tears running, I begged her.

"I have no choice," she said. "I am sorry. Nobody wants to make anything worse for you, but this is important." Dr. Kerrow looked up at my mother, and then said, "Although, you know, I'm sure the school has already reported. You've talked to them?"

"Oh, yes," said Mom. "They are well aware."

The doctor returned to me, and set a hand on my shoulder. I noticed this because it was something my mother did not do— she did not touch me much that summer. We had never been a family of huggers, but now I wondered if there was judgment in the withholding, or fear. Dr. Kerrow said, "Your headmaster will already have called the police. He is mandated by the same law I am. So they will already know everything I have to say. Nothing will happen that isn't already happening."

"Then you don't have to tell them," I tried.

She was firm, and gave me another piece of news. "You were fifteen, and that makes you a minor. In fact, I'm surprised you haven't heard from the police or child welfare by now. Have you?"

Mom shook her head.

"Well, you will. I am so sorry."

I felt betrayed by this kind lady in the white coat. She had stickers on her stethoscope for the littlest kids. There seemed no end to how many mistakes I could make, how much worse I could make my life. Telling my mother, starting this cascade— the police? The state? All anyone needed to know was that I was ruined. There was nothing more to see or learn.

The car ride home was particularly awful. Anytime I was alone with Mom, that summer, I burned.

"Well," said Mom, eyes straight ahead, "I'm glad that's done."

I could not make sense of comments such as this. She spoke as though there were a trajectory here, some linear logic. I was engulfed.

I would not have said much in reply. My throat was killing

me. Mom, manicured fingers on the wheel, would have run her other hand over her mahogany hair, ending with a strand for idle twisting. Her beauty had not even considered beginning to fade. She was forty-one that summer, younger than I am now.

Our squat little pediatrics office, an energy-efficient shoebox from the seventies, was becoming part of a "health care complex." Giant construction vehicles dug and clawed behind the fences. Alongside a pillared assisted living facility, developers had put in a fake pond and a fake path between transplanted trees. Mom pointed this out. I thought that if I had to get so old and sick that I had to live in a place like that, I'd rather it be in a meadow. What was wrong with the meadow?

How sour I'd become. Rolling betrayal like a candy in my mouth. Whether I had betrayed everyone I loved or the world had betrayed me, I couldn't tell. It all felt the same. Everything in flames. The neat arithmetic of two-parent Protestant diligence left me nowhere to put catastrophes such as this, a battery of STD testing at the old pediatrics office where I'd gotten my ears pierced three years before. I remembered all the times I'd been a passenger on this winding lane. The woozy ride with a fever or the agony before shots. I remembered the time Mom sped wildly because my brother had cut his finger on a biscuit tin. His baby blanket was soaked in blood and he was eating the crackers Mom had given him to distract him— large table crackers blooming pink like carnations in his hands. I was in the middle seat, unbuckled. It was great fun, peeling around the turns. I had said so, and Mom had scowled at me. Because my brother wasn't crying (the tin had cut him without his noticing), I hadn't bothered to think about why we were going fast. I just loved the ride.

Mom was excited about the idea of the Concord Police knowing what had happened to me. I don't think she'd known that the school was required to report to them.

"Wait till the rector takes *that* call," she said. "It'll be good to have law enforcement involved, don't you think?"

I couldn't imagine what would be good about this.

"Don't you?"

What had I imagined would happen once I told her? Nothing. I had failed to anticipate and now I'd lost control. People were taking it up and carrying it forward. There was nothing I could do to stop it.

The report of a sexual assault triggered blood tests and criminal reports—a forensic process that followed my disclosure of the event, my representation of what had happened to me, in the only words I could find and at the only time I could manage. The witness lights up the grid of response. Which means feeling responsible not only for what happened to you, but for everything that follows, too.

It was strange, because none of my parents' calls were being returned. They'd left a message for Ms. Shay, my fourth-form adviser, because Mom had always felt a special affinity with her and had thought it mutual. They'd called my fifth-form adviser, Mrs. Fenn. They'd called Reverend S. again. Nobody called back.

On the suggestion of Dr. Kerrow, Mom made an appointment for me with a rape crisis counselor. She found this person about forty-five minutes away, in Evanston, working out of a women's center at Northwestern University. I drove there myself in Dad's little stick-shift car. Though the cast was off my hand, I couldn't grip with much force, particularly when the gear stick was rattling with highway speed, so instead I just bumped the stick in and out of gear with the base of my palm, the way my father did.

The counselor's office was in a small cottage behind a tidy lawn. I parked on the street. Walking in, I pretended to myself that I was a college student entering the facility to work on a college project: women's rights, maybe, or feminist critiques of fairy tales. I wondered if the few women I saw in the building were students or rape counselors or real live rape victims. Clearly I did not belong there, and the counselor, when she greeted me, nailed this point home. She was a woman of color with excellent hair that corkscrewed and tumbled to uneven lengths all around her head. She demonstrated a physics of presence that defied everything I'd been taught. She sat squarely opposite me. Nothing crossed. Feet on the floor. I must have looked limp as a switch to her, assembling myself there.

She said, "Do you want to tell me what happened?"

God, I wished I could have laid before her a different tale: something nice and binary, maybe involving a dark alley or a country road. A snarling white man missing half his brain. Something to earn my place in this chair before this woman.

I don't remember how I replied.

"It may be that you're not ready to talk about it yet," offered the counselor.

Nonsense. I had talked about it plenty, I thought: *I'd told my parents, the pediatrician, and now I would tell this kind woman.*

I impressed upon her my awareness that something troubling had happened and that it was important to be mindful of its impact on my thoughts and feelings. I nodded to her assertions about self-care. I should keep a journal, yes. Absolutely I ought to consider long-term counseling support.

What she didn't understand, I was convinced, was that I was a rising sixth former at an elite boarding school where you could either get counseling or be perfect, but not both, and that if you were not perfect, you were not safe. People would know you needed help. A psychiatrist visited campus one day a week and I'd never asked for a meeting with him, but I knew most of the kids who did. Success at St. Paul's was not predicated on resilience or transcendence but on destiny, which meant you did not show defeat, not ever. In any case, the boys had graduated. Also, I explained, polite and patronizing, I was very close to my parents and had good friends and a great boyfriend, so I was very well supported. To show how serious I was about recovery, I drove directly from this little cottage to a huge Barnes & Noble to purchase a copy of a workbook she had recommended, *The Courage to Heal*. A workbook. I can still feel my sneer. I tossed the book beneath the window seat in my room, which Mom had made Dad build out for me just that year, though I never sat there. I preferred to wedge myself against the window screen, feet high on the frame, and wonder what it would take to fall out.

This was an idle consideration. The screen was sturdy.

"Was it helpful?" Mom asked. When I said that it was, she dropped the subject out of respect for the therapeutic experience.

Mom filled those first days repairing obvious defects. I got a haircut, saw the dermatologist about my adolescent acne, and had my eyes checked. A surgeon evaluated the tendon in my right hand for potential surgery. This involved laying a protractor on my open hand, aligning zero with my fingers, and then bending my thumb as far in the direction of the injury as it would go. I had to recline during the procedure because patients often passed out from it. My temples filled with snow, but I didn't lose consciousness.

The surgeon was jovial, full-bellied, and chatty. My thumb was definitely loose, he said, but there was some resistance there. I should heal just fine in time.

By now the St. Paul's School year had officially ended, and everyone had gone home. The egret would be fishing by himself beneath the falls. The soccer fields would be unmowed, the meadow quiet.

One afternoon, an old friend from my elementary school called the house. My mom came bounding up the stairs to my room to tell me. She made the wide eyes that were meant to suggest extra importance: a friend was calling! An old friend! I should not miss the beneficence of this.

Natalie was herself just home from Deerfield, a noble boarding school that had gone coed with her class. She had been praised for the independence and confidence she demonstrated in being willing to break new ground. Deerfield was in central Massachusetts, too far from St. Paul's to be part of our regular sports competitions—we drove to Andover and Exeter, Groton and St. Mark's, but we played against Deerfield or Choate only when a team or a player rose to a regional level of competition we called New Englands.

"Hey!" said Natalie. I warmed to her. She seemed exceptionally kind.

We exchanged awkward pleasantries about being home. Her brothers were driving her nuts already. I said my own was obsessed with baseball cards. I asked after her dogs, Bucket and Rose, and she asked after mine. Hearing her voice was as if in a dream. Boarding school had divided us. She did not know me, nor I her. It seemed more likely that somewhere the two of us were playing together, still aged nine, trading stickers and practicing bubble letters with paint pen on our Trapper Keepers.

"So," said Natalie, after a pause. "What's this I hear about St. Paul's?"

My heart pounded. "What about St. Paul's?"

"Just that something happened."

"Nothing happened."

"No, I hear that you had to come home."

"It's summertime. We're home."

"But I heard it was about something sexual? A sexually transmitted disease?"

"There's nothing," I said. "I'm fine. I have to go."

"No," she said. "There are all these people saying that—"

I hung up the phone and went downstairs.

"How's Natalie?" asked Mom.

"She's fine."

"Are you two going to get together?"

"She's traveling."

"Oh. Well, it was nice of her to call. You girls used to be so close."

So it was there, then, in Lake Forest too. I didn't know how this nightmare had traveled, and I did not yet know how the gossip had begun. But the speed of the secret's spread felt to me like an enormous tension, a coiled potential. There was nowhere I could go to be safe from it. What were they going to do, burn me at the stake?

Here the cruelty of girls at school had been useful: I was already quite skilled at self-exile. My old friend Natalie and I never spoke again.

In the second week of June, Dr. Kerrow called my house. The culture from my throat had tested positive for herpes simplex virus. She was very sorry.

My mother put her back to the kitchen cabinets and slid to the floor, like her bones had gone to powder. I looked at her down there, and then I took the phone from her hand and talked to Dr. Kerrow myself. We had a cordless phone in the kitchen, so I could carry the handset into another room. I walked quickly and with purpose.

"Please, could you tell me?" I asked the doctor.

Dr. Kerrow explained. It would never go away, but after ten or twelve years, most patients found that their outbreaks ceased. I could learn over time how to stay healthy and have the least chance of discomfort. The good news was that everything else was negative, so we didn't have to worry anymore.

"Is that why I had a fever?" I asked her. "Why I couldn't eat?"

All of those things, she said. But my body would rarely be that sick again. That was just the initial onset of the infection. The virus would hide in my nerve endings and be reactivated periodically, but never systemically like that, and probably not as painfully.

I was pacing the border of my great-grandmother's dining room carpet, boxing the room: wall, wall, wall, window. Wall, wall, wall, window. I asked the doctor, "Can I give it to other people?" What I was picturing when I asked this was Scotty and an ice cream spoon.

She waited a long moment. "It is contagious, yes, of course. But honestly, your infection is so far out of the way, I'm not sure how you *could* transmit it to someone. You'd have to really work at it, I mean, to get that deep. And I can't imagine . . ."

Wall, wall, wall, window—

She said, "I don't think you need to worry about that right now."

"Do I need to tell people?"

Again she waited. "The only person you might tell about it, I think, is your husband."

My eyes filled at the thought. The simple certainty the doctor evinced in saying the word.

"But," she continued, "*I* need to tell someone, I'm afraid. I have to call and add this to my report."

"The school?" I squeaked.

"No, no. The police. It's up to you what you want to tell the school about your own health. That's private. But I really don't think you should hide this from them. They ought to know what's going on on their campus."

The disgust in her voice at the words *school* and *campus* would become familiar to me. For a long time I didn't understand why people intoned the words this way, and I assumed it was because they thought St. Paul's was full of snobs. Which of course it also was.

But for now, I thought it was in my control what to say

about my throat. Because Natalie's call had been simply too awful, and too extraordinary, to consider, I removed it from my consciousness, setting it aside as a curiosity, like a museum diorama: What if everyone in the world of New England boarding schools knew about this? What if saber-toothed tigers had survived? Shiver. But here in the real world, no one could know, because I myself had only just found out! Dr. Kerrow offered to see me again to discuss my throat further, if I wished. She called in a prescription to prevent future outbreaks. She told me to take good care of myself and call her anytime.

I went back into the kitchen, where my mother was still on the floor. Her face was streaked with red.

"Give me the phone," she said, staring straight ahead. "I need to call your father. The shit is about to hit the fan."

But my parents' version of *shit* was not all that impressive, or else they didn't have much in the way of a fan. We didn't even have a lawyer. My father walked down the hall to the den where he kept his home office to call the vice rector and tell him this latest news.

Bill Matthews responded calmly: "How do we know she didn't give it to the boys?"

I didn't hear these words the moment they were spoken, but I saw my dad hearing them. His body seemed to pause in its animation, and he wore a look I had never seen before. His mouth funneled down into jowls previously invisible, and his eyes shrank not by narrowing but by deepening into his skull. I saw this look once again a few decades later, when my father was trying to handle a large and terribly anxious dog. Dad was enormously fond of this dog, had raised it, and without provocation it came back up the leash and sank its canines into Dad's hand. I watched my father curl in pain. He made no sound. He did not discipline the dog or defend himself or even look angry. This was the way he looked after Bill Matthews said what he said.

Matthews went on. "You don't want to go digging, Jim," he told my father. They had not previously been on a first-name basis. "Trust me. She's not a good girl."

Dad ended the call.

Up in my room I wrote longhand letters to Scotty, at home in Pennsylvania. I had always wanted a love interest I could write to, and it didn't matter to me that Scotty wasn't the epistolary sort; there was a fair chance my envelopes were stacked up somewhere on his mother's kitchen counter, collecting toast crumbs. I suspect I even found it liberating that he wouldn't take seriously any of my posturing, my writing about summer moons or locusts or being sixteen. He wouldn't even have recognized it as posturing, because I wasn't professing anything untrue—I was just allowing the characters of the books I was reading to bloom into being, then writing as though I were those women: zany or careless or devoted or stifled, but always with the self-possession of a character whose relevance is assured.

That spring the perennial books of Tom Robbins had swept through the fifth-form girls—*Even Cowgirls Get the Blues, Jitterbug Perfume*—and I finished them at home. How could we not have loved madcap mentions of hot, unpunished sex and actual menstrual periods? These books were ziplines over the tundra of the theologian Paul Tillich—look, there's grief, there's death, there's faith! Everything in the Robbins canon signified, in a zany way, and I tried to imagine that this kaleidoscopic scattering of meaning could extend to the entire world. For example: the heroine in *Jitterbug Perfume* receives curious deliveries of beets, and I had read, in English class, Louise Erdrich's *The Beet Queen*. Therefore, beets. A small confluence had to mean something—whether it was about crops and sugar, sweetness and sun, the relevance of the earth to writers, or something else entirely, I didn't ask and I didn't care. Ideas were roads out of town. Where next?

I drove myself everywhere, preferring to be out of the house, where I couldn't sense my mother's agony. I leaped at the chance to pick up two onions for supper and drove three towns over to buy them. I entered a large tennis tournament—one I'd done very well in the year before, held on concrete courts behind a prairie high school two hours west of the city. The fencing around the courts was twelve feet high to keep the wind from blowing balls a mile east, and crabgrass bowed against it. The other competitors were all regulars on the scene. My first-round match was at eight a.m. I met my opponent, set up my rackets and water bottle, and lost the toss. She served. A not particularly strong first serve, hard and flat. I was ready. When the ball hit my strings, my hand failed. My racket flew, twirling, and clattered on the ground. The ball lolled at my feet.

I picked it up, walked to the net, and waited for her to approach. When I shook her hand, my thumb was shaking so hard she jerked back, as though I'd stung her.

"That's it?" asked the girl, a leggy fighter with a low ranking from a southern suburb.

I said, "Congratulations."

"But you don't even want—"

"I can't."

She had twin ponytails and the hair leading to them was ribbed with bobby pins. Sweatbands on both wrists. Some good-luck charm glinting around her neck. "You're a terrible sport," she said, more curious than cruel.

"You won. Be happy."

I retrieved my things and walked back to the car.

In town one day I ran into the mother of a grade school classmate. Phoenix Weinberg had joined our class just before we all scattered for high school, but I'd liked her, and I'd really liked her mom. Like my mother, Mrs. Weinberg had been a model before having her daughter. Unlike my mother, she'd married a Jewish architect and moved into a rural farmhouse where the displayed prints from her modeling years included a nude photo of her draped by a python. Mom never saw this, but she didn't have to. Mrs. Weinberg told people she had only one child because she would "try anything once." She'd survived late-stage cancer before having Phoenix, and her daughter grew up knowing it might come back. Fee was a girl in a hurry, the first to have a boyfriend, the first to flirt and flatter. She was also the first in any moment to laugh. To the farmhouse Fee's father attached a lofted great room with globe lights and slices of sky. In the raftered kitchen, from a free perch, a parrot teased the dog by name. The original butcher block still bore a fretwork of ax marks. Mrs. Weinberg had pointed these out to us when we were in the seventh grade: "You'd hold the chicken's head right there."

Even more fantastic to my eleven-year-old self had been the multiple ropes of pastel fairy lights in Fee's room. Mom scowled. "But why? Do they even celebrate Christmas?" Dad suggested these likely posed a fire hazard. I didn't bother describing the long, ribboned mobiles that hung ceiling to floor and which Fee passed through like a fish does a wave.

Mrs. Weinberg was running errands in town, heading straight for me on the sidewalk, statuesque as ever. In equal measure I wanted to hug her and I wanted to hide.

"Please call me Barbara!" she said, seeing me. She still had her aviator sunglasses with laced-leather guards at the sides, the ones she might have taken off the face of a fighter pilot. Her tulip lipstick broke around a smile I studied but could not crack. She seemed genuinely happy to see me. She must not have heard a thing.

"Where's Fee?" I asked.

She was traveling with her dad. Phoenix was fine, Phoenix was great. How was I? How was school? A senior now! How could that be?

I must have shown her something, because she pulled off her sunglasses and lowered her head to me. Her beauty was almost awkward up close—the size of her lips, the planes of her cheeks.

"What's happened?" she asked.

Something bad, actually, I said, almost involuntarily. Something actually pretty bad had happened to me at school, and now the police were getting involved, and I didn't know how to talk to my parents about any of it.

We were standing in front of the bank in my little town. Mrs. Weinberg didn't shiver and she didn't look around. She said, "Would you like to come over sometime and have a cup of tea and talk about it?"

I drove out to the farmhouse without telling my mother.

Driving those roads and highways on which I'd only ever been a passenger wasn't unlike all my running at St. Paul's. I was making places mine, practicing being alone in an uncharted world. I saw a dead raccoon in the middle of Waukegan Road that had been painted over with a fresh double-yellow line. I passed the Sara Lee factory that had been built hard by an old church graveyard. Once, when we were little, Dad told us that was where they buried you if you ate too much pound cake. It didn't occur to me until that summer—the summer I was sixteen—that this was a joke, that he'd looked in the rearview mirror and told his children this because he was bored or frustrated or sad, some tiny cruelty nipping at his thoughts.

Mrs. Weinberg came to her door in tight jeans and motorcycle boots and seemed unsurprised to see me. Mr. Weinberg was in his studio, she explained. The parrot liked to hang out with him there. The dog was asleep on the planked floor. Mrs. W. set a mug in my hands.

I told her about Rick and Taz.

"Well, what fuckers," she said. "How dare they."

I wanted to push against this to see if it held. "But then I went and lost my virginity to a guy I don't even talk to. And I've made some bad decisions since then."

"Well, of course."

She had enormous eyes, lashed like a cartoon.

"Of course?"

"Sure. You're devastated. They stole your self-respect and ruined your sense of boundaries. It's natural to take some time to get those things back."

I sipped my tea. It had a complicated taste, like a burned garden. "How long, do you think?"

She watched me. She'd considered it a good sign that I had shared what had happened, but now she was seeing chaos.

"I think it can take a long time. But I also think there are things you can do to help yourself."

I waited.

"You need to take care of yourself, Lacy," she said.

"I don't know how to do that."

She smiled. "First of all. Where are you going to school next year?"

"I'm going back," I said quickly.

She smooshed up her lips in a fierce, quizzical smirk.

"No, it's best. Really. I have one year left, I have friends, I have a boyfriend." I knew better than to mention college applications, because Mrs. Weinberg wouldn't have cared about those the way my family did.

"I can't imagine you won't find those things somewhere else."

Helpless, I told her, "There *is* nowhere else."

"I see. Well, then, you're going to have to get a bit creative, aren't you?"

I thought of the Tom Robbins books—which were silly, I knew they were, but they enveloped me in a fantastical trance that allowed me to think, for a period of time afterward, that the world was wider and sparklier and less threatening than I knew it to be. I could coast for an hour or longer after a good run of pages. Was this what she meant?

"I'm doing an independent study project with a teacher I really like."

She nodded. "Tell me about the boyfriend."

"Oh, Scotty." As though he were a known quantity in the world. "Well, he's really sweet. Mellow. He used to go out with my close friend, but she left the school, and we just kind of came together."

"More tea?"

I was failing her. The elixir was too strong—she was offering me a form of care I could not yet accept. And I was beginning to have the strange sense that I was betraying my mother by being here. I didn't share this stuff with Mom. I did not think there was any way I could.

"And he knows? The boyfriend?"

"About what happened? Yes. Well, the bare bones of it, yes."

She nodded again. "The school must have been flat-out stunned when they heard those assholes got you sick. I bet that shocked them, huh?"

I didn't want to admit the truth, which until now I had not considered—that no, actually, Mr. Matthews hadn't seemed shocked at all.

"Yeah," I said faintly.

"So. How are you going to get through?"

I said I didn't really know, but that I was sure I'd be fine.

"Are you reading?"

"Yes. A lot."

"Journaling?"

No. My own voice was to be avoided in all forms.

"Praying?"

Um.

"Meditating?"

I shook my head.

"Energy work? Dream work?"

I set down my mug.

"Hang on," she said, tapping the kitchen table. "Be right

back." I was left with the old sashed windows. The farm was fallow but the fields hadn't yet given way to subdivisions, so the wavy glass revealed two blocks of color, land and blue. The birds over the fields were starlings. Phoenix had told me this when we were younger.

Mrs. Weinberg returned with a few dog-eared paperback books. Her bracelets and boot buckles rattled. I'd never seen Manhattan and I didn't read *Vogue,* so I didn't know what to make of her clothes or buzzed hair. She might have been an assassin.

"You know, I'm kind of a hippie," she said. "And this is a little bit woo-woo, but if you're going to go back there, you're going to have to find some faith." She set the books on the table.

"Carlos Castaneda," I read, mispronouncing the name.

She corrected me.

"Sorry."

She touched my arm. "You're not always supposed to know."

"Okay."

"Ever met a shaman?"

I shook my head.

"You sure?"

"Pretty sure."

"Borrow these. If they work, great. If not, just set them aside. But I've found some of the ideas here to be very helpful at times."

When she said *at times* I thought I heard the memory of cancer. I wondered for a moment if it pained her to give away these books, even if she trusted me to return them. Might she need them for her own daughter? Or had my old friend

Fee already transcended these sorts of challenges, finished her growing up?

"Are you sure?" I asked.

"Very sure." The bright tulip smile. "Take your time. Enjoy them."

She had a set of clear beads on a string around her wrist, and she was rolling and smacking these softly as she considered me. I worried that Mrs. Weinberg would give me the bracelet too, whatever it was, but she kept that for herself.

After the call with Bill Matthews, my parents began holding conversations related to St. Paul's together in my dad's office, in the den down at the end of the hall, with the phone on speaker. Dad took notes on pads of graph paper. He wrote with a mechanical pencil that had a little silver cap he removed to expose the eraser. Everything was replaceable—eraser, lead, even the tiny cap—and he kept the same utensils, one blue and one red, for years. He was a lefty, producing a tiny line of lead on the page, and the little boxes on the graph paper helped him square his script.

I was not supposed to be around for the St. Paul's phone calls. Mom and Dad were protecting me. But because the subject matter was so floridly intimate, I felt cored every time they sequestered themselves to talk. I wedged myself into my window upstairs or paced the border on the dining room carpet. They would either come find me immediately, or they would say nothing at all. The issue never for one moment left us alone. My advisers refused to call us back, and my parents were walking around red-eyed. Mom insisted that the school was engaging in a cover-up, but I blocked her out. What was covered up?

I couldn't have felt more exposed. Her ferocity frightened me. Dad seemed to agree with me: "Let's just see how they respond," he counseled her. "Let's just see what they do."

It didn't help that I did not yet understand how the school was handling our affairs. Nobody had filled me in on what they should have done legally, and I'd had little hope for any moral remedy in the first place.

"I'm telling you," she'd say, Cassandra-like. "They will bury our daughter before they let this get out."

I didn't understand: get out where? Bury me how?

My parents figured they were sparing me by not filling me in on every detail. I thought I was sparing them by not letting them know anything about how I had survived. That the former would soon collide with the latter was inevitable and obvious. And as much as I dreaded it, I almost wished for the arrival of the reckoning I felt I deserved.

One day Mom came bashing through the dining room door and said, as though the room were waiting to hear it, "The district attorney said he's had enough with St. Paul's School."

In the summer our dining room table was empty. The silver candlesticks were on the sideboard, everything else tucked away. A foxed mirror from my great-grandmother's house reflected the backyard. Suburban green.

I stopped pacing. "What does that mean?"

"It means he wants to bring charges against those...boys, because they were of age and you were fifteen, and because things like this have been happening at the school for years and the school has been burying it. He's been waiting ten years to go after St. Paul's. He said that. You are the smoking gun."

I understood language like "burying it" and "smoking gun" to belong to my mother—some fire and brimstone came naturally to her, and never more than when she felt wronged. So I discounted this news a bit, automatically, on account of rhetoric.

But Mom had new authority now. She repeated, "The *district attorney,* Lacy." He was the rook behind the queen. My dad had taught me to play chess when I was tiny. You can clear the board with that combination.

My voice sounded small. I was still hung up on *smoking gun.* "Does that mean I can't go back?"

"They're going to take on the school. No, you can't go back."

It was the end of June. "But where will I go?"

"I don't know. Sally Lane says Thacher is wonderful. That's in California. She says it couldn't be more different from St. Paul's. We can call them this afternoon and find out if they have a place."

"I'm going back," I told my mom. "I am going to finish."

She spat out air. Her hands flew up. "I don't know that I can send you back. I don't know that I can stand that."

The moment she started to cry, I dried up like a stone. She kept at it, adding a wail here and there, her forehead against the dining room wall. "I don't know how I'm going to make it through this!"

I wanted to shake her. *Tough shit,* I'd have said.

She turned back from the wall to try again. "Lacy."

"What."

"The school never told the police. Do you understand that? They never reported. They let the boys graduate. They let them go home. Do you get that?"

Of course I got that. What of this was news to her? What was so astounding? Rick had won the top athletic award. On Prize Day, he would have hoisted the silver plate high over his head right there, alongside the flagpole.

"They are going to start college in the fall just like nothing happened."

I thought, *Good riddance.*

"The Concord Police would like to investigate with an eye to pressing charges. It is a statutory claim and there seems to be little dispute about what, um...went on. You know, what they did." She gripped her throat to demonstrate.

I felt a small surge of courage. Since Dr. Kerrow had explained to me about statutory consent, I'd held the idea like a fabulous gemstone—too precious to trot out, almost vulgar to wear, but a resource that might buy me passage in war. The law, it turns out, anticipates naivete, or at least allows that when a child and an adult engage in a sexual act, power will occupy so much of the province of desire (if indeed there is any) that wanting would be inauthentic. Consent is not possible. No matter what anyone else claimed, the law said it was not my fault.

"Well, that's fine," I told my mom. I would be happy to tell the truth. "What do I have to do?"

"They'll put you on the stand and ask you to testify against the boys. And maybe against the school. I don't know yet. We'll have to hire a lawyer."

"Why do I need a lawyer?"

"To protect you. The district attorney told me that this has happened time and time again. That a child is assaulted on that campus, and the school covers it up."

I did not care about other children. I didn't know who

they were and I figured they'd have to take care of themselves, just as I had.

She was steeled almost to the point of delight. "Angel, I think it's time to blow this thing sky-high. I really think it's time."

Whose time, exactly? They'd sent me to St. Paul's, and they'd made me stay, and now I'd be damned if I gave all of that up—watched the school transform into something not just challenging but antagonistic, with its sights set on my future. No, ma'am. I was going to graduate if it killed me.

"I don't want to do anything," I said. "I just want to go back."

"Just think about it," Mom pleaded. "Please just think about it?"

I told her I would.

Dad then had a difficult conversation with the rector. My father prided himself on sensibility and calm. He was not impulsive or hotheaded or easily swayed. He set up his pad of quadrille paper, clicked out a few millimeters of lead, and told Reverend Clark that we weren't making progress. Would any notice be sent to the boys' colleges? Would the school be talking to the parents of the boys?

Why wasn't any of that happening?

And yes, Dad said, his daughter did wish to return for the sixth form, of course, as planned, and he and Mom were sure the school would do everything in its power to welcome me back—as a community of faith, as a community of scholars. I was an excellent student who contributed across a range of sports and activities. Every single report attested to this.

The rector didn't have much to offer. The boys had graduated and were no longer under the school's supervision. I was not on campus. By all accounts save mine, the encounter had been consensual. I'd waited so long to say something. If I'd been so upset, why hadn't I alerted a teacher or adviser straightaway? Dozens of teachers on campus knew me and would have been in a position to help. I'd had literally hundreds of occasions to speak up. And I had chosen not to until now? Perhaps this was best left to the adolescents to understand. Perhaps the adults might acknowledge, with deep regret, that there really was nothing to discuss.

The rector did not admit that only one side had a legal obligation to report the assault to the police, and it wasn't me. The school had failed this first test. The Concord Police knew nothing about it until my pediatrician called them. It just so happened that the delay meant they couldn't interview the boys before they left the state.

The rector only said, *Why didn't Lacy tell anyone?*

Dad replied, *She did. That's why we're having this conversation.*

Even he, who habitually saw the best until his face was smashed up against the worst, began to think the district attorney was on to something.

"I think we should sue the school," said Mom. "It's the only way to force them to admit what happened."

My father sighed. "You might be right."

My brother, coming up that summer on his twelfth birthday, raised his red hair from his dinner plate. Where had he been all June, all July? I have no idea. Day camps, friends' homes, down the hall sorting baseball cards.

"What does it mean to *sue?*" he asked.

"It means take them to task," said Mom.

"Your mother means to say that it's a legal proceeding whereby we seek redress in the courts for a dispute the two parties can't solve themselves," corrected Dad.

"Oh."

I said, "But then I can't go back."

"No," said Mom.

"No," said Dad.

My brother said, "Will you come home?"

I told him no.

"Well, you *could*," said Dad, half-heartedly.

"But what about Princeton?"

Dad pressed his mouth into a line. His chin crinkled when he did this, like a little boy just about to cry. "We'll just have to try to explain it in your application."

"So I have to write about this? And have everyone there know about it?"

I imagined a future where I might be just a new kid at school, trailing no scandal. But St. Paul's had already taken care of this. I was trapped. It had been genius to gather up my schoolmates, tell them I was sick, then send them out into the world for the summer. How quickly their words spread. My freshman year in college, late one night, a sophomore I'd never met emerged from the other side of the road, calling to my companion, "Hey, she's got herpes." Years after graduation, the man I was dating out in California attended a major theatrical opening in New York City directed by a close friend. The director also taught, and a few of his students were there that night—much younger, they had overlapped with me at university. My boyfriend mentioned my name. One of them replied, "Oh yes, she's cool, but watch out: she's got herpes."

I would always be the one left gasping, wondering how on earth to reply. What should I say? Yes, but it wasn't my fault? Yes, but you could never catch it from me, unless you did *that?*

My brother, James Ellis Crawford IV, was heading into the sixth grade. Already my family was talking about whether to send him to Groton as a second former, in the eighth grade—Groton was one of the few schools that still accepted boys so young. They were assigned little curtained cubicles like the sleeping car of a train. We'd seen these spaces on our tour years ago when I'd gone to look at boarding schools.

Groton was the only school one might, with a certain lens, consider on a par with St. Paul's. Andover and Exeter were rigorous, sure, but they were huge. The rest were lovely. But Groton was tiny and old and it was where Jed Lane had gone, and all the rest of the Lanes too. My brother would have felt it mandatory that he take his place in this precious and arcane little world. So the castle shaking for me meant the castle shaking for him—already he'd have known that.

He asked, "Why would you sue St. Paul's?"

And my mother replied, "To make them tell the truth, sweetheart."

"About what they did to Lacy?"

"Well, yes. About what was done to Lacy."

"By two boys."

"Men," said my father.

"Yes," said Mom.

"Which was very bad," said my brother.

"Yes," said Dad.

"A sexual assault," said James, the words unfamiliar in his mouth.

My parents looked at each other.

Dad said, "That's right."

My brother, knowing not to ask any more questions, nodded. Then he gave me his version of my father's flat-line, wrinkly-chin sympathy sigh.

"Got it," he said.

Mom, crying again, excused herself to go upstairs.

Up in my room, I imagined a courtroom: dark-paneled, not unlike Coit Dining Hall at school. Benches like pews. I had the pacing attorneys, for and against, borrowed from television dramas. They asked me what happened. Rick and Taz were seated across the way, shoulders rounded, heads hung in a simulacrum of humility. My mother cried somewhere beyond my line of sight. The lawyers would ask me: *But you went to their room, did you not? Against school rules? And you did not run away or scream or punch them, am I correct? Yes or no, Miss Crawford. Yes or no.*

And onward from there, to Budge, who would appear now a few rows back, his coxcomb hair bleached with summer, sidekick at his shoulder. Beside him, Johnny Devereux. Then dear Timothy Macalester, the wide-smiling, clear-hearted hippie. Like Scrooge's ghosts, they'd show who I was and how I'd come this way. My parents would understand they'd raised a slut. I was almost reconciled to this discovery; I was almost certain there was no escaping it. But the telos of my agony that summer was not, ultimately, my parents' idea of me. It was the Möbius strip of logic that would give my behavior since the assault as proof that the assault was not an assault at all. They'd say, *You wanted this. Even if you didn't think you did, even if you didn't say so, you wanted it.*

Take away anything, I thought. My school, my friends, my parents' love. But do not dare tell me what I wanted, who I was on that night when I took your call and thought that you were sad.

That's why the memory of Rick carrying me after the bike accident had moved me when nothing else could. I saw myself in his arms: a girl who was hurt and needed help. No one would deny it. He—even he—had seen it too. That's why he'd picked me up and brought me up the hill.

Once I'd been reminded of her, whom I had banished all year, something low in me started to burn.

In July, a formal call came in. The school, in concert with legal counsel from the well-regarded Concord firm of Orr & Reno, wished to communicate a few things.

My father got out his graph paper. I was not invited into the library for the call, so I stayed upstairs in my room, with my door closed, and stared out the window over our drive-way. It was short and opened onto the central artery through town, a two-lane country road lined with mature trees. In the summer you drove in a tunnel of green. I heard cars whoosh-ing through and saw the shudder in the leaves above the fences a second later.

A knock at my door. My parents came in, looking pale.

I moved from my window to my twin bed and folded myself up in the middle of it. My parents stood side by side in front of me. Sitting small, I said, "What's up?"

Dad was the only one of them to speak. "The lawyer for the school says that you are not welcome to return to campus."

"What? Why?"

"Well, they have a list of things here that they are prepared to say about you. That is, if you agree to press charges against the boys, they will get you on the stand, and here's what they're going to say."

He held up his graph pad and read.

"One, Lacy is a drug user.

"Two, Lacy is a drug dealer who has sold her Prozac and other drugs to students on campus, endangering them.

"Three, Lacy regularly abuses privileges and circumvents rules on campus.

"Four, Lacy is a promiscuous girl who has had intercourse with a number of boys on campus, including the accused.

"Five, Lacy is not welcome as a student at St. Paul's School."

Dad lowered the page and aimed his eyes at me, querulous and hard, with my mother beside him avoiding my face. The moment when he might have laughed at that drug-dealing bit had passed. The moment when we might have started punching out windows had passed too. They just stood there, opaque, like a Wasp update of that exhausted hardscrabble couple in *American Pastoral*—graph paper instead of pitchfork clutched in Dad's hand.

I could not get past *Prozac.* I was hung up on that word. It sounds ugly to begin with, inorganic and cheap, and I had to dig a bit to think why I was hearing it now. Nobody knew I'd taken the drug. Who told them? Why did they care? I'd never lost a pill, never given one away. The idea that I had sold that or any other drug was insane. There was not a shred of evidence of that, not the smallest whisper.

Unless, of course, you were willing to flat-out lie. Unless you were willing to access a girl's medical records without her consent and share what you found there with the administration (and all of her schoolmates). Unless you were willing to manufacture accusations to poison the place for her and poison her for it. Then you could say whatever you wanted.

Who were these deans? Or doctors? Or lawyers? Or priests? Who were these *people?*

"Oh my God," I said. My throat was hard against the threat of vomit, which would have burned terribly.

"Basically," my father said, his voice rasping, "they're promising to destroy you." The rasp terrified me. My dad sounded so old.

I hadn't, up to this point, wanted to think of St. Paul's School as *they.* I'd fought the dissolution of the lawns and classes and people I knew into a faceless institution, monolithic and cruel. That had felt too easy to me, too binary—what you would say if you'd never been a student there. But I was the fool. This was not the game I'd thought it was, a civilized dance of virtue and discretion. I'd been so careful and so worried. They'd just quietly been taking aim.

Now my mother was looking at me imploringly. I tried to understand her meaning: What did she want? The fight, or not?

Dad continued. "Lacy, they're saying that you've had sexual partners."

I dragged my mind from the thought of being a Prozac dealer to the far less interesting accusation of teenage sex. *That's* what bothered him most?

He said, "That the two boys were not the only ones. Is that true?"

When I did not reply, my mother burst into tears. My

father turned and took her into his arms. He looked over her shoulder at me and shook his head.

I said I was sorry.

Mom sobbed. He held her.

"It's not what we wanted for our daughter," he told me, and they left my room.

My mother did not come downstairs for dinner that night. She cooked and left bowls on the counter for my father to serve. My brother was unusually chipper, half as a defense and half to claim his advantage. My father was polite but cold.

I replayed his words in my head. *It's not what we wanted for our daughter.* It seemed to me that all I had ever done was try to give them what they wanted. This, our mutual disappointment, might have given us an opening to talk to one another. But nobody started that conversation, so we never did.

The school's characterization of me as a drug dealer was the boldest lie I had ever encountered. Like all lies of its degree, existing wholly without truth, it felt violent. Discourse was now impossible. The conversation we'd been having with the school ceased. All speech that followed was cannily performative, every line parry or thrust. I imagine I could have convinced a court that I had never sold drugs. Any student caught doing so was immediately expelled; besides, there was a tight ecosystem of students involved in illicit substances, and not one of them would claim membership with me. The assertion that I was selling Prozac rather than, say, cocaine is laughable. But the intent of the accusation was not to posit fact. It was to threaten me.

And, of course, they'd changed the subject. Nobody was talking about the boys or what they had done. It would take all my energy to reclaim myself from the wanton, derelict, criminal blow-up doll of a girl the school had dropped over the side of their ship, and they knew this. They weren't playing for justice; they were playing for reputation. Which means one deploys not evidence but innuendo.

What college looks mildly on the application of a student accused by her prep school of dealing drugs? My parents, meanwhile—creatures of their own time and culture—would have preferred a drug dealer to a whore. A junkie can be rehabilitated, after all.

Decades later, reading my pediatrician's report of my account of the assault, I was surprised to realize that the story I was reading had a genre. Plain and simple, it reads like the synopsis of a porn flick. I had never seen pornography when I was in high school, so I could not have recognized it then, but now it was obvious: the summoning-the-nurse setup, the buzzing-the-secretary setup. The men the girl doesn't know call her up and tell a laughable lie, which she falls for. When she arrives, they are all business. First one cock, then the other. She doesn't ask any questions and they don't offer any explanations. She needs to keep quiet because she might get caught. Once they've both gotten off so deep in her throat that she can't breathe, they tell her, "It's your turn now." Only when I refused and climbed back out the window would the clapper have come down. In the movie they would have fucked me again, and I'd have performed multiple screaming orgasms.

As an adult still searching for some understanding, I allowed this question: Could the boys have believed that would happen? Is there any possibility they imagined that pornography might be real, that I was in on the lie from the beginning?

Did they think we were sharing something after all?

Of course, there's nothing intimate about the sex in porn. The story the school told about my using and dealing drugs was just another version of this, squarely in keeping with the genre. An absolute, boffo lie, lewdly fictitious. We all knew it—they did and we did. My protesting ("Oh, but I'm *not* a drug dealer!") would be little more than foreplay. Their lie was meant not to convince, but to compel. That's how it works. That's the entire point. Nobody cares about how you get there; details are a waste of time. The story has one end: no matter what, the girl is going to give it up.

My parents did not speak to me again about what happened at St. Paul's. The conversation simply ended.

We managed logistics the way people do when planning a trip, referring to possible pitfalls like weather or delays, preparing mindfully. At some point I made the necessary formal statement over the phone that I did not wish the police to move forward with criminal charges. It would have been hopeless to try to support their investigation without my parents supporting me.

As soon as it became clear that there would be no charges, the school, which had been so certain I was a criminal drug dealer, found no reason not to enroll me for the sixth form. I was welcomed back. Here was the contract, as I understood it: I would not speak of the assault, and they would not do anything to interfere with my applications to college or my progress toward graduation. My father had made it very clear to the school's lawyer that he expected this.

That was all just fine with the school. The damage to me

was done. It had reached my old friend Natalie even before it reached me.

My father tore the sheets of conversation notes off his graph pad and placed them in a red folder and put the file away.

Almost a decade later, when I was in graduate school in Chicago, I was home for the weekend. My parents had recently moved houses. Dad was clearing out files.

"I have no reason to hang on to this," he said, holding out the red file. "Would you like it, or should I shred it?"

I opened the cover and saw the five accusations, in my dad's line-of-ants hand. I began to shake. This surprised me—I had no idea so much force remained. It had been a long time. I closed the file. I'd never considered that this document might still exist, but of course it did—and here it was. *Drug dealer.* A bolder version of me, an older one, would have laughed. *Maybe I'd have been a lot happier if I'd done a few drugs,* she might have said. *Maybe I ought to go find some right now, roll a fat one with this here graph paper.*

I carried the red folder as if it burned, and I brought it with me, buried in my bag, to my next appointment with the therapist I was seeing. Margaret was a PsyD who specialized in Jungian analysis; she and her husband, also an analyst, worked on gender archetypes and roles in relationships. He had published several books on masculinity and ran workshops on manhood. Margaret was reputed to be very good with survivors of sexual violence. Both therapists practiced out of a beautiful home in Hyde Park, a few blocks from the campus of the University of Chicago, where I was in the Department of English Language and Literature. Despite my affinity for narratives, I found Margaret's Jungian approach unsatisfying—we were constantly extrapolating from my experience to something universal, which erased details and dovetailed too nicely with my own impulses to denial. I was quite self-destructive in those years and had been for some time, though this could be hard to see. (A PhD program is an excellent place to mask self-hatred.)

I told Margaret about the file, holding it quivering between us. She had a suggestion: leave it with her. A safe, third space. If I wanted it back, it was there; if I didn't want it back, I didn't have to do anything at all. This suited me.

Periodically, once we'd stopped meeting, Margaret would email me to ask about the file. I was never ready for it. I moved overseas, changed my life, met my husband. Started a family.

Many years later still, investigators sought to corroborate my account of what the school's lawyers had said to my parents, because it sounded to them like a possible obstruction of justice. They proposed that it might reveal an attempt at witness tampering. Could we retrieve the file?

Of course we could. I looked up Margaret to make sure she was still at the same address before giving her a call. Not long before I typed Margaret's name into Google, her husband had shot her in the head. He then killed himself, too. I read her obituary instead. They'd had no children, and there was no clinical executor of her estate.

I called the Cook County Department of Justice, but they rather understandably had better things to do than help me track down my old red file. I spent an hour on the phone, being passed between departments. *Oh, domestic violence,* said one woman. *Let me put you through to someone else.* She clicked, and the line went dead.

10

Fall 1991, Sixth Form

My mother flew with me back to New Hampshire to begin my sixth-form year. She did not wear what she called her dog collar, though she'd floated the idea. She was imperious in her planning, laying hard generosity on every aspect of getting me settled: new sheets and blankets, a bedside lamp, an account with a local deli so I could order soup when my throat was bad. This fierce focus was all she betrayed of her terror at bringing me back. That, and the way she'd clutch my arm, just above my elbow, whenever we passed through a doorway. I ended up stepping into new spaces half a stride ahead of her, my arm dully aching in her grip. This is how we presented ourselves on a hot afternoon to Brewster House, where again I had been assigned to live, to search the bulletin board for the number of my room:

9.

I knew it already. The smallest room in the dorm, in previous generations a storage space, fit only for an anchorite who might receive handouts of food through her half-panel window, which was adjacent to the dorm's back door. There was a Room 9 in each of the four buildings on the quad, and by unspoken law it was always given to a third former. We all felt tender for the freshman who had drawn the short straw. It was almost a badge of honor.

"Maybe it's a mistake," said Mom.

My friends were all in Brewster too. Caroline and Sam had the long, bowling-alley double on the third floor, with the dormer windows. Brooke and Maddy had sunny singles on the second floor, Meg and Tabby the equally sunny singles beneath them. Obviously the school had granted my wish to live with my friends, but the room barely fit a bed. I saw it and understood that St. Paul's had not been planning on my return. My mom saw it and understood that St. Paul's was intent on punishing me, and she turned on a Ferragamo heel in the direction of Mrs. Fenn's open door.

"We're going to change this right now."

I'd never seen this version of my mother before. Mom could be arctic in her expectations, but she was never a *pushy broad*.

Mrs. Fenn, ever mild, followed us back down the muggy hall and peered into the gloaming of Room 9. What she said next was the last thing I expected:

"Yep, I agree with you. Let's just go on up and make a change."

And like that, I had a sunny single on the top floor, right near my friends. The third former who'd originally been assigned my room got the storage space. She never knew what she'd lost. I could not believe what I had gained. Not the real estate—though that was wonderful, I had room for a dresser *and* a chair—but a sense that the school would comply.

"All right, then," said Mom, hands on hips, looking around the bright surfaces. "See? Things are looking up. Things are going to be different now."

This sort of vague injunction to fortune was the closest we came to talking about what had happened. I felt it would be cruel of me to raise it, and besides, here Mom was with a motel room in Concord, spending two whole days shuttling me back and forth from campus to town. At a housewares store down by the river she bought a spring-loaded curtain rail and hung little sheers over my twin dormer windows, which had a view of the quad. I missed the meadow and wondered about my ingratitude. Her ministrations made me feel newly vulnerable, as though the impression of plenty might invite attack.

Take the room. Mrs. Fenn's willingness to give it to me didn't seem to emerge from her own measured constitution. I sensed some precondition, and though it was ostensibly working in my favor, that it existed at all hardened my defenses. It proved there was indeed an entity on the other side of the scrim, an adversary I was going to be wrestling with all year. Who was it? The rector? The trustees? Some composite figure of priests and lawyers? I sometimes imagined I'd caught a glimpse in certain features of the landscape, such as the thrust of the chapel tower and the occasional downspout gargoyle. This anodyne body of history and power, previously blind to me, was now, I knew, aware. And angry.

Mom watched me skid my school-issue dresser across the floor until it sat as close to the door as possible, perpendicular to the entry. I moved my bed alongside the wall behind it. When I opened the dresser drawers, the door to my room slammed into them and opened no further.

"Won't that drive you nuts?" asked Mom. "Your door is going to bang into those drawers all the time. What if a friend is coming to say hi?"

I didn't tell her. It would have caused her heart to seize in her chest. Instead we went into town and bought a bright wall calendar to attach to the back of the dresser. I told her I would lie in bed last thing at night and count the days.

"I will, too," she said, soft tears now finally in her eyes. "Goddammit, I will, too."

Those first days, life at school came together. My room, my dorm, my friends. Soccer and singing. I ordered up mountains of books and articles from the thrilled librarian at the desk for my ISP. Scotty returned from Philly. I buried my prescription for my throat deep in my footlocker, a large bottle filled at the pharmacy at home so nobody would know.

To the world, as to myself, I attempted to appear blasé. I remembered the dismissive hauteur of those senior girls back in my newb year, and sometimes I wore that cloak now, shivering into it and shivering out. It wasn't really in me to be cruel. I advocated mercy for the third former from the Upper East Side who walked into Meg's room after sports and helped herself to face cream—an unimaginable crime in the days of our youth. We considered ourselves gracious and nuanced. The newb was let off with nothing but a firm scolding (which seemed to shock her nevertheless). But sometimes I also pretended not to see these young girls from my dorm, passing them on the way into meals or to Chapel. I saw them abort their greetings, just as I had, being met with blind eyes, and I pretended not to see this, either.

I wondered what they knew. I wondered what anyone knew.

Then, a few days into our return, Scotty invited me after supper to the Tuck Shop for ice cream. I nestled on the bench opposite him and raised my spoon. It was all the same—the warm night, the meadow air, sweet Scotty there—and I was stronger now.

Scotty said, "Hey, Lacy, I'm going to have to stop, you know, hanging out."

My spoon was still aloft. But I was very cool.

"You're breaking up with me?"

"Yeah." He winced, and then smiled a bit.

"Why?"

I was almost inured to surprises by now, but this one got me. Scotty *had* written back over the summer. It took a few weeks, but a note had arrived. If you'd smashed three cellar spiders on card stock it would have been more emotive (*love, Scotty*), but he wanted me to come visit—our mothers worked it out, with the result that I had spent three August days floating around in a little boat with an outboard motor at a summer paradise called Thousand Islands.

I threaded worms onto his hook while Scotty drank beer and smoked. His older brother was a phantom of cool, delivering pot and beer, sometimes pizza. His sister had fetched me at the airport, barefoot in a leaf-green MG. I thought I pleased his mom with my conscientious manners and the little cachepot I'd brought on the plane as a hostess gift. Scotty had been furloughed from his job over at the marina for filling the water tank of a yacht with gasoline. Or it might have been vice versa, he wasn't sure, but anyway they got really mad. So we puttered around, the two-stroke engine giving us an excuse to fail to make conversation. The islands we skirted were discrete and tiny, some of them holding only one house, ringed by gravel and pine trees, a gentle wash of wind and wave like a halo around each one. We motored somewhere and went cliff diving. We motored somewhere else for sandwiches. Scotty pointed out Skull and Bones Island. I had already been thinking it looked spooky, but a lot of those little islands did, so I didn't understand he was showing me the territorial home of the powerful Yale secret society. I figured someone had died there—maybe it was the site of a Native American massacre? A cholera outbreak? Scotty wasn't interested in Yale—Thousand Islands was filthy with Elis, in their faded blue caps, but he was the tail end of old money's ambition-quashing habit, his the generation that gives up entirely on private docks and heads out west to major in ceramics.

It's what I liked about him. I had thought we understood this about each other. He'd settle my jumpiness about what came next, and I'd keep the tiniest bit of fiber in his routine. I'd zoom and he'd dawdle. He'd get high and I'd read novels, and we'd eventually just watch a movie instead of trying to have sex. I thought it was going to last us all year.

"Well, it's just..." Scotty said now, his ice cream untouched, hand scratching at the back of his head, "it's just the things people are saying, I guess. It's too much."

In three days? Four? Five? We'd only just returned to campus. "I don't understand," I said. "Did you talk to someone?"

He nodded, his arm going up and down with his head.

Nothing had happened, nothing new. I'd marked every threat. I knew them all.

"Who? What did they say?"

"Aw, come on," said Scotty. "I don't want to say it."

"Say what?"

His hand landed with a thud on the table. "Lacy."

"Okay, then who. Who was it?"

"Wyler," he admitted. Who had graduated the year before. Though he'd dated my friend Brooke, he had avoided me until his good friend Scotty and I had started seeing each other. After that he'd said hello to me a few times. That was the most we'd ever spoken.

"I don't talk to Wyler," I said. "He's not even here anymore."

"I know."

"All he's got is gossip."

"Well, okay."

"What is it?"

"Just, you know ..." Scotty was miserable, shifting around on the seat of his faded jeans. "Just you're sick and all."

I felt my stomach harden. The old not-eating was back again. A year lay ahead, and the place was closing around me like a trap.

"I'm sick," I repeated.

"Well, yeah. Sorry. Coach told them about it, I guess, some sixth formers, and it just got around, talking and stuff, and Wyler called."

Coach. Coach. I burned to know which *coach* this was. They were talking about my throat?

"Last year?" I asked him. "They were talking about me? Last year? Who? Where?"

"Aw, Lacy, I don't know. I don't know ... anything. Look, I'm sorry. It's just more than I can deal with."

There were a hundred arguments—what it was, where it was, how it had gotten there, and why Scotty never needed to worry about it—but I could see that it was done. *We* were done.

"Okay," I said.

I left the table, half expecting Scotty to come after me, shaking his shaggy head and saying it was all just a joke.

Walking back through the meadow alone, I did not permit myself to cry. The wildflowers were as high as they'd be all year, clambering piles of green and gold, vibrating with insects, smelling of mildew and sage. *Coach.* Gillespie? Was it Coach Gillespie—he of the sodium ball? Was it Coach Matthews—he of "She's not a good girl"? Coach Buxton? Someone else? Which players had heard? What did the coach say? And how on earth did he know?

To hell with Scotty, then. I was invincibly alone. The little light was on in the anchorite's room. I marched up to my airy single, grabbed a jacket, told Mrs. Fenn I was in for the night, and went back out. My friends were on their way home for check-in, and I passed their curious faces. They waved but did not ask—they never asked. It was part frost and part care, I think. But I never told them, either.

For more than an hour, I walked. I watched lights coming on and wondered who had which rooms this year. I stayed out as long as I dared. They'd told the lacrosse team I was ill? Could that be true?

If so, I blamed my parents for telling the school I had contracted herpes. To do this I had to remove from consideration my old friend Natalie's call at the beginning of the summer, and also the lawyers' threat about my Prozac. There is no way I could have stayed at school if I had let myself see what these lawyers, teachers, and priests had done. But I don't think I could have figured it out even if I had been willing, because as far as I knew, the school had found out about my herpes only after my doctor had tested me for it at home. And by then the previous sixth formers had graduated, and everyone else had gone; there was no one left to gather and tell.

I decided to bait the place, just to see if things were as animated, as complicated, as I sensed they were.

Outside the art building, where the streetlights were brightest, I encountered a tall master I'd never had in class. He was startled and asked if I needed help, and then his agitation became clear. I should not have been out of my dorm. This was cruising and it was an obvious D.C. He peered at me hard. "Is that Lacy?" he asked. "Crawford?"

"Yes," I answered.

"Oh," he said. He held his head low, wished me good night, and hurried away.

I tested my limits a few more times before I forgot about limits altogether. One morning I went for a run before dawn. I had streetlights on the road up out of campus, but then followed long stretches of vertiginous, shoulderless black. I wanted to check on my woods. By the time I reached the return paths they were pearled and soft with dawn, nearly unrecognizable after a summer of growth. A master from a boys' dorm, making coffee in his little kitchen, caught me returning. He leaned across his counter to push open his window and summoned me.

"Where have you been?"

I told him.

"A run?"

I gave him my whole face. I was aching for him to get mad.

"And where did you go on this run?"

I could dimly see his T-shirt, presumably the one he slept in. I pitied this man, living alone in an apartment attached to a dorm full of teenagers in the New Hampshire woods. "Blinking Light and Boat Docks."

"How far is that?" he asked.

"I think almost five."

"And did you run it alone?"

I nodded and smiled wide, to show him I hadn't been alone, though of course I had been. There was a little flare in his face and his nostrils widened, but then he blew across the top of his coffee and let his eyes settle derisively on me.

"Are you going to be doing this often?" he asked.

"Dunno." As bratty as I could be.

It was sad, because I'd been such a good girl before—I'd been so eager to make teachers feel important. Now he would know me only as a spoiled delinquent.

"Perhaps you should wait until you have a little more light," he said finally. "You might trip. You might get hurt out there."

I turned without being dismissed.

But I wasn't, at heart, a rebel. I didn't go into nearby towns and pay men at the bus stop to buy handles of booze. I didn't have connections to the kids who brought gallon bags of weed from their houses in Bermuda and the Bahamas, much less the few moving cocaine from Manhattan. I was more inclined to put my advantage into service on behalf of my friends. When Caroline's Dave came back from Brown to visit, I let him hide under my bed until check-in was complete and all the teachers' doors were closed for the night. When Brooke scored a fifth of vodka for a boring weekend, I let her keep it in my footlocker.

Our favorite way to alter consciousness was to do shots of vodka as quickly and surreptitiously as possible. The bottle was restowed after every pour, the shot glass shoved beneath a mattress or behind a stack of books after each swallow. No more than four of us gathered to "pound" so we didn't seem suspicious to a teacher passing in the hall. After we'd had as many shots as we could tolerate, we'd eat tablespoons of peanut butter straight from the jar, thinking this masked the smell.

But drinking was risky beyond the threat of getting caught. I got soused and I was at the mercy of internal tides that came on with shocking force. I'd sit on my bed, watching Brooke and Sam convulse with laughter, hearing Maddy tell yet another wild story about what finally happened that night she and Brophy hooked up, and inside me would be the smell of diesel and pine. I'd be rocking in a boat with Scotty at the stern, tiller lightly in his filthy palm, pointing out cabins and deer. I'd be feeling the way our small wake moved the gravel shores, making a sound like money, heaps of money, piling over itself. I had borrowed from him his way of holding the world so loosely, the way only the truly privileged can, detached and indemnified from his own outcomes—not that I wished to exist in the world without responsibility, but that around him I had been able to pretend not to care. This pretending went so deep it changed how much I really did think. Ideas loosened around Scotty. Words got up and drifted away. But still there we were, with everything we could ever want at our fingertips.

Now that he'd dropped me, I was at the mercy of my own thoughts again: I was diseased, I was disgraced, I was alone. I had no idea how I would survive college. If I could even get in. Teachers refused to punish me, which was another way of saying they refused to look after me. I could do anything here, because nobody was willing to see me anymore.

I heard the chapel bells. My friends laughed. I counted. It was late. Once papers were assigned and exams loomed, we would not be able to waste time like this. The girls were laughing so hard their faces shone. One of them—I will not say who, but it was a friend I loved—hopped onto my bed and bounced a bit to jolly me up. Someone else cracked that this was a Brophy move, that I should take shelter immediately, and someone else made another joke about another boy, about all boys...

"And then they do this"—sticking a tongue out like a cartoon ghoul—"and then this"—squeezing her own tits—

"And this"—ramming two fingers up, up, up in the air—

"And this—" Maddy, pantomiming the eyes and reaching arms of the boys contemplating her rack, backing up slowly, hands out ahead of her, as though threatened with death—

Caroline was bent over, laughing. Sam said she had just peed herself a little bit, and someone was shushing us—we were drunk, we could all get caught, and fuck college and fuck life and fuck it all—when the friend next to me, her arm heavy on my shoulders, turned to me and gave a little sob.

"Oh, Lace."

We quieted.

She said, "I have it too."

Her laughter had dissolved to tears, similarly loose and overwhelming, and I put my arms around her. We were lying together in each other's arms on my bed, crying. "He said he had no idea. He swore to me."

It didn't matter, to us, who *he* was. *He* was every boy in our world. He was the world. We understood.

All of us in that room wept. "I'm sorry," I told my friend. "I'm so sorry."

• • •

Two more girls knocked on my door that fall to tell me they had herpes. I dug out my bottle of Zovirax and showed them the label so they could ask their physicians, once they worked up the courage, for a prescription of their own. We walked together to the old white pages in the common room, a paper slab with lines of mold through it like a Stilton, and searched for clinics close enough to reach by taxi without being gone so long a teacher would have to know. I stopped short of giving them my drugs, because I knew this was illegal, and I was not about to make the administration right. Not even for free, not even for this.

Then a third former, devoted to her third-form boyfriend, approached me for advice about birth control. And someone else asked me how to handle the situation with her mom's new boyfriend. There were other questions too, more benign but no less important: How to tell my parents I won't apply to their college? How to drop this class, quit that sport, break up with him?

Hester Prynne, Hawthorne writes in *The Scarlet Letter*, "did not flee." She moved with her fatherless child to a "little, lonesome dwelling" on the outskirts of town. Of course she did. One step shy of the witch in her cave, our Hester, marginalized by an entire community.

I learned that while the fallen woman may keep her unloved door plain and her drapes drawn, her circle small and her fire low—if she's wise, I suppose, she will—the path to her back stoop will be well-traveled. I guarantee it.

Then in October I was contemplating its having been a year, and Brooke put Alannah Myles's "Black Velvet" on the new music player in the newly redesigned student center, where we were all bored out of our skulls—sixteen and seventeen and wild for something other than track halogens and a quarterless jukebox—and I was fed up and wanting to go back to my room to read when I passed a fifth-form jock who said, "What's up, you freak?"

I turned to where he was sitting, propped on a ledge with a bunch of similar goons. It was astonishing how these things reconstellated themselves, the microcycles of high school life— here the seedling assholes all in a row, coming up to take the place of the guys who had graduated just the year before. Already they knew to mock me. Couldn't even let me walk by. I narrowed my eyes on the one who had spoken to me. His name was Alexander Ault. He was hugely strong, but not tall. Handsome, but I did not care. The usual football–ice hockey–lacrosse type. The monkeys flanking him let their lips flap in cruel grins. These were boys with names like Grant and Sebastian.

"What did you call me?"

"What you are. A freak."

"Fuck you." These students were a year behind me. I might have recently been a pariah, but hierarchies were hierarchies.

"Oh, come on," said Alex lightly, and he patted the ledge beside him, forcing Grant to scoot over. "I'm just giving you a hard time."

I glared. He made honest-dog eyes.

"Please? Have a seat."

I did not sit. I looked at this enormously well-built guy, who was smiling broadly—beautifully—at me, and wondered if there might be something there. As I've mentioned, "freak" was a complicated term.

I asked, "Why?" He played on the lacrosse team. He knew Scotty.

"Because you're cute," said Alex. "You're really, really cute." He patted the ledge again. "Will you sit down?"

I perched.

"Good," said Alex. "I've been waiting for a chance to talk to you all year."

I waited. When he didn't say more, I asked again, "Why?" and held my breath, because of what he might say next.

I noticed him not noticing, or not caring, what the goons were doing, jabbing each other and slapping their thighs. "Do I have to say it again? You're the best-looking girl here."

Kindness was confounding. I was aware of where our hands met on the ledge.

"If you really think that, then why did you call me a *freak?*"

He leaned left and right to get his buddies' attention. "Hey, will you guys fuck off?"

They grew solemn and slid off.

Alex looked back at me. "It just seems like nasty gets a lot more done in this place, you know?"

I did know.

"And besides, it worked," he said, again with the smile.

We walked through the meadow. He didn't try to touch me, but when it happened accidentally, just at the arm or hip, I felt like yelping. Some knot was unloosing inside me and this was terrible. Then I remembered who he lived with, showered with, ran wind sprints with. I was confused and frightened. But then I heard his voice and I wasn't afraid. This reversal happened, quick oscillations, in sub-seconds. Ever seen the inside of a pocket watch? It was exhausting.

Alex had a warm, deep voice, and he was articulate. "Glad to find someone who appreciates that cruelty is currency," he said. "Not easily admitted around here."

My body was swimming beneath my brain. "No, it's not."

He hated St. Paul's.

"Why do you stay?" I asked.

"My dad." Alex's father had grown up poor and had achieved, via football and a Rhodes Scholarship, top corporate positions. Cultural leadership would follow. Alex worshipped him. His dad had augmented his son's early ice-hockey talent with ballet lessons to improve his balance. He'd raised a boy who had read the Federalist Papers by the ninth grade and kept them, along with other key works of constitutional law and history, in his room, above the moldering heap of hockey pads in their rotten bag on the floor. Alex had been a top recruit to St. Paul's. I saw, immediately, that this weight was burying him. The father was exceptional. The son was gifted and terrified.

"My dad and hockey," Alex said. "How about you?"

He hadn't meant to, but already we'd come to it. With hockey he'd summoned the ghost of Rick. It was unavoidable. Alex wasn't a giant, like Rick was, but his talent was commensurate—he was one of the stars in his year. They filled the same roles at the school, had the same coaches. Over ice and turf, much would have passed between them.

"I guess I haven't left because I refuse to give up," I said.

Alex was quiet. I needed to know right away, so I said, "Rick Banner fucked me up last year."

But Alex said only, "I know."

"And Taz."

"I know."

"I wanted to kill myself."

"I'm glad you didn't."

"Maybe I should have, though," I said, feeling swamped again.

"There's still plenty of time."

I laughed.

Alex said, "Stick with me."

I could not stop my smile. "Why should I?"

"Because I, my dear, will beat the shit out of anyone."

"Anyone?"

"Anyone. I can travel if I need to, too. Just give me time to sign out for the weekend."

"Deal."

"Though I'd rather we sign out together and go hang out somewhere."

"Like where?"

"I dunno. Somewhere I won't get busted for murdering Rick Banner in his sleep."

"Paris?"

"Done."

"Alex?"

"Yeah?"

"Was he always like that?"

"Who. Banner?"

"Yeah. Was he always such a dick?"

Alex stopped on the path and turned me toward him. He took my hands in his hands, and when I was still he said, "Oh, my god, Lacy. You didn't think it was *you*, did you? You thought it was *you?*"

•　　•　　•

That spot in the meadow thereafter has, in my memory, a tiny light, a little firefly point I'm sure I could still see if I ever went back. Other places on campus lit too, that fall, one by one. The pillar at the front of the math building where one day I realized, ten seconds then thirty seconds then five minutes late to class, that I felt an actual pain in my chest when Alex and I parted. There's a light at the step up into the dining halls, where he waited for me. There's one where I sat in the choir stalls. One at the spot where he broke away from football practice to find me up on the soccer fields, grown men howling his name at his back. Above all a glow from the cramped single at the back of the top floor of Foster House, where in the evenings I'd lie for hours on Alex's chest and he would stroke my hair.

He loved to discuss history and nation-states and the collapse of empires and macroeconomics, but mostly he told me about his family. One sister was brilliant, at Harvard Law School, and he intended to follow her there. His other sister was not as bookish but had a gift with people, just wait and I'd see it myself, and indeed I did. His mother was a warm Southern belle with extreme smarts. Alex was born of these women, shaped by them such that with his teammates he could be a hockey thug tumbling toward the locker room grab-assing and gassy, badgering through a half-maw of chewing tobacco, and still shower, put on a pressed button-down, and arrive at my room to walk me to Seated Meal, because that's what a gentleman did. And while I heard him vulgar and puerile plenty of times, never once did I hear him deploy the feminine as insult. He could hit hard enough to leave girls out of it.

There lived, in Foster House that year, a critical mass of hockey players, whose stench began at the base of the grand staircase (the dorm had originally been a mansion) and boiled, once the radiators came on, into a carpet-based airbroth that made it almost intolerable to be inside those walls. During intervisitation hours, girls stood blushing at the bottom step with hanks of hair drawn across their noses, waiting for some younger jock to go fetch their friend. Had Alex not been Alex—my Alex—the place would have been a lion's den to me. But as a sixth former I could stay out half an hour later than Alex could, so I would huddle with him there in his single room with its lone window cracked to the pine air until well past ten, when I was supposed to leave.

One of the masters in Foster was too old to climb the three flights of stairs. Another—the young and handsome English teacher—was routinely racing the clock too, parking his little blue sports car with its long-haired passenger in the treed lot beneath Alex's window. The third was a Japanese instructor whom the hockey thugs could not resist abusing. Caught with mouths of chewing tobacco, they stared and gawked when Mr. Hayashi asked why they were talking strangely, until the question, in its reflexivity, seemed absurd. They liked to leave their windows wide open and spread peanuts across their dressers so they could run yelling down the stairs that a wild animal was in their room, come quickly, what was it, what could it be? Mr. Hayashi would get caught in the double rhotic consonant of *squirrel* and spend whole miserable seconds trying to deliver his verdict.

Late one night that fall Alex and I were lying in the dark, as we did, when Mr. Hayashi pushed open the door. Surgical light spilled in from the fluorescent hall. Mr. Hayashi saw us and blinked, trying to find the words.

"Mr. Hayashi," said Alex politely, "please go away."

The door closed.

Alex had not come to St. Paul's a virgin. He was old for his class and his girlfriend at home had been older still. He was not, with me, in a hurry. As I've said, he was terrifically strong. In the dark his arms looked as though someone had hurled muscle at him and it had stuck, mounding every stretch of skin and bone. I lay inside that strength. It was threat turned inside out, given to me handle-first. It is possible that I owe Alex Ault my life. I resist the tale that has the maiden rescued by the warrior, not least because it is dull—though if I am going to call hockey players *thugs,* I must admit a landscape of *maidens,* too. I was not among them. And I would not call it *rescue,* because once I was in college and Alex and I were no longer together, I felt the old powerlessness return. I had learned nothing at all.

But while we were together, it held.

Because he was a male tri-varsity athlete of a certain sort—football-hockey-lacrosse, with weight room and sprinting records, and an easy, popular way about him—he had heard all the news about me.

"Scotty dumped me because of something Wyler told him," I said, early on in our relationship. We'd have been talking in the meadow, or walking the long footbridge toward Chapel, or sitting on the porch of his dorm while the air was still mild.

"I heard that," said Alex. "What an idiot."

"Apparently Wyler said something about the coach telling them I was sick."

"That's true," said Alex.

I got vertigo in moments of revelation like this. The collision of shame and rage spun in me like a cyclone, an unholy storm. But I tried to keep my voice light. "Was it Matthews?" I asked. "Gillespie? Buxton? What did he say?"

"Oh, Lace."

"No, please."

Alex put his head down. He had a wide, masculine jaw, and I could see its outline even when he ducked his face. "I don't care," he said, and took my hand. "You know I don't care."

"What did he say?"

Alex sighed. "They asked if anyone had ever been, you know, intimate with you. I guess some guys said yes. And then they said that anyone who had should head to the infirmary to get checked for . . . diseases."

I didn't ask anything else. Alex wasn't looking at me, and I didn't look at him. The bile in my throat burned, and it felt, in that moment, like a betrayal by my own body. *See?* said the pain. *You* are *sick. They weren't wrong.*

I had the scene from last spring in my mind, these young men out on the lacrosse field, sprawled in the sunny grass, helmets in their hands and sticks by their sides, and their mentors issuing their warning in low tones. Or it might have been in some coach's apartment: men's bodies on sofas and chairs, the loose, sophomoric gathering marked by a surprisingly sober moment. And then these boys had threaded campus with the warning about me. I imagined their jokes, the innuendo, the bluster. It infected everyone and everything, so that I could never enter a room and not wonder who was thinking about my body and considering me either dirty or dangerous.

"But you really don't care?" I finally asked Alex, unbelieving.

He raised his head. He was angry, and I thought I'd pushed

him too far. Of course he cared. My reputation, my history at the school, caused him shame and embarrassment. He'd just been ignoring it, and I'd forced him right to the heart of what was abhorrent about me, and now he'd turn on me too.

"Don't *ever* do that," he said. "Not ever again."

I was already starting to sob. I'd have to leave school if Alex broke up with me—it would be the loss too great. I was almost afraid to speak. "Do what?"

"Think I'm like those guys. Those schmucks. Do not ever."

I gave him my word.

A curious thing happened. By the start of hockey season, the campus had become aware that we were an item, and Alex, for the first time in his life, was benched. The coaches wouldn't play him. There seemed no reason. Alex talked to Bill Matthews, who had recruited him. Matthews had a problem with Alex's skating, his stops, his turns, his stick handling, his slap shot. Or he had no problem, or he was just working out the lines, or Alex was overreacting. Mr. Ault took time off from work and came up to New Hampshire to try to sort it out. Alex spent extra hours in the weight room, missing Seated Meal and earning detentions. He sent me home early so he could get a good night's sleep. Mr. Ault was reduced to headshaking scowls. Nothing added up. How could Alex demonstrate his worth if they never played him? A fourth former took his spot on his line. Matthews couldn't seem to explain the problem in a way that could be addressed. A school change was discussed. The pounding, jocular crash-greetings I observed when Alex came across his teammates, or they him, started to lose their force. At first these players called me Hockey Yoko, but that quickly stopped—they understood that Alex's performance on the ice had not changed. They lowered their eyes and set callused palms for long moments on Alex's shoulders.

After Thanksgiving I paid a visit to Ms. Royce, who had asked every returning member of the varsity girls' hockey team to drop by her apartment after supper because she was gearing up for the coaching season. She put Marvin Gaye's "Sexual Healing" on the stereo in her little apartment, and tittered with us cool sixth formers about how she shouldn't do this, but wasn't it a great song? I told her I'd be sitting out the season, and she was unkind. "You're leaving me in the lurch," she said, which was ridiculous—we all knew I was a terrible hockey player. "I'm disappointed in you. That's a mistake. What are you going to do?" Even my friends showed their surprise.

Avoid the rink was the answer; work on my ISP; gain a little too much weight; walk Raspberry through the snow. Try to figure out how to help Alex.

But fate had begun its cascade. Kept from the ice, Alex lost his courage in classes. He started papers and could not finish them. Teachers gave him the highest grades on the first eight pages but had to fail him anyway. I spent hours in the library, finding books for him. When he told me, stricken, that this didn't help, I'd clean his room for him while he worked alone somewhere else. It was a poor instinct, to mother him. But neither of us knew what demon this was or what it could do.

Alex began an unraveling. I've wondered since if it was that only one of us could survive, as if we were in a lifeboat too small for two. Or was it a snakebite, and he took from me the poison? Or something other—some biological force as powerful as his intelligence but latent, that would, before he finished college, undo his academic gifts, and that had nothing to do with me?

How he shook my grandfather's hand, when Big Jim and Ginny arrived in Concord, looking awkward as shell-less snails, to sit in the gymnasium for my interminable graduation ceremony on a day of relentless rain. How he tousled and thumped my little brother, who could be observed dropping back to hold his breath and peer down at his own chest, trying to isolate his muscles, to find the strength in himself that was so clear in Alex. How Alex, his own athletic career stalling, cheered for me when I, having played in the top singles spot all spring, won the tennis prize. How he laughed with my mother about electoral politics and the church. How my father nodded and inquired about Mr. Ault's Rhodes—maybe they had friends in common?

I have no idea how Alex tolerated any of this. How he took up my shame and magicked it away. Somewhere between rescue and self-sacrifice is simple accompaniment, of sufficient force to bring a person back into her life.

I graduated from St. Paul's. Alex did not. He has made his way, but he is lost to me now. Still, there is a light at the cold door to Foster House, in the St. Paul's map of my mind, where I arrived at a dead run with my Princeton acceptance letter clutched in my hand so Alex could be the first to know. He held me hard and his eyes shone. For Christmas, because I'd wanted it, he gave me a little silver ring.

11

Alumna, SPS Form of 1992

For the next twenty-four years, I paid no attention to St. Paul's School, with the rare exceptions of tragedies that shook me into communion. The summer before our senior year in college, Sarah Devens, the superstar athlete who had comforted me that cold hockey afternoon in 1991, shot herself at her father's house. She'd been a rising senior at Dartmouth, captain of everything. I was a student at a writers' conference in upstate New York when I heard this news, and I went out for a very long run, through rolling horse pastures and past sunset, as though in extremis I might meet up with Sarah's spirit and understand why.

Later that summer I received a form letter from her closest St. Paul's friends inviting donations toward a girls' hockey changing room to be dedicated in her honor. I remembered the rink, I remembered Royce's ice-skating drill, Categories. That moment with Sarah was as clear in my mind as the day it happened: we had just left the drafty trailer where we changed when Sarah broke from the pack and jogged up to embrace me. I didn't want to put her back in that locker room any more than I wanted to go back myself. I wrote to her friends somewhat haughtily that I would have preferred to give money toward something that was a more human honor—a scholarship, or a fund to endow a school counselor. I meant to celebrate Sarah, but my intentions were not pure. I had begun to hate what seemed to me another expression of almost unbelievable privilege: an uncomplicated relationship to institutions. These girls and their guileless trust. That trust had once been mine. Who wouldn't want to write a check to St. Paul's? Who wouldn't want a new locker room for girls? What could be wrong with that?

Sarah's friends replied that her family had made their decision to honor Sarah in a certain way and I could participate or not. I sent a check.

After college, another form-mate, a brilliant and wry writer, finished up his master's at Stanford and died in a car being driven by his best friend from St. Paul's. A third classmate barely cleared forty before dying of chronic disease. The Jesus painter's redheaded brother drowned. A student who had been a year ahead of me died of cancer. Stewart, the son of the scion, who had teased me in his limousine, choked at a restaurant and left behind two little girls. A student who had been a year behind me, a wide-smiling classics scholar, killed herself.

I considered each tragedy an education in perspective, and told myself I had nothing to begrudge the school, or fate. I had made my choices.

Occasional reports of turmoil at the school rose to national media prominence, but I hardly registered that Bishop Craig Anderson, the eleventh rector, was forced out amid investigations into the misuse of school funds. Bill Matthews succeeded him as the twelfth. While Matthews was sitting rector, he oversaw the construction of a new hockey center. The trustees of the school decided that it should be named after him. The

Sarah Devens Locker Room, I supposed, would sit inside the Bill Matthews Hockey Center. Two gorgeous new rinks. New stands. I pictured the spot back in the pines, behind the dining hall and Kittredge House, over an icy bridge: the enshrinement in physical space of the man who had said, to my father, *She's not a good girl, Jim,* and inside it spotlit playgrounds for boys like Rick Banner.

I did not spend time reading news reports about the girls who were suspended from school in an ugly hazing scandal in the early 2000s or the one who was sexually assaulted on a rooftop just a few days before the end of her third-form year, in 2014. There was an element of self-protection to my disinterest, of course—not just that I did not wish to revisit old feelings, but also that I knew there was nothing I could do about any of it. To risk the rise of indignation or even sympathy would be to experience all over again the powerlessness of the girl who was told that the lawyers were ready to destroy her.

But it was not my choice to be uninformed about the dogged group of alumni from the 1970s who submitted to the school in the year 2000 a list of shared accusations of sexual harassment and assault by faculty members, with a request for investigation and response. The school handled their request silently, so nobody knew about it except a lawyer at the venerable Boston firm of Ropes & Gray, whom the school tasked with addressing the alumni request. The firm declined to investigate all but three accounts. No action was taken on any of those three cases. Subsequently the rector, the vice rector, and the chairman of the board of trustees together concluded that "an explicit confession of past sins...would be unjustifiably destructive to the interests of the School."

One of the faculty members Ropes & Gray declined to investigate was Mr. Katzenbach, who had taught me Modern Novel. He died five years after I graduated. In those five years, at least three substantial allegations of sexual misconduct were made against him. Over the long course of his employment at the school he had not only grabbed a student's breast but exposed himself to other girls, propositioned them for weekends away, and consummated at least one relationship with a student. I had known he made wildly inappropriate comments, but I knew nothing of his predatory behavior. After I graduated, a female vice rector had brought witness accounts, along with her concerns, to the rector and the board of trustees, and argued to remove Katzenbach from the school community. The school responded by firing her.

Mr. Katzenbach ultimately resigned of his own volition, citing health reasons. Mr. Gillespie—The Rock—wrote him "glowing" recommendations so that he might teach to the end of his life at another school, in Virginia.

All I ever learned during these years is that poor Mr. Katzenbach had died.

Meanwhile St. Paul's wrapped up its investigation with form letters of apology to the alumni who had sought it. "The Trustees are satisfied that the School has acted swiftly, fairly, decisively and appropriately," they wrote.

This group of alumni pushed back, requesting an open call for accounts from anyone who had been victimized at the school. They were refused.

How might my life have been different if that call had gone out when I was still a very young adult?

I was devastated during those early years of adulthood, but

it was as if I were still gagged. Three weeks into my first year in college, the underclass dorms were alive with talk of the "face-book party," an upperclass event held off campus to which freshman girls received invitations, slid under their doors, issued on the sole basis of the *hotness* of their photographs in the student directory. I'd heard it said that Princeton was a men's college that admitted women, and this felt right to me—I relished saying it—but when a sleepy-eyed blond classmate approached me that fall, beer in hand, and said, "I've heard you think women are not equal here. Why is that?" I could not answer her. The girl who asked me this question was dating one of the men who hosted the face-book party. I had been invited, too, and I'd gone. It had seemed a triumph. I felt grateful to these college men I didn't even know for overlooking the gossip about my herpes. I was still smarting about high school face-book ratings. With what clarity, what empathy, could I explain to the drunk girlfriend that this was not what equality looked like?

My education should have helped, and to some extent it did. I read Susan Sontag's *Illness as Metaphor* and found language for the vice rector's choice to tell a group of boys that I might have gotten them sick. Sontag writes, "Nothing is more punitive than to give a disease a meaning—that meaning being invariably a moralistic one." But the culture on Princeton's campus—or at least the culture whose validation I longed for—did not emerge from the scholarship I approached in class. Rather it seemed to repudiate it. I wrote about Sontag and then went to dine in an eating club, newly coed, where men in formal wear raised glasses of whiskey to roast a young woman in absentia for having had a yeast infection. I was disgusted, yes, with their words, but more than that I was grateful they weren't roasting me.

My sophomore year, by grace and proximity, I met a philosophy professor, Susan Brison, who was completing a fellowship. Brison is a survivor of rape and attempted murder. At Princeton she was working on philosophical expressions of the catastrophe experienced by victims of trauma when they report what has happened to them and are not believed. I told her a bit about St. Paul's, though not much. What had happened to me paled beside her attack—and in any case I did not yet understand how the school's silencing of me had been, in its way, the greater crisis. But Susan must have, because she gave me a copy of a paper she'd written about the importance of being heard. It was due for publication in a major journal. She gave it to me in manuscript form, and those paper-clipped pages felt to me like a secret.

"The denial by the listener inflicts... the ultimately fateful blow," Brison writes. If nobody believes you, part of you cannot survive. I grasped this instinctively. I carried her paper everywhere, keeping it in my bag beside my calendar and my notebooks and my student ID.

But I felt I did not deserve her insight. Brison's primary archive was Holocaust testimony, and with the Holocaust as referent, an experience such as mine becomes vanishingly insignificant, except—for me at least—inasmuch as the banality of its cruelty seems to bloom: This happened in a *school?* In a *church school?* In a cosseted New England boarding school? It's not historic evil, it's everyday evil: it's wasteful, churlish, absurd.

There was nothing I could do about what had happened to

me. I read as much as I could. I saved Sontag's essays, I saved Brison's paper. I did not know how to change my life because of what I found there.

Twice a year, St. Paul's School asked me for money. There were invitations to receptions in Hong Kong and Hobe Sound. When the jewel-toned *Alumni Horae* arrived, thick and matte, I tossed it immediately. I moved cities, on average, every two years. When I interviewed after college to teach high school English, twenty-one years old and quivering, the department head who eventually hired me told me that I should find a way to make myself sound at least neutral about my own high school experience. I'd thought I had.

In addition to teaching, I tried being a reporter for public radio, but I hated coaxing people into sharing things they did not wish to say. I started work toward a doctorate in English and wrote a master's thesis on metaphor in the rape testimonies of small children. I turned twenty-four, twenty-five. I hitched my wagon to the star of a lying man who looked good on television, and followed him to London. There I sat on the floor of an overheated charity office that had run out of chairs and wrote reports to tie together information coming in from the field, where staffers were using brand-new GPS technologies to identify illegally felled trees on the Thai-Cambodian border and illegally mined diamonds in Congo and illegal bribes to agents of U.S. oil companies in Niger.

But they couldn't pay me, so I got a job with a British lord, writing his correspondence, and when I'd wobble down the stairs in the heels they'd requested I wear, summoned in sonorous tones to take a note, I'd find some of the dodgy corporate leaders I'd profiled in my charity reports waiting to go in: Kazakhs filling their three-piece suits like envelopes of cash, two or three matching monsters with fingers in their ears lingering in the vestibule. While the lying man was away, reporting on foreign wars, I met an English fighter pilot who shared his taxi in a downpour. He rang me up at the lord's office and nipped over from Whitehall to take me for a drink— and then for an entire winter of chaste drinks, followed by supper and walks in the park, all under cover of the London night because of course he was already married. In this way I managed to pretend I was not alone, while not actually having to be in a relationship at all. No man touched me.

Everything glistened but nothing grew. I lived alone with my dangerous-looking Belgian shepherd and failed, year by year, to build a life. The plan was to drown myself in the Thames, though I left the door open for other actors to play the water's part. It is an oversimplification to say this was all the fault of what happened at St. Paul's. But the problem found its teeth there.

Not long before I turned thirty, I received a phone call from a strange number: a guy I had dated briefly, without intention or intimacy, a decade earlier, at the writers' conference in upstate New York. He'd been living that summer in a rented house with five buddies and a lizard called Gandalf they kept alone in a room, lashing and hissing, at the top of the stairs. Once a day one of these college kids would crack the door and throw in a bag of frozen vegetables. I'd been working at a café, where I arrived before dawn to meet the baker's van and her warm trays of pastry. Nights Ted was a valet parker. We made up stories about the people whose cars he drove. You could tell from the dash what lives they led. The key chain, the cupholder, the scents that remained. All of this ten years before. "Hi," said Ted. "How are you? How have you been? Funny, yeah, gosh. Time!" Turns out he lived in Los Angeles now, where his sister the screenwriter had gone to a bar and heard from someone that I had herpes, and did he have to worry?

"Ted," I said, in flames. "Are you serious?"

"Very."

"Do you have herpes?"

"Uh, well, no," he said.

"Are you sick?"

"No. I'm great, actually."

"Then why are you calling me?"

"Because my sister said that a guy at the bar said you'd had it in high school, and I just didn't remember what you and I did, and maybe if I still could have caught it—if I'd know by now—"

I would drown myself at dawn. As soon as I found someone to take my dog.

I said, "Ted, if you are unwell, I think you should call your doctor. Otherwise, I think you should leave me alone."

"Oh," he said. "Okay."

"Thank you."

There was a pause. I went to disconnect us. "I'm sorry," he told me. "It's just that I'm in love. I've met...the one. You know. And I don't want her to get sick."

It would be another year before the spring morning when I returned in light rain to my little flat and found a letter from the other woman my then-fiancé was engaged to. I remembered Budge's Candace as I rang up the letter writer.

She revealed that while I'd been wearing his diamond in our home in London, he'd gone to Israel to ask her dying father for his blessing on their wedding. Just then our cell phones pinged, this woman's and mine, at exactly the same moment with exactly the same text from the lying man, saying how much he missed each of us. He was still in Iraq, reporting on a war that was itself based on a lie. Together, we confronted him upon his return. Six weeks after that, he was engaged to a third woman, whose name we had never heard.

How carefully I had denied myself truth, companionship, a future. My devotion to shame, to the St. Paul's depiction of me, had taken precedence over everything.

I sold the lying man's ring and rented as many months as it afforded me in a haunted basement flat with its coal scuttle still visible on the street-side wall. I was close, then, to meeting the people who would help me begin to live, but I did not know it yet. When the dog and I walked across London to our new home, I wore a backpack containing my most precious things. I might have been fifteen. On my way to the Schoolhouse, on my way to the rink, on my way home from Rick and Taz's room.

When the boys did what they did to me, they denied the third person on that bed. I had no humanity. The impact of this violation only sharpened with time. My careful distinctions of injury and responsibility—the difference I imagined between *what they did* and *rape,* between terrible things you should put behind you and truly hellish things no one would expect you to bear—allowed me, for many years, to restore that third person in the room in my mind. I could pretend that having been permitted to keep my jeans on while being choked by cocks was something like agency, that it meant that at least they saw and heard me, the girl beneath them. I worked—I still work—to restore the boys' humanity as a way of restoring mine: they were symptoms of a sick system, they were tools of the patriarchy, they were fooled by porn.

But then the school went and did the same thing, denying my humanity, rewriting the character of a girl and spilling all her secrets to classmates to tempt them into shunning her. The teachers, rectors, lawyers, and priests of St. Paul's School lied to preserve their legacy. It would take decades to learn not to hate the girl they disparaged, and to give her the words she deserved.

It was the school's inhumanity I could not—cannot—overcome. Because now I was up against an institution that subsumes human beings and presents a slick wall of rhetoric and posture and ice where there should be thought and feeling. Thus is the world, this world, made.

I saw it everywhere.

12

Investigation, 2016

By the time I turned forty, I had found safe harbor in marriage to a kind man who was unimpressed by Wasp wealth and had had a fine time attending the public high school a mile from his house in Los Angeles. His immigrant parents could not imagine what would cause a family to send its child across the country for high school: *What had I done?* My husband and I laughed and left it there. My family never talked about what had happened at St. Paul's, and our new friends in new communities would never know. There's no tidy way to tell the tale, no obvious antecedent that requires explication, and the result of any such revelation in an otherwise civil relationship is to coat everything with a sticky alien muck that might or might not linger in the form of shame or timidity. With my husband the event was dropped into the well we tend, where our courtship resides, too, and the births of our sons, along with the premature deaths of loved ones and my husband's experience as a first responder at the World Trade Center. There are things he saw there that he will not tell me of. We hold these stories not in how we talk about them but in how we talk to each other about everything else.

I had finally outrun St. Paul's. The alumni office had even lost track of me—I no longer received solicitations for money, or the *Alumni Horae*. My eldest child was almost ready to start exploring online, and on the day he'd think to pick out the letters of his mother's name, I realized gratefully, nothing about any of this would come up.

Then in August of 2016, my oldest friend, Andrea, called.

"My God. St. Paul's. Those motherfuckers. Can you believe it?"

In spite of steady headlines about the latest sexual-assault trial, I'd been ignoring the news out of New Hampshire. It was easy to do. Not my life, I'd decided. Not anymore.

"I'm sure I could believe it," I told my friend, "but I don't know what it is."

Andrea explained that the school, facing a civil lawsuit from the assault victim's family, had filed a motion in U.S. District Court in Concord to force the release of her name. By universal convention, the names of underage victims of sexual crimes are redacted in court filings. Her attacker had now been convicted on multiple counts. A handful of powerful alumni had fund-raised to pay his legal fees. Now the school did not feel it fair that everyone should know the name of the institution accused of failing to protect the young people legally and ethically in its care, but not the name of the girl who was assaulted there. So this Episcopalian school, with an endowment at that time worth well north of half a billion dollars, meant to force the teenager to defend herself to the world. They meant to intimidate her, perhaps to silence her.

It was such an astonishingly nasty legal action that Andrea, who is a lawyer, could not at first believe it was true. She'd gone so far as to find the motion on the court website to be sure.

"It's such a dick move," she said.

Is the term itself a cheap shot? A generalization, certainly. We let it stand.

The girl, Chessy Prout, outmaneuvered St. Paul's. Composed, articulate, she went on television and "outed" herself.

I recognized the school's act, of course. Its precise cruelty, the fanged transformation of private pain into public shame, turned a key in me. I sent a note to the Prout family's lawyer. When he called me, I asked him to please tell Chessy that they had done something just like this to me. I asked him to tell her she was not alone.

Then in July 2017, the State of New Hampshire announced that it was opening a criminal investigation into St. Paul's School. The investigation would consider first whether the school had ever engaged in conduct endangering the welfare of a child—putting or keeping us in harm's way—and second whether it had obstructed the course of justice by failing to report crimes or by interfering with the investigation of those crimes in order to protect its own reputation.

I read this and thought, *Hmm*.

Anyone with information regarding criminal conduct at the school was urged to contact the attorney general's office. I sent an email without thinking what might follow, as though intention were nothing but reflex, and then all but forgot I'd done it. So practiced was I, still, at banishing the assault from my mind that I was puzzled for an instant when the attorney general's office called me. A detective with a voice like a granite shore told me they'd pulled my criminal case file from 1991, and would I be willing to talk with investigators?

The measure of how young I was in 1991 is that I'd had no

idea a case file existed. The measure of how close I still was to that girl in 2017 is that I was shocked to hear there was a case file now. If I'd not had a two-year-old clinging to my knees when the call came in, I might not have believed myself in the world.

I gave a recorded interview to the female detective in Concord assigned to my case. Julie Curtin had been working sexual assault cases at St. Paul's School for a dozen years. "It's not all she does," joked her supervisor, Lieutenant Sean Ford, on speakerphone, "but it seems like it is." I told Detective Curtin what I remembered. When I hung up I was shaking, and it was difficult to place my finger over the correct button on the phone to end the call. The linking of memory to memory felt violently interior, as though I were making a chain of my own internal organs. Everything tethered to the same ugly gut hook, my own small history.

On the call I had stressed that I had no wish to speak about the assault in public or to press charges, having learned the hard way decades before that speaking up only made things worse. My intention was simply to bear witness to the way the school had treated me. Detective Curtin was quiet for a while. I thought I knew why. I'd given her—this careful, victim-centered professional—the story of a crime, then asked her to do nothing about it.

At the very least, she said, she would work up my case and add it to the list of offenses being considered by the attorney general's office. The AG had brought out of retirement a seasoned detective whose last project had led to the exposure and dismantling of the institutional harboring of child sexual abusers in the Catholic Diocese of Manchester. He would be the one to try to act on everything Detective Curtin and Lieutenant Ford were able to pull together on my case.

Detective Curtin—I began to call her Julie—interviewed my parents and attempted to get hold of my red file from the murdered psychoanalyst's estate. I told her I was quite sure the school had failed to report the assault. "Oh, yeah," she said. "We got that." But failure to report is a civil not criminal crime, and the statute of limitations is only two years. Still, the attorney general's office could certainly use my case to help argue a pattern of behavior on the part of the school.

That sounded fine, I told her. That sounded good. I admitted to Julie that I sometimes fantasized about knocking on Bill Matthews's door. He had since retired from the school, after the celebration of his leadership and of the opening of his eponymous hockey center. I imagined approaching his house, wherever he lived now. In my fantasy it was springtime and I stood boldly on a front stoop to knock. When he appeared at his door I would ask him, on behalf of the girl he had slandered, "Why did you hate me?"

But I had no desire to turn over rocks. Any case I initiated would be tried in New Hampshire. I pictured myself kissing my little boys goodbye and flying across the country. The motel room I'd stay in, the testimony I'd be required to give. The way defense attorneys would seek to discredit me, and how I'd have to protect my memory of the girl I had been from their assertion that they knew her better than I did.

The child I had been was gone. I had my own children now, who needed to be raised, and to stay with them seemed the better remedy.

●　●　●

In a later conversation, Detective Curtin and Lieutenant Ford discussed the ways the school had worked to shut down my testifying about my assault. I told them about the unspoken contract that if I asked the district attorney not to press charges, St. Paul's School would let me return for my sixth-form year. *Did I have that in writing anywhere?* they wanted to know. Because that would be huge for the attorney general's investigation—a smoking gun.

Of course I didn't. I could never prove a thing.

Julie had gone carefully through the criminal-case file from 1991, which I still had not seen. "It looks like nothing was ever done in response to the boys," she observed.

We called them *the boys* even though they are, like me, in their fifth decade now. I am raising sons, and *man* is an honorific in my home. So is *woman*. I do not like to think of those two as *men*. This might be a way to continue to contain and reduce them in my mind. Nevertheless, Detective Curtin and Lieutenant Ford were careful to follow my lead with language, introducing new terms only where legal diction required it.

Sometimes they introduced other terms, such as when Lieutenant Ford explained to me that for complicated reasons, the statute of limitations had not expired on prosecuting Rick and Taz: we could still bring a case against them if I wished.

"Speaking as a cop," said Lieutenant Ford on speakerphone, "this is predatory behavior. And a tiger doesn't change its stripes."

Predatory. Yes. I admitted one shivery thrill. This was a new feeling, to have someone fighting for me.

But the boys weren't monsters, and they weren't tigers. They were men out there living their lives, and I was living mine.

I had looked them up in a half-assed way—not going to the second page of search results, not trying alternate terms. Never on social media, ever. I found only one. I learned he had a daughter. What good would come of her daddy being taken away? How on earth could this help me?

"No," I told the police officers. "Thank you, but no."

"We support your decision, whatever it is, one hundred percent," said Julie. "But you also said that you might reconsider if it was to protect other girls."

Now I felt a new queasiness. Could it be that by exercising my right to keep my private life private, I had failed to offer witness to other victims?

"Would you be comfortable with us just talking to the boys, to ask some questions?" asked Julie.

It hadn't occurred to me until now that nobody had ever done this. I'd been having this complicated and brutal one-sided conversation for decades, and the boys might not have had any clue.

"Yes," I told her. "I'm okay with that. I don't even know where they live."

"We do."

"Who will go?"

"Detectives."

"What will they say?"

"They will have a conversation."

I told her I didn't see any value in revenge. I didn't feel vindictive. I didn't want anyone's money. I didn't want anyone to go to prison. "One of them has a daughter," I said, to prove this point.

"Right," said Julie, turning my point. "A daughter."

• • •

I would have these exchanges with Detective Curtin and Lieutenant Ford, and when I hung up the phone I'd go back to my
life, heading downstairs to start dinner for my children. It felt
surreal and I wanted it to stay that way: St. Paul's had receded
in my mind to a span of gothic misery that was tangled in an
adolescence and a certain narrow class consciousness I'd done
my best to leave behind. I did not tell a single friend about my
involvement in the investigation of St. Paul's. The school itself
had hired a new law firm, Casner & Edwards, to produce a
fresh set of reports about faculty misconduct. The firm's first
report, issued in May of 2017, revealed much of the failure of
response to the initial alumni allegations of 2000 and indicated
that the firm was continuing to solicit accusations of faculty
abuse from victims and witnesses. Once the AG opened its
investigation in August of that year, this meant both Casner &
Edwards and state investigators would potentially be talking to
the same witnesses. I saw the school's call go out over email,
to all SPS alumni, for witnesses to "boundary violations," and
I laughed with my friend who had also been raped at St. Paul's
about what a fool's errand that would be—to trust a firm on
the payroll of the school with your story, rather than going
straight to the police. "They're beating the bushes," said my
friend. "Driving out all the victims before the cops can get
there." The current rector, we heard, was delivering heartfelt
apologies by phone to survivors who offered their stories.

"Yeah, that'd help," deadpanned my friend.

Even so, I didn't tell her that I was talking to investigators
in Concord. I wasn't sure I would ever tell a soul outside
my family.

But at the end of August 2017, I got a personal email from Casner & Edwards anyway. In cold and officious tones, I was informed that the law firm wanted to speak to me. The email did not indicate how they'd gotten my name or what they wished to say. I forwarded the email to Detective Curtin: *What was this about?*

She called me immediately. "It's go time."

She drove up to the campus that afternoon to request my student files. I had faxed her written consent to receive my documents, and on the St. Paul's map in my mind I saw her car approaching the school, taking the left off Pleasant Street, and nosing into a spot in the empty lot behind the Schoolhouse, where I imagined records were kept. I felt guilty and wondered why. The rector at the time, Mike Hirschfeld, happened to be in his office, and he handed Detective Curtin my file. She photographed every page, both covers, and the little thumbnail photograph of me, aged fourteen, pinned inside.

The next day she called me again. Did I have any idea why someone would have been working in my file in the years after I graduated? Ten, fifteen years afterward?

I did not.

Did I have any idea why members of the administration would have wanted to go back through all of my documents? Did anything happen subsequently?

No, not that I knew.

There was something else in the file, Detective Curtin told me, that she and her fellow investigators had not expected to find. Something she was sure the school would not have wanted them to find.

She did not say this triumphantly. She said it with the air of a surgeon who bustles out of the operating theater to let you know things have become a bit more complicated.

Oh, I said. Okay.

She thanked me for my time, said she would be in touch soon, and ended the call. That's how investigations run, I've learned: you're given a set of questions that feel like someone peeling back your sky, but just before you see what's causing the constellations to turn, the detectives ring off, protocol being the necessary precondition of justice. And then you hear nothing for a long time.

Weeks went by. Sometimes I had the feeling that my story about what happened at St. Paul's, which I had tried so hard to tell these investigators truthfully and plainly, with accountability for my own actions and my own forgetting, was like a child—my child, dear to me, imperfect but uniquely mine—and I was now finally sending it into this edifice of criminal and civil justice like a kid into school for the first time. Would it stack up? Would it sit correctly, stand correctly, walk in a line? Would it fit with what the system required?

I waited to hear what they'd made of what had happened to me.

That fall, I started getting emails from people associated with St. Paul's School. Just trying to confirm my contact details, they wrote. Just trying to "reconnect." I did not respond.

The school's alumni office resumed sending me the *Alumni Horae* magazine. But the address label bore only my husband's title, plus his first and last name, which I do not use—I was indicated only as *Mrs.* The first time it arrived, I was sure it was a mistake, and that some man in the area with my husband's name must have gone there.

Finally, in early November, Detective Curtin wrote to set up a time to speak. Lieutenant Ford joined the call. Their voices echoed on speakerphone from Concord, hollowed and abraded by the room I imagined them in—metal chairs, faux-wood table. I paced my carpet at home, seeing nothing.

"This is one of the hardest calls I've had to make," said Julie, to open.

I couldn't think what she could tell me that would make things worse. The worst part was all way behind me, long since over.

"What's happened?"

"I'm very sorry, but I can't work on your case anymore," she said.

"What? Why?"

"We've been severed from the investigation," explained Lieutenant Ford.

I told them I didn't understand.

"Well," said Julie, permitting an edge in her voice, "neither do we. This has never happened before."

Julie talked for a few moments, delivering stilted sentences. They had been working up various aspects of my case, but now, for reasons Julie described as "murky," the attorney general's office had instructed them to stop working with me entirely.

"So what do I do?" I asked.

"The last thing I would ever ask of a victim is to have to go through the process of giving testimony more than once," said Julie. "We don't do that. Even in cases with multiple jurisdictions, we don't make a victim testify twice. To be frank, any difference in what you say could be used by the defense to discredit you. Anything at all. So if the attorney general's office asks you for an interview, I recommend you consider that."

I thought I was beginning to understand: these detectives empathized so thoroughly with victims that they hated to suggest I might have to live through the retelling another time. *It's fine,* I thought, *I'm tough, I can do that once more.*

"Am I going to have to give a taped interview again?"

There was a pause. "Well, we don't know," said Ford.

A longer pause.

"The attorney general's office doesn't want your file," said Julie.

I began to feel wild. "Why?"

Ford again, strained: "We can't say."

"So my case won't be included in the cases they are considering against St. Paul's?"

"We can't say." But the attorney general's office was not interested in my case or in any of the information that had been collected by the Concord Police.

Wildness moved from my fingers into my palms, lacing my wrists, rising up in my belly. The school was at it again—the school was manifest again, had reconjured itself as an entity I could not see or name or talk to but that would force me to be silent. The cascade returned and it was roaring right behind me.

"They're covering it up," I said. My voice cracked with anger, and I felt, hearing myself, that I would lose credibility all on my own. "St. Paul's is covering it up again. They are powerful and they are enormously wealthy and they are going to make it go away."

Nobody said a word.

"They're making *me* go away," I said.

"We're not giving up," said Julie. "I will call the investigator, Jim Kinney, in the AG's office myself and tell him to talk to you. I already have. I will do it again."

I rebounded. I was not fifteen. I was in my forties, with a home and a husband, a base from which I could work.

"I will call Jim Kinney," I said. Knowing his name felt like a foot in the door.

"Good," said Lieutenant Ford.

"Good," said Detective Curtin.

Four months had passed since I'd first contacted the authorities.

"I'm sorry I can't work with you any further," said Detective Curtin. "I'm so sorry."

That afternoon I called my pediatrician's office back in Lake Forest, something I should have done decades before. As a matter of policy, I was told, they destroyed medical records when a patient turned twenty-seven. I had missed the mark by almost fifteen years. But the woman on the phone asked me to hang on, and when she returned she was humming. "Whoo-ee!" she said, all music. "You got lucky!"

She printed it all off microfilm and sent it to me. This is how I saw, for the first time, my pediatrician's written report of my account of the assault, and the positive culture for herpes. Also included in these documents were pages faxed from St. Paul's School. The school had destroyed my health files after I graduated—or so they told detectives. But at some point the health center had faxed to my doctors at home pages of progress notes from 1990. This is how I learned that the school's pediatrician had known my diagnosis and failed to disclose it to me. He clearly failed to reveal it to my Chicago pediatricians too, because there are pages of notes detailing the Chicago doctors' conversations with colleagues, making careful lists of differential diagnoses and trying to figure out what was ailing me.

At no point had anyone suspected that canker sores were the answer. Nobody was even fool enough to write that down.

I paged through these documents sitting on the floor of my bedroom, in front of a white cardboard file box I had commandeered to contain them. Old work files were unhoused to make room. This felt like a regression. The pages began with my infant vaccinations. First well-child checkups. That time I had an infected spider bite in second grade.

As I read them, the person I ached for was my mom: the woman who kept calling, as these pages noted, the one who brought me in every single time, the unseen person behind all these details, trying to make and keep her daughter well.

I was at St. Paul's in the first place because I had parents who believed, above all, in the education of a girl.

"Mother called again," reads a note from November 1991. "Child in infirmary. Fever, losing weight. Mrs. C very concerned."

I contacted Jim Kinney in the New Hampshire attorney general's office and was told politely that they intended to investigate every case and that they would not overlook mine.

• • •

Then, on the Friday before Thanksgiving, Detective Curtin and Lieutenant Ford called again. It was the end of the day in New Hampshire when they rang, and the upcoming holiday had taken from the workweek its momentum and its obligations. The timing of their call was worrisome. Didn't they want to get started on their weekend, head out, head home?

Ford spoke first. "I've never seen anything like this."

I hovered patiently. "What's happened?"

Though they had been severed from my case, Detective Curtin and Lieutenant Ford had been called to present their early findings to the attorney general's office. It had not gone well. "They called us in," he explained. "It felt like the Inquisition. We almost felt like *we* were the suspects. I've been doing this for twenty-five years and it's the most difficult experience I've had in that time."

Both of them were quiet for a moment.

"They're rejecting my case," I said, so they wouldn't have to. Silly seasoned detectives—they'd thought the law would prevail. "They're actually going to cover it up again."

"We're all in agreement that there seems to be some collusion or incestuous relations between attorneys here," said Julie.

I did not know at the time, but there was certainly a case for incest because the lead counsel for St. Paul's happened to be the former attorney general of New Hampshire. He'd be working with his former colleagues on which documents would be admitted into the investigation. Anything related to me, apparently, would not.

"It's attorneys tipping off attorneys," said Lieutenant Ford.

"Put it this way: If I'm the San Francisco Forty-Niners and I'm playing the New England Patriots this weekend, I don't call up Bill Belichick and tell him what plays I'm going to run."

I was too upset during the conversation to work out immediately that this was likely how Casner & Edwards, the firm working for the school, got my name. Once Julie and Lieutenant Ford had begun presenting my case to the attorney general's office, the information had gone to the school's attorneys—and Casner & Edwards had contacted me to try to get their piece of my participation in the investigation.

"This is like that movie *The Pelican Brief*," said Lieutenant Ford. "You know, the St. Paul's pelicans? I mean, you can't make this stuff up. We should retire and write a book."

The pelican is the mascot of St. Paul's School. An icon of early Christianity, the pelican represented martyrs in their faith because mother birds appear to violently tear flesh from their own breasts to feed their young. In fact, early Christians misunderstood what they were seeing: adult pelicans hunt other birds' nestlings, eat them, and regurgitate them for their own chicks.

"The way we were treated up there is shocking," said Julie. "They won't include, will *not* include, anything from your file. They have specifically instructed us not to send them anything else. And I think what we have with your case is the smoking gun."

Smoking gun. I had heard this before, from the pediatrician decades earlier. She'd used the phrase to explain to my mother how the sores in my throat were so far down that they all but precluded the possibility of consensual activity—never mind that my age negated consent altogether. When the doctor had said this, my mind had conjured a hot gun shoved in my mouth, muzzle right where it hurt.

"What's the gun?" I asked.

Julie finally explained. When she had driven up to the school to request my file, the documents the rector handed her contained, right near the top, a letter written in the summer of 1991—the summer I was accused of being a drug dealer and so on. In this letter, the school's attorney laid out for then-rector Kelly Clark his formal advice for how Reverend Clark should handle "any further communications" with my family.

"I don't want to read it to you," said Julie, "because it will make you crazy."

I appreciated her concern, but *crazy* was not a useful barometer at this point.

The lawyer made three points in his letter, and Julie, with Lieutenant Ford listening, read them to me.

One: Rector Clark was advised to say that from the beginning, the school had acted in concert with legal counsel, which Julie interpreted for me as potentially providing cover for the school's failure to report.

Two: Clark should be sure to say that the school "stood behind" my family. ("I *really* didn't want to make you listen to that one," said Julie wryly.)

Three: But that "it would be very difficult to admit Lacy to reenter the school" for sixth form "under current circumstances."

"'The Crawfords,'" read Detective Curtin slowly, *"'first must resolve the charge of a cover-up which they communicated to the State of New Hampshire.'"*

I copied down these words as quickly as I could. Then I read my handwriting.

"That's what I told you," I said to the detectives. "They would not let me come back unless I agreed to drop the charges."

"In writing," said Julie. "We think that's witness tampering."

"Only if we can use it," said Lieutenant Ford. "And they're arguing that we didn't come by those pages correctly, because the school's attorneys, if they had known they were in your file, never would have given them to us."

"But the rector gave them to Julie!"

"Exactly," said Julie. "And I had the proper consent. But the AG's office was very unhappy we had it, and severed our case. They did not want us to use those pages."

"So that's it?" I asked. We had found proof, and in the same conversation I was being told it could not be allowed to do its work?

"We'd like to act on it," said Ford. "We'd like to do right by you. By all of the many victims of the school. But they have severed us."

"From my case."

"Yes."

"My case alone."

A pause. "Yes."

The Crawford Curse.

"Why? Why?"

Well. The detectives didn't like to guess. They hated to speculate. But the attorney who wrote the letter in my file was still alive and kicking. "Don't Google him," said Julie (the thought hadn't occurred to me). She knew I would find that he was a prominent and respected lawyer.

I still didn't get it. "So?"

"So he wrote the letter," the one she'd just read to me, the one she felt reflected "counseling failure to report and witness tampering in the investigation of the statutory sexual assault of a fifteen-year-old girl."

I asked if they thought my case had been severed in order to prevent this letter from coming to light, in order to protect the lawyer who wrote it all those years ago.

"We can't say why," they told me, carefully. They were not privy to those conversations in the attorney general's office. "We're disgusted with the politics of this," said Lieutenant Ford.

It seemed unimaginable that we had finally found incontrovertible proof of at least the nature of the wall of men who had worked to silence me when I was a teenager, and we could do nothing with it. I asked if I could do something myself. Specifically, I asked if I could run screaming down Main Street, shouting it to the void.

"Oh, please don't do that," said Julie.

I'd been kidding. She was not. I said, "Why not?"

"Because victims of St. Paul's are still coming forward." And if something happened to damage their impression of the integrity of the investigation, "they won't keep coming forward."

#MeToo had six weeks prior to this conversation begun to sweep social media. Tarana Burke's movement using new media to publicly align voices against shame was a phenomenon now. *Here, tell—we believe you.* All over the world, victims were being encouraged to share their stories in an effort to embolden other victims. I was being asked to keep quiet about mine so as not to discourage them.

So many people demanded my silence. The list begins with my own denial. But of all the manipulation, slander, and failure, this reasonable request from a kind investigator devastated me most of all.

I got hold of my records from the ear-nose-and-throat clinic in Concord. The outpatient report of my herpes diagnosis—the one the pediatrician at school had referred to—was not among them. It has vanished entirely. The records that remain of my visit appear woefully incomplete.

But what was there struck a note so sharp I could hear it, a chip of ice so cold it must be the hard center. It's small, not much. Just a phone message taken in the middle of the summer in 1991. This was a few weeks after the school lawyer issued his letter of guidance for the rector. I'd have been taking my Zovirax and writing letters to Scotty, driving myself around Midwestern roads with failed desire and a still-healing hand. John Buxton, the vice rector of St. Paul's School, had called this doctor in Concord to talk about me.

"Would like to speak with you about a patient," reads the message. He got his wish. "Returned call," noted someone else. "Sensitive matter."

John Buxton, the vice rector with whom I had never had a conversation and never would, had known that I had visited this clinician in town and had called him directly to discuss my private medical records.

And as I would hear later, from records Julie read to me, the 1991 police file reflects that the school's lawyer informed the Concord Police that the clinic in Concord had diagnosed canker sores. *It wasn't herpes,* this lawyer told the police the summer I was sixteen.

There could not have been a clearer instance of the ravenous paternalistic entitlement of this school, to help itself to my doctor and my privacy even in my absence. The boys fucked my throat, and then another guy went down there too, just to tidy things up.

In the last days of 2017, Detective Jim Kinney from the New Hampshire attorney general's office scheduled a time to interview me.

He did not ask me to repeat my testimony about the assault. Instead, he asked about the school's response: whom I told and what was done. Because he didn't have my file, he hadn't seen any of the medical records or read the reports. But as I talked, Kinney was doing the math ahead of me: "So the students knew about the herpes before you did," he said at one point.

Yes, they did. And now I could prove this. The administration had gone through my medical records. They had revealed private details to my peers. They had failed to report. They had invited their lawyer's advice on how to silence me, and they had followed it. They had threatened to call me a drug dealer. They had said that unless we told the police nothing had happened, I could not come back. I talked for two hours.

"I don't mean to hurt your feelings," said Detective Kinney when I was finished. "I don't mean to undermine what you've gone through. But your piece is one of hundreds of pieces. This goes back to the nineteen-forties. I don't even see the end of this investigation."

I felt him deflecting, and I did not want to let this deflection proceed. "What is sad," I said, "is to hear about everyone else."

"Of course."

"That's why when the detectives in Concord tell me they have a letter that documents the school tampering with a witness and failing to report, it seems important to include that. It's exactly what this investigation purports to be looking for if you are going to be able to bring charges against the school."

"Yes," he told me. "I hear that. But we have to do things properly. Even though I don't like it, it's the right thing to do for the case."

"I know the letter exists," I said.

"I do too."

"Is it true that it's being suppressed to protect the attorney who wrote it? That the lawyers in the state office are too close to the lawyers for the school?"

"The bloodlines do cross over," he said.

"So that's it? Silence again?"

"I can't introduce it into the investigation without going through the proper channels."

"Which are?"

A grand jury had been empaneled, he explained. Subpoenas were being issued. He could not tell me this yet, but in a few months the investigation would lead to the arrest of a teacher who had initiated a sexual relationship with a student and then suborned her to perjury when they were found out. I read about this in the news. After they caught this teacher sleeping with his student, but before the police found out, St.

Paul's School ensured his safe landing at another private school in New Hampshire. Rector Bill Matthews wrote the abuser a stellar recommendation. The firm of Casner & Edwards reported this itself.

I would also read the statement given by the state's deputy attorney general, Jane Young, later that summer, expressing her frustration that Casner & Edwards had continued to contact survivors and witnesses during the state's investigation. "It was well-known by the school and their attorneys that this criminal investigation was ongoing," she told a reporter for the *Concord Monitor,* "so the fact that they were speaking to witnesses, interviewing witnesses...is baffling and quite frankly disturbing."

Detective Kinney assured me that his job was to protect the investigation by doing things by the book. That's what was happening now, he said, and it was the only reason detectives in Concord had been severed from my case. We had to do things properly. I sent him the records I had gathered myself—the medical reports, the phone message proving the vice rector had called my private physician. The grand jury would hear about me, Detective Kinney assured me. I chose to believe him.

13

Summer 2018

It took some time, but Detective Curtin managed to inter-view both boys. She wrote to me to say so and suggested we speak.

"I can't tell you much," she told me, over the phone. "How much do you want to hear?"

I had thought about this. I was shaking, moved by a core-born shiver that you could hear in my voice. "Enough so I don't imagine something worse than what it actually was."

Julie spoke carefully and gave few details. One of the boys, she revealed, had been calm and almost conciliatory. The other was ferocious. I had predicted this—I had, foolishly, I suppose, advised her to take a man with her if she interviewed Rick in person. I was worried for her safety.

"In fact, I made a note of that in my report," said Julie. "That you said what they'd be like."

The enormous kindness of a small affirmation like this. I was not crazy. I described things the way they were.

Then she said, "Neither of them denied it."

I let this sit. I waited for it to grow, like a bit of kindling trying to catch.

"They didn't deny it?"

"Oh, they said it was consensual. You know, *we were all*

teenagers, and you were a willing party." (It was a party!) "But no one disputed what happened."

I felt a powerful alignment. The revelation that they had not denied the assault was more important to me in this moment than my own memory. I thought it would sound undignified to say, "Wow."

"But isn't that an admission to a crime? A statutory crime?"

"Yes," said Julie.

"He was pretty angry," Julie added, of Rick Banner. She did not give his name, but I knew which one she meant. "You know: 'That was 1990, this is 2018. Why now?'"

A typically defensive question, and I could dismiss it for its insinuation that I had some underhanded motive whose tell was my delay in availing myself of the criminal justice system. I'm not sure what motive that would have been—I wasn't suing, wasn't pressing charges. But that wasn't the point of the question. The question tries to portray the victim as the predator, the one with a clever plan. It aims to throw the whole circumstance on its head.

"Sure, sure," I replied to Julie. "Why now."

Of course, I'd talked about the assault back in 1991 too, and had been assured that if I did so in the context of a criminal investigation, I would be expelled from school and slandered up and down the Eastern Seaboard. I wished Julie had said this to him, but that was not her job.

I thanked her. Because she was not preparing my case for charges, we would have no reason to speak again. It was strange to think of hanging up after having told her as much as I had. Over the last year, I'd told her everything. I apologized for this and said I hoped I hadn't wasted her time.

371

"You have *not* wasted anyone's time," she replied. "In fact, Lieutenant Ford and I agree that you have taught us a lot about what happens to girls after something like this."

Happens to girls. Not *what girls do.*

I thanked her again, quickly. I did not want her to hear me cry.

Julie said she'd write up the case report to relate the new information she'd gathered in the last year. The report would have to be thoroughly redacted before it could be released, and though I understood that this document was born of and belonged to the legal system, I found it incredible that it should be combed for inappropriate revelations before I could see it.

My story was mine, but the law's version of it was not.

I had already made my formal requests for this police file and the original from 1991. There was space for these documents in the white box with my medical records and conversation notes.

But I was sure this was not the end. I imagined I would meet Detective Curtin in Concord when I flew to New Hampshire at Jim Kinney's request, to testify before the grand jury. How could I not be summoned, especially now? The boys had not denied my account of the assault. No one at the school or in the AG's office could say it hadn't happened. There was no *she said, they said.* Mine was a textbook case, mine the smoking gun. I looked forward to meeting Julie, though I didn't say this out loud.

While I waited, I searched online for the boys again. I was emboldened by Julie's conversations with them. Their admissions made me brave.

Pretty quickly, Taz's mug shot appeared.

More than one mug shot appeared.

His arrest record was not short and included jail time. I read that he had first been arrested six months after he graduated from St. Paul's, for carrying a handgun.

I thought, *So there's the gun.*

But in his mug shots was the boy turned to misery. I'd never really looked at him at school—not in the face, not before, and not after. We had never spoken. But there he was. And what did I know of the world he'd returned to after St. Paul's? What did I know of what he was handling while he was still at school?

When St. Paul's let Taz graduate without a word after he'd assaulted me, it was not only me they failed.

I noted that Taz had not also asked Julie, *Why now.* For him, maybe, it was not so long past. He might have understood how crisis endures.

I calmed myself by thinking about the answer to Rick Banner's query. *Why now* is a bullshit question, but I found power in thinking about it anyway. I was going to give the grand jury my answer. I'd be ready for it. Why now? Well, because the state launched an investigation into the school, of course. But also I would tell them how at least one of the young people in the room that night had spent half a life entangled in the criminal justice system. I would tell them about my own years of arrest—not that I had broken any laws, but that it had taken me almost two decades to begin to live. I would tell them how it had felt to read the unabashed statements of the Prout family, followed by news of the school's efforts to shame their girl. I would tell them about the chain of custody of my nascent feminism, which began with the queer female priest who showed me the spare room where I could safely sleep and the black woman counselor who urged me to take seriously my loss. I would describe Mrs. Weinberg setting tea in my hand and books on the table when I was too frightened of upsetting my own mother to dare to talk to her. I was going to read to them Professor Susan Brison's words about what happens to a survivor when you refuse to believe her. I was going to elevate every single person whose words, clarity, and courage had elevated me.

I prepared for what would happen next.

14

September 2018

Detective Kinney did not call.

Instead I received a mass email from the president of the St. Paul's School board of trustees—who happened to be Archibald Cox Jr., the son of Watergate prosecutor Archibald Cox Sr.—writing with that year's interim rector to communicate to the entire St. Paul's community how "pleased" they were that the school had reached an agreement with the New Hampshire attorney general's office: the investigation would end. No charges would be filed. The school had agreed to install for "up to" five years a compliance officer on campus to ensure that the school leadership obeyed reporting laws for sexual assault and other crimes.

The attorney general gave a press conference to explain that while the state had enough evidence to bring charges of child endangerment against the school leadership, these charges would have led to only misdemeanor convictions, whereas his office wanted to ensure institutional change.

I thought that institutional change and misdemeanor convictions could coexist quite happily. I thought, in fact, that the latter might help effect the former.

Archie Cox Jr. told the media he didn't believe the school had acted criminally. But, he said, "we're not going to debate that point. It's in the interest of both parties that this thing get settled."

So my story vanished. Was finished. Went cold.

It was hockey I thought of when I read about the agreement. I pictured two teams of young men scraping and slamming on the bright new ice, and how we imagine they are rivals when really they're kings. This is their game. So the school scrimmaged the state, and delivered the outcome. I was never going to have my chance.

How many experiences like mine have been similarly secreted away? Detective Kinney had said there were dozens and dozens of incidences of assault on campus, but I did not have the chance to ask for details, and he would not have answered if I had. We did not speak again.

It was a ringing quiet. Fool girl, I had trusted that documents and perpetrator admissions and the fullness of time would suffice.

As it happened, on the day the New Hampshire attorney general announced his deal with St. Paul's School, the senior United States senator from the State of California, where I make my home with my husband and sons, forwarded to the FBI a letter from a woman detailing a sexual assault committed by a male nominee to the United States Supreme Court. The woman's name was redacted, but she could not be protected. I thought I knew how the Brett Kavanaugh matter would unfold, and that is how it happened. The feeling was of concentric craters—mine, and then the nation's—giant blast zones we could not seem to climb out of.

•   •   •

I spoke to Detective Curtin once more, to follow up on a few last pieces of her department's investigation, which she was closing.

"The attorney general's office ended their investigation," I prompted.

"Yes." Julie waited a moment. Then she said, "We thought about you around here, when we heard that. We thought of you."

I was surprised by how this moved me. I wished I could go back decades and tell myself as a girl about the two detectives in Concord who would be waiting to listen when I was ready to talk.

When she'd asked to interview my parents about the assault, Julie had suggested I might contact them first to let them know she'd be in touch. My parents and I do not speak easily or often, and we have not for many years. But when I wrote to them about St. Paul's, they called immediately. We spoke with a formal dignity, as one would of a diagnosis or a loss.

I had explained the state's investigation, and that I had come forward as a student who was victimized—was raped—on campus. Would they be willing to be interviewed?

"Yes," said my father. "Yes, of course."

I thanked him.

"That whole thing was so excruciating," Dad said, "that I haven't thought about it in *years*. I've really just sort of blocked it out."

My father has a gentle voice, warm and musical. He sings tenor in the same church choir where I soloed on Christmas Eve when I was nine. I leaned into the familiar tones even as his words caused me an old, deeply known pain. My father did not think about what happened at St. Paul's and he had not in years.

Maybe I should have been happy for him to have forgotten, to have that shadow lifted. But I was not that generous. I wanted so much from his words. I was still looking to be redeemed by him and for him. I reminded myself that I was an adult, and that it was up to me now.

"But the thing I will never forget," he added, "is Bill Matthews's voice, saying, 'She's not a good girl, Jim. You don't want to go there, Jim.'"

I had taken my phone outside and was standing next to the raised garden bed I tend with my sons. The garden was trampled and sprawling, full of bright fruits they'd missed. I counted tomatoes. Dad remembered Matthews, of course. How could a father forget? I waited for him to keep talking, with his next breath to go on to disparage Bill Matthews and restore me—*that asshole, can you imagine, I hope he's dead, my wonderful girl.* Maybe Dad thought it unnecessary to say these things. Maybe all of that was clear.

Still, the only words between us were the ones Bill Matthews spoke. We weren't remembering what had been done to my body, but what had been done to my reputation. Maybe, by a set of hellish degrees, it was somehow less painful for Dad to recall his daughter's slandering than her violation.

I am a parent. I think I understand.

"I'm sorry you felt so much shame," I told him. "I'm sorry that is still there for you."

Mom came on the line. "Oh, yes," she said. "And I will never forget"—she said a priest's name, someone with powerful connections to St. Paul's whom she had approached, devastated—"I will never forget him telling me, 'Oh, no, this is on Lacy. This is really Lacy's doing.'"

I hadn't known this about this priest, to whom our family was no longer close. It made sense that she would have appealed to him for help, that summer I was sixteen: he shared her vocation, knew her daughter, knew and was known by the school. I was not surprised to hear that he seemed not to have believed that my assault was real. Mom, like Dad, was remembering the agony of her own abandonment, but I had long preferred to imagine that the people who might have helped us simply did not believe. I had always liked this priest. He'd met me when I still wore ribboned barrettes in my hair. If he had known what the boys had done, if he'd known what St. Paul's had done, wouldn't he have fought for me? If not that horrible year, then during all the years since, when wave after wave of allegations about the school rose to national prominence? This was one small refuge of the survivor, to grant to the silent the grace of ignorance.

I was counting globe tomatoes and feeling off the ground, finding it all a bit funny. *Lacy's doing! Not a good girl.* How powerful they had made me, these men, in denying the truth. How much they imagined I could choreograph in their storied New England boarding school. I had been a fifteen-year-old girl in duck boots. Many days, I could barely speak.

I did not know, when I first told my parents about the brand-new investigation, that I would write about St. Paul's. I had spent so much time considering the challenge of bearing witness, of finding ways to transcribe experience so other people would understand. The work of telling is essential, and it is not enough. There is always the danger that the

energy of the injustice will exhaust itself in the revelation—
that we will be horrified but remain unchanged. The reason
for this, I suspect, is that these are stories we all already
know. *A girl was assaulted. A boy was molested.* The producer,
the judge, the bishop, the boss. To hear these stories spoken
aloud is jarring, but not because it causes us to reconsider
who we are and how we are organized. It is only when
power is threatened that power responds.

After all, the boys told everyone the story of our bodies
in that room. The school took the news in stride. Despite
their precious patter about goodness and virtue, my offense
wasn't what I did, and it certainly wasn't what the boys did.
It was that I showed up in a pediatrician's office in my hometown with the clinical evidence of a crime. It was not until I
challenged the school's reputation that the school decided to
care about mine.

I didn't think I would change the school by writing this
account. I did not think I would change the nation over whose
leaders-in-training the school presumes to preside. We talked,
my husband and I, about initiating charges against the boys:
What would that do to our family, to our lives? How could
that help others? We talked about suing St. Paul's School—
with my documentation and their fear of exposure, I was almost guaranteed a settlement of some sort. The school would
pay me in exchange for my continued silence. We could fund
college accounts for our kids. I could repay my parents for
all the therapy of my youth. Detective Curtin and Lieutenant
Ford had met with a local prosecutor in New Hampshire, who
had been appalled by my case and had recommended I hire

lawyers to seek redress. I could do these things. Most victims cannot. Not only most victims from St. Paul's, I understand, whose experiences might not be as well-documented as mine, but victims from every place—every survivor who has been made to carry the blame.

What I wanted was to find some way to release my peers from their shame. I wanted to show them the secret letter buried in each of their files, the one where the institution aligned against them determined how to keep them quiet, this blueprint of patriarchal silence. So that voices like the vice-rector's—*you are bad, your family must not look closely here*—will roll off them and onto the grass, and they will tell, and tell, and tell.

I talked with my husband about writing about St. Paul's. It would expose me, I said. It would expose him. It would plant in the world these words *(herpes, slut, rape)* associated with my name, and these events for our children to discover. Their friends, their communities. Our community. Would it salt the fields? How large was the danger of regret?

My husband had been waiting for my question.

"Love," he said, "you want to know what I think?"

I did.

He held me and said, "Burn it all down."

It's so simple, what happened at St. Paul's. It happens all the time.

First, they refused to believe me. Then they shamed me. Then they silenced me. On balance, if this is a girl's trajectory from dignity to disappearance, I say it is better to be a slut than to be silent. I believe, in fact, that the slur *slut* carries within it,

Trojan-horse style, silence as its true intent. That the opposite of *slut* is not virtue but voice.

So I've written what happened, exactly as I remember. It is an effort of accompaniment as much as it is of witness: to go back to that girl leaving the boys' room on an October night, sneakers landing on the sandy path, and walk with her all the way home.

15

I don't remember during which of my three years at St. Paul's it was that in the springtime a lone goose landed on the library pond and haunted us. Geese passed through in the fall and spring by the hundreds, but this one year—late April or May it would have been, when the air was soft—a solitary goose appeared and honked, riotously, as we streamed to Chapel in the morning along the brilliant water.

I remember laughing. Laughter rolled down the line of us. The bird, when we passed it, nearly barked, sounding an uproar, like an angry person caught in traffic, sputtering and cursing. Who couldn't find a reason in her own life to yell like that? The laughter lifted us—we were always groggy on the way to Chapel—and caused us to look at the pond. The spring trees. It was so good to be reminded that we were young.

The goose talked throughout the day. *Honk, honk.* Other geese would arrive, we figured, or it would eventually leave. Some natural agenda would have its way.

At night, though, the bird kept calling. From midnight to 6 a.m. the chapel bells tolled only the hour, single bongs without melody, and the bird punctured those hollow hours erratically, enough to keep a lonely or frightened or sad student from sleep. In the morning, when we funneled to

Chapel, it again made a riot. Even the teachers were discussing it. The drunk goose, the lonely goose, the seriously confused and disruptive goose.

A plot was hatched. An old Irish setter lived in a master's apartment in Wing, the dorm adjacent to the dining halls at the top of the hill. We called the dog Murphy. Except in the deepest freeze, Murphy sat outside the front door all day long. He held his chin high and let his auburn ears feather in the breeze. We patted Murphy on the head for good luck, the way tourists rub the foot of Saint Peter in Rome. The dog's head was burgundy where we stroked it as we passed, heading into and out of the dining halls for meals.

Every year, newbs squirreled bits of food out for Murphy and were frustrated when he wouldn't eat. Nobody understood why he refused, but the running theory was that someone had fed him LSD back in the seventies—hence his preternatural calm, too. I don't think anyone worked out that dropping a tab in the seventies would have made this dog Methuselah, but the explanation had become axiom long before I arrived.

Murphy, it was decided, could handle the goose. He was a setter! Against all evidence, students figured that he would spot the goose in the reeds and go bounding in, scaring it off to haunt some other pond. After lunch Murphy was led by his soft collar down to the spot closest to where the bird's calls were coming from. Its cries increased in frequency as the students approached.

But Murphy was unmoved. So a student picked up a rock and tossed it in the direction of the goose, to alert the dog with the splash. Murphy barely widened his eyes. His ears hung still.

Another boy threw another rock. And a third. It was only a matter of time before someone hit the goose, and the miserable squawk it made gave everyone a chill. Still, more rocks followed. How could they not? There must have been something wrong with the bird in the first place, of course. *It was probably already close to death,* said the few boys who would talk about it later. *That's why it was stuck there, making that racket. It was a mercy, frankly.*

We were all grateful the honking stopped.

We had all read "The Lottery," of course. It was a staple of fourth-form English class, along with Fitzgerald and Hemingway, Hawthorne and *Hamlet.* But nobody *meant* to reenact Shirley Jackson's horror story. We were as blind to allegory as we were to privilege. Consequences were not our concern. The school's rules were not even called *rules*—they were formally known as *expectations.* Here the children of the elite were trained not in right or wrong but in projections of belief.

Once the dead bird began to smell, the maintenance crew drove their cart down the path and waded in. Murphy, failed setter, resumed his spot at the door to Wing, overlooking his grounds.

When I was a sixth former, my parents, pleased that it would soon be over, suffered a convulsion of thanks and made a cash contribution to St. Paul's. They had noticed that the school's banner was in tatters. This was the gilded tapestry hoisted by an acolyte in formal chapel processions, just before the high cross. The red stitching of the crest was dulled and loose. You could barely make out the pelican in the corner. I'd seen the banner looking like a sail after a storm and not even guessed what it was. Mom, alert to parish pageantry, rang up the development office and commissioned its renewal.

For the final service of my sixth-form year, with my parents and all the graduates' families teary-eyed in the pews of the magnificent chapel, the restored banner was revealed. I watched it come down the aisle, shining like a wing. That was our part, I thought, the Crawford part, though nobody knew. I felt neither anger nor pride. It was enough to know that I had been there, and of my time this silk would remain. Alex was beside my family, watching me sing. My parents I could barely look at, so I focused on my fellow choristers—their mouths framing sound, their faces docile, grateful.

Acknowledgments

Thank you to Detective Julie Curtin and Lieutenant Sean Ford of the Concord, New Hampshire, Police Department, whose honesty and consistent focus on victim-centered discourse were transformative. Almost alone among administrators and authorities who were involved with my case, they saw through bureaucratic obstacles, diversion, and obfuscation and worked to restore truth and integrity. Where there cannot be justice, there is sometimes clarity, and this is its own mercy.

This book would not have a voice were it not for the leadership of Tarana Burke and the advocacy she has inspired, or for the example of fortitude and fierce care offered by Chessy Prout and the Prout family. Every survivor and witness of abuse at St. Paul's School who spoke up, anonymously or otherwise, helped generate enough interest and anger to rouse an institution slumbering in its pride and reach those of us who had resigned ourselves to silence. Thank you.

After this book was completed, the trustees of St. Paul's voted to remove Bill Matthews's name from the hockey center. This decision was made without consideration of how Matthews treated me and my family, but stemmed from his handling of more recent events. Archibald Cox Jr., as board chair, and Kathy Giles, current rector, presided over a decision that was, and remains, highly contentious among alumni and trustees. The symbolic removal of Matthews's legacy bespeaks good intentions, but I find cause for hope only in the fact that current leadership is willing to tolerate antagonism to force conversation about change. I wish them courage.

I first wrote about St. Paul's in a writing seminar led by Toni Morrison, who encouraged this work in its very earliest form and beyond the seminar's end. The staggering privilege (in all senses) that put me in that room of six women, in the space she created, is in my mind dwarfed only by Professor Morrison's generosity. In the years since, I've been lucky to be encouraged in this telling by wonderful writers, particularly Russell Banks, Carol Edgarian, Tom Jenks, and Mark Strand. Thank you especially to Meg Howrey and Sameer Pandya, who offered essential support through multiple drafts of multiple books.

There are several people who, quietly and with kind patience, offered me words, books, and examples of awareness and advocacy. Thank you to Susan Brison (and to Eva Feder Kittay, for the introduction), Molly Bidwell, and Marva Butler White. I am indebted to the philosopher Heidi Maibom for her insights regarding nonhuman expressions of shame.

Thank you to Jeffrey Baron, Andrea Bent, Alexia Brown, Kendra Dobalian, Melissa Floren Filippone, Margo Furman, and Nelson González for critical conversations about gender, sexuality, boundaries, privilege, and violence during these few years, and for decades of friendship besides.

Thank you to Stephen Grosz.

Thank you to Maggie, whom I miss very much.

I wrote these pages knowing Sarah Burnes was waiting to

read them. Her advocacy has been irreplaceable. Thank you to Seth Fishman for opening the door, and to Julia Eagleton, Rebecca Gardner, Will Roberts, and Anna Worrall at the Gernert Company.

Sarah and Asya Muchnick have been as supportive as it is possible to be, and offered a collaboration that is the only cure for the loneliness of sending a revealing book into the world. They have never confused the book for the writer or the writer for the girl, and this clarity allowed for consistent expression of care and respect. Thank you also to the entire team at Little, Brown, especially Terry Adams, Reagan Arthur, Ira Boudah, Sabrina Callahan, Allan Fallow, Evan Hansen-Bundy, Shannon Hennessey, Pamela Marshall, Elisa Rivlin, Maggie Southard, Massey Barner, and Craig Young. Thank you to Elizabeth Garriga and Nicole Dewey for their instincts to both publicity and protection.

Robin Troy and Mimi Munson, girl on the rock, girl in the pew: you have meant life since I was fourteen. "Alex": may you have everything good.

Thank you to my parents, who have always sought out the best schools, books, cities, churches, words, stories, adventures, mountains, and people they could to help me build a life and a self. What was glamorous taught me ambition; what was eccentric taught me wit; what was passionate taught me devotion. Here we are.

Finally, to my husband: your courage is my torch. I love you, and our boys, with everything I have.

About the Author

Lacy Crawford is the author of the novel *Early Decision*. She lives in California with her family.